About Paul Willia...

"*The* pioneer of modern rock journalism."   —*Twilight Zone*

"A major talent."   —*Publishers Weekly*

"The best writer around today whose subject is rock and roll."
   —*Rolling Stone*

Library Journal calls Paul Williams "one of the architects of serious rock criticism". He is the author of fifteen books, including *Dylan—What Happened?*, and the founder of *Crawdaddy!*, the first American rock music magazine.

About BOB DYLAN: Performing Artist:

"Anything Paul Williams writes about Bob Dylan—and always in his wonderfully unpretentious, conversational, and heartfelt manner—is worth reading. *BOB DYLAN: Performing Artist* immediately enters the canon as one of the few necessary books on Bob Dylan."   —Jonathan Cott, contributing editor, *Rolling Stone*

"Bob Dylan's one of the greatest blues singers of western world; ancient art, on-the-spot improvisation, mind quickness, endless variation, classical formulae, prophetic vision, mighty wind-horse. Paul Williams's *BOB DYLAN: Performing Artist* historicises Dylan's genius of American tongue."
   —Allen Ginsberg

"No one has before attempted a critical appreciation of Dylan's recorded work with close reference to all the extant material. This book makes it clear why Dylan deserves such careful attention; Paul Williams, a perceptive critic, is better equipped than most to fathom the deep heart of Bob Dylan's mystery."
   —John Bauldie, editor, *The Telegraph*

Bob Dylan

Performing Artist

1960 ★ 1973

The Early Years

by Paul Williams

Bob Dylan

Performing Artist

1960 ★ 1973

The Early Years

by *Paul Williams*

OMNIBUS PRESS
LONDON · NEW YORK · SYDNEY

Cover designed by Pearce Marchbank, Studio Twenty
Cover photograph by Val Wilmer, Redferns

ISBN: 1.84449.095.5
Order No: OP 49852

Exclusive Distributors
Music Sales Limited,
8/9 Frith Street,
London W1D 3JB, UK.

Music Sales Corporation,
257 Park Avenue South,
New York, NY 10010, USA.

Macmillan Distribution Services,
53 Park West Drive,
Derrimut, Vic 3030,
Australia.

To the Music Trade only:
Music Sales Limited,
8/9 Frith Street,
London W1D 3JB, UK.

Every effort has been made to trace the copyright holders of the photographs in
this book but one or two were unreachable. We would be grateful if the
photographers concerned would contact us.

Printed in Great Britain by Cox & Wyman Ltd, Reading.

A catalogue record for this book is available from the British Library.

Visit Omnibus Press on the web at www.omnibuspress.com.

this book is dedicated to
Bob & Susan Fino
Paul Loeber
Jim McLaren
Jerry Weddle
and all the other generous friends
who have dedicated themselves
to appreciating and sharing
this music

thank you for your support!

Contents

Bob Dylan

Performing Artist

1960 ★ 1973

The Early Years

by Paul Williams

Introduction

"I See Why He Had to Keep Going"

It's hard to know where to begin, because the only place to begin is
the present, and it's damn hard to know the present. And on the
other hand to be deaf dumb and blind to the present is a crying
shame, because it only goes by once. This is a book about a living
artist. The present as I begin is September 1986. In Bob Dylan time
it's the time of *Knocked Out Loaded* (his 32nd album, released in July),
the time of Robert Shelton's long-awaited Dylan biography (published this month), the time when audio- and videotapes of Dylan's
triumphant summer 1986 American tour with Tom Petty & the
Heartbreakers are starting to circulate among the faithful. The man
himself is in England being filmed as an actor in somebody else's
movie. The central song on Dylan's latest album, written a few years
ago, is about identifying with an actor in a film—not with the
character the actor plays but with the actor at the moment of

portraying the character. It was cowritten with Sam Shepard, a playwright who has become a screen actor himself. A million people saw Dylan on his recent tour. Not even a quarter of 'em have bought his new album.

Who is Bob Dylan? This is not a meaningful question, but it has a wonderful resonance and a remarkable endurance, all the same. What has Dylan done, and what's he doing now? These are questions I consider appropriate to an investigation of the work of a living artist. I have been in love with Bob Dylan's music for twenty-three years, and my experience of and with it becomes richer and more rewarding all the time. This to me is extraordinary, there's nothing else quite like it in my life. At the same time I'm aware that people have similarly intense and enduring relationships with the works of creators like Shakespeare, Picasso, Beethoven, Duke Ellington, James Joyce. The general heading of these experiences is, I believe, "Great Art." This is a book about great art. It is a personal report, a subjective investigation. So is all history, all scholarship, all criticism. The best any of us can do is to tell the truth as we see hear and feel it.

Something else we can do is stay in touch with the joy and the wonder of it, and let that come through in our reports. Wish me luck.

What Bob Dylan has done already, as of this date, is staggering, difficult to contemplate. I am referring to the sheer quantity of works he has produced, as well as to their quality (and of course the quantity would not be significant were it not that the quality is so consistently high). The only point of reference I have is Picasso, another impossibly prodigious artist. I doubt that there are many people alive who have seen all or even most of Picasso's significant work; to set out to do so, giving oneself adequate time to contemplate and actually see, appreciate, feel each painting, drawing, sculpture, could easily be a lifetime task. Similarly, as much as Dylan is loved, even worshipped, there are probably not many people who have actually listened to, spent time with, all 32 of his "official" albums; and those albums, with their hundreds of songs and performances, are only the tip of the iceberg of what Dylan's done.

Even after the release of *Biograph* (a five-record set that includes many previously unreleased Dylan recordings), there are hundreds of unreleased outtakes and alternate takes from Dylan recording sessions circulating among collectors, and many more are still locked away. The book *Lyrics, 1962-1985* includes 67 Dylan songs that are not on any of his albums, and at least another 60 are known to exist. There are movies by and about Dylan, and many recordings of television appearances. There are some published short writings, a book of prose, and a great many fascinating interviews. There are drawings and paintings, some glimpsed by the public, most unseen.

And most of all there are the live performances. Dylan has been performing for audiences all his life, and professionally since at least 1960. Audience audiotapes exist of many performances from the 1960s, and of almost all the performances of the 1970s and 1980s (this means tapes of more than 500 Dylan concerts, with Dylan performing for an hour and a half or two hours in many cases). Some audience videotapes exist. In addition Dylan is known to have made audio recordings of virtually all of his live performances from 1974 on (and has filmed or videotaped dozens of these shows)—a fabulous archive one can only hope and dream will someday be available, preferably through legal, commercial channels, to the general public.

Dylan's "torrential flow of work" (the phrase is Roland Penrose's from his biography of Picasso), then, is not only remarkable in itself, but is also uniquely well-documented, to a degree inconceivable in the performing arts before the latest breakthroughs in audio and video recording technology. It is not widely appreciated what big news this is in the history of art as we know it (i.e., western art during the last dozen centuries or so). For individuals to have access to as much different work by one contemporary performer as is available to you and me in the case of Dylan is something new under the sun, suggesting whole new possible realms in the relationship between artist and audience. The documentation of performed art via sound recordings and film/video also makes possible a kind of immortality for performed art that before this century was available to the work of composers and playwrights but not to singers, musicians, or actors. Now performances as well as compositions are able to endure across time.

This is the sort of thing that fills me with wonder, and makes me glad I'm around at this difficult, rewarding moment in human history. But it is not just the newness or the revolutionary quality of the experience that gives it its specialness. Being the first white man to gaze on the Pacific Ocean may be a powerful romantic image (for white men); but that body of water hardly needs historical context to be awe-inspiring. It is wonderful simply to be alive at a time and place where one can see, hear and smell the thing, be it the edge of an ocean or the edge of one person's everchanging creative expression.

I don't know for sure that it's "good" to have access to so much of one artist's work. What I do know is this is reality. The material exists and draws me to it (and I'm hardly alone in this)—the more attention I give it the more I am repaid, and so I want to hear more Bob Dylan performances, and hear the ones I've already heard again, and again. Having art like this in my life, that engages me because I *want* to experience it, not because I think I should, is my idea of wealth.

Performing arts, according to my dictionary, are "arts, such as drama, dance, and music, that involve performance before an audience." Implicit in, but missing from, this definition, is the fact that a performance exists at a particular moment in time. It is always, from the artist's point of view, "live." It is shared at the same moment that it is created. There may have been all sorts of preparation, including the writing of a script or song or score, rehearsals and so forth; but the actual performance occurs in a moment and necessarily expresses that moment. It is also noteworthy that the performing artist retains no control over his or her performance; as soon as it is brought into existence, it is given away.

Performers, however much they may try to hide in their private lives, always give themselves away at the moment that they perform before an audience. This is perhaps the one necessary thing to understand about an artist like Bob Dylan; and the purpose of this book is to explore a little bit of what Dylan has given away in the thousands of performances that make up his career, his work, so far.

My preparation for this book began in the summer of 1963, when my friend David Hartwell, fresh from the Newport Folk Festival, turned me on to *Freewheelin'*. I first saw Dylan in concert in the fall of that year, in a theater in Boston. He couldn't remember the words to "Blowin' in the Wind." It was a wonderful show. I've kept up with him fairly steadily ever since, and this past summer I fulfilled a longtime fantasy by following a Dylan concert tour around the United States, ultimately catching 30 of the 41 concerts

he did with Tom Petty & the Heartbreakers between June 9 and
August 6, 1986.

Following the tour, seeing essentially the same songs in a series
of different performances night after night, was for me an opportunity to get to know Dylan the performer in an intimate and
affecting way. Friends ask if I met or interviewed Dylan during the
tour. I didn't, this time. I made a decision before the tour started
that it would be better for my book not to talk with Dylan, not to go
backstage, but to stay focused on what I heard and saw and felt
from him as a member of the audience.

I have spent time with Dylan backstage, in Philadelphia in
1966 (an afternoon and two evenings) and in San Francisco in 1980
(four visits of a couple of hours each, after his shows at the Warfield), and on both occasions he was friendly and generous with his
time and attention, perhaps because I wasn't trying to get anything
from him (it would have been different this summer, me with a
book to write). But the illusion we all suffer under, as we go to do
interviews or read stories about our heroes, is that the person
backstage, the private person, has the answers, holds the key, to the
mysteries of the public person.

This is not so. The two are related to each other, but in ways
that the artist as much as the observer finds difficult to understand.
The man on stage speaks to us constantly of his inner life; the
private man, on the other hand, seldom knows much more than we
do about the mystery and power of his public self. When he does
have something to say on the subject, he says it in performance
(Dylan's interviews, for example, are always performances). The
other state, the private person you might meet if you lived or
worked with the man or got to him backstage, is, in relation to the
performer, a state of rest. There is beauty in the performer at rest,
beauty in what is different and unique about him, and beauty in his
very ordinariness. But meeting him as a man at rest, you only meet
the man at rest. To get to know the person on stage you must watch
him on stage.

Having said that, I'll share a backstage story about Dylan. My
then-wife Sachiko and I were visiting him backstage in November
1980, during his series of concerts at the Warfield Theater, and one
night I brought along a book of Picasso paintings, the catalog from
a recent retrospective at the Museum of Modern Art. (The fore-
word quotes Picasso on plans for a 1966 exhibition of his work: "In

short, it's the inventory of someone with the same name as mine."
A very Dylan-like comment.) There were fifteen or twenty pieces of
paper sticking out of the pages of the book—I had marked paintings from throughout Picasso's career called "Guitar" or "Guitar
Player," and I wanted to show them to Dylan.

My thought was that here was Picasso painting the same
painting over and over again, over the course of years, and having
it come out different each time, just as (in my view) Dylan has sung
"It Ain't Me Babe" and so many others through the years, not as
the same song again and again but as a hundred different songs
that happen to have the same name and similar lyrics. Variations
on a theme, the full sequence of which adds up to an artist's oeuvre.
I guess I wanted, in the context of critics and fans bitching about
Dylan's new arrangements of his old material (on the 1978 tour in
particular), to express my support and approval. And I figured
Dylan might at least get a kick out of the subject matter.

But I chickened out, and removed the placemarks from the
book, and then Sachiko took the initiative to hand it to him anyway—"Paul wanted to show you this." It was too late for the guitars,
but I suddenly had the inspiration to accomplish something similar
in a capsule by showing him a two-page spread, eleven progressive
states of the same lithograph, worked on over the course of six
weeks, called "Bull." The first lithographs are realistic sketches,
and then they change in a variety of radical ways, becoming more
abstract, as the bull devolves or evolves towards its essence. Each
lithograph, each state, is fascinating and complete in its own right.

At first Dylan protested that he wasn't interested in that kind
of art at all, but he looked at the page and seemed to be pulled in.
Staying with his initial (it seemed to me) anti-intellectual stance, he
pointed to the second earliest of the drawings and proclaimed it as
the best: "He should have stopped at that one." Then, looking
closer: "Oh, but I see why he had to keep going ..."

Electricity hung in the air. Dylan asked if we intended to give
him the book; I said no. Other distractions in the room rushed in.

My plan for this book is a fairly simple one: I intend to
describe and discuss a significant number (though by no means all)
of Bob Dylan's performances, in chronological order, from
throughout his career so far. For the sake of clarity I've made a
somewhat arbitrary division of his life into sections (in the later

years the sections are his major tours and the periods between the tours, which seems appropriate for a performing artist). All performances, whether on stage or in a recording studio or in front of a television camera, are identified by the time when they occur (rather than, in the case of recordings on an album, the time of their public release). In a few cases the date is not known; and in other cases, for example the film *Renaldo & Clara*, a choice has to be made as to what constitutes "time of performance." In the case of *Renaldo & Clara*, I will discuss the filmed musical performances in relation to the time when they were filmed, fall 1975; but the movie as a whole belongs to the year 1977, when Dylan devoted himself to the task of editing a mountain of footage into a finished work.

A few years back Dylan mentioned that he might write an autobiography; more recently he's told interviewers he's given up that project. But of course Dylan's true autobiography, as with any artist, is his work, in which he consciously and unconsciously shares everything that occurs in his inner and outer life. It is my hope that by discussing Dylan's performances chronologically this book may serve as a kind of catalog, the merest beginnings of a guide, to the story of Bob Dylan that he himself has told and is still telling, every time he sings, every time he steps up to a microphone, every time he lets the music flow through him.

It is a story that matters not because of what it contains but because of the way it is told: with anger, love, honesty, passion, wit, humility, arrogance, and heart. With integrity and spirit. With enthusiasm, pain, curiosity, and doubt. Human qualities. Even as we stand in awe of his gifts, it is the humanity of the storyteller that endears him to us. We like the sloppy spontaneity of his power. We are terrified and fascinated by the risks he takes.

The nature of the artist is that he keeps going. The paradox of the audience is that we love him for this, and yet we want him to stop and stay in the place where he touched us last, or most.

But he can't. And as he keeps moving, a body of work accumulates. It is the nature of an artist to drop work behind him like a balloonist trying to stay above the trees. "Oh ev'ry thought that's strung a knot in my mind/I might go insane if it couldn't be sprung/But it's not to stand naked under unknowin' eyes/It's for myself and my friends my stories are sung." (Dylan, "Restless Farewell," 1963)

Who are those friends? We are, if we choose to be.

"And I'll tell it and think it and speak it and breathe it,
And reflect from the mountain so all souls can see it"

—Bob Dylan, "A Hard Rain's A-Gonna Fall"

I. Child

May 1941 — August 1959

"*The town I grew up in is the one*
that has left me with my legacy visions"
—Bob Dylan, 1963

1.

Bob Dylan was born May 24, 1941, and left home for good eighteen years later, in August of 1959. This long stretch in Bob Dylan's life is a short chapter in this book, a chapter that may serve primarily to call attention to the book's basic concept: these chapters are not about periods in Dylan's life but rather are examinations of the performances that took place during each period.

To be true to this structure, I have to avoid the temptation to talk about Dylan's childhood here (that subject can be explored more appropriately when Dylan raises it, for example in 1974 when he sings, "Used to play in the cemetery/Dance and sing and run when I was a child," or in 1977 when he says "I had some amazing projections when I was a kid"; an artist is best understood, I think, by treating such statements not as data about an earlier time in his life but as expressions of what he's feeling at the moment he's speaking or singing), and stay instead with the content of his performances.

But I can only discuss the content of performances if they've been recorded (with the exception of the few unrecorded performances at which I was present), and even then only if the recordings are available to me in some way. This limitation is most striking in the present chapter, but it is important to remember that it persists throughout Dylan's career, and that our picture of the performer is always necessarily distorted by the fact that we do not and cannot have access to the entire range of his work. Mikal Gilmore in the July 17, 1986 *Rolling Stone* describes Dylan making music in the studio with the recorder turned off: "In one particularly inspired moment he leads the four singers through a lovely a cappella version of 'White Christmas,' then moves into a haunting reading of an old gospel standard, 'Evening Sun.' [Tom] Petty and the rest of us just stare, stunned. 'Man,' says Petty frantically, 'we've *got* to get this on tape.' " Gilmore also tells of Dylan suddenly creating a new version of "I Dreamed I Saw St. Augustine" at a rehearsal. "Five minutes later, the moment has passed. According to Petty and [Benmont] Tench, Dylan's rehearsals are often like this: inventive versions of wondrous songs come and go and are never heard again." There are a few tapes of Dylan rehearsals circulating, but they only serve to remind us of how much of his work is out of reach of even his most dedicated fans.

At the present time, there are no recordings of Dylan performances from the first eighteen years of his life circulating through the network of Dylan tape collectors. Robert Shelton's book (*No Direction Home: The Life and Music of Bob Dylan*, New York, 1986) informs us that Dylan gave his first public performances at the age of three, in his father's office, "talking and singing into a Dictaphone." His career as a performing and recording artist began early. Shelton's book does not say whether Dylan's mother, Beatty Zimmerman, might still have some of those old Dictaphone wires, but Shelton does describe Dylan's parents in 1968 playing him "old practice tapes of his various high-school bands. Bob's young, harsh voice belted out 'Rock and Roll Is Here to Stay.' " So it seems likely that at least some recorded documents of the performer as a child survive, and may even be available for public scrutiny someday. Meanwhile this chapter must necessarily consist of hearsay.

Shelton, basing his comments on his interviews with Dylan's parents, describes Dylan at age two and three as the center of attention in his father's office, surrounded by secretaries and clerks, and suggests that he sang for the crowd as well as alone with his father and the recording machine. He reports, "the boy marveled at the recorded sound of his own voice." Shelton then de-

scribes a pair of dramatic public performances just before and after
Dylan's fifth birthday, at a Mother's Day celebration in Duluth and
at his aunt Irene's wedding reception. He quotes Beatty Zimmerman on the Mother's Day performance: "He stamped his foot and
commanded attention. Bobby said, 'If everybody in this room will
keep quiet, I will sing for my grandmother. I'm going to sing
"Some Sunday Morning." ' Well, he sang it, and they tore the place
apart. They clapped so hard that he sang his other big number,
'Accentuate the Positive.' He didn't know much more than those
two songs."

First poem: age ten, almost eleven. Many more followed. Two
years later, an important performance: the recital of the Torah at
his Bar Mitzvah. There were four hundred guests at the celebration in his honor. Dylan learned a simple lesson, at three, at five, at
thirteen: to perform was to be received as a star. That was his
experience of his public self.

Age ten, fooled around on the piano but rejected lessons. Age
fourteen, discovered the guitar. Those are Shelton's dates; Anthony Scaduto, in his 1971 biography, has Dylan playing piano at
eight or nine, harmonica and guitar by age ten. They agree (which
doesn't make it so) that he was fourteen when he started playing in
a band, the Golden Chords: Dylan on rhythm guitar, Monte
Edwardson on lead guitar, Leroy Hoikkala on drums.

Some bands like to practice privately for years, worrying all
the while about whether they're good enough, but that was never
Dylan's style. The Golden Chords apparently played in public
every chance they got: Moose Lodge meetings, PTA meetings,
talent contests, dances, open rehearsals, local restaurants. Other
bands followed. Dylan's biographers place him a year later in a
nameless band with a drummer, a bass player, an electric guitarist,
and Dylan on piano, guitar, and lead vocals. Your basic Chicago
blues band, soon to be your basic rock and roll band (Beatles,
Stones). One wonders if the band had no name because Dylan (still
Robert Allen Zimmerman in those days) saw the other guys as
back-up musicians. Larry Fabbro, the guitar player, told Scaduto,
"Bob was very much the leader. He had an exact thing he wanted
us to do, some little *doo dah, doo wah* in the background, but
otherwise strictly his singing. We were his accompaniment. It
wasn't a matter of trying to be a group. It was Bob being pretty

much of a personality. He was Little Richard, with rhythm in the background. This was strictly Little Richard."

Little Richard. Little Richard was sexual, Little Richard was self-confidence, Little Richard was a wild man. And he was something else: a brilliant intuitive musician, experimental, out on the cutting edge. He let a natural (maybe supernatural) spirit come through his voice, and he pushed his piano and his rhythm section to go out and find the place where certain previously unknown but palpable laws of sound and music demanded they be in relation to that vocal. Dylan caught on right away and was inspired to work that realm, the realm where he later discovered "Like a Rolling Stone," a realm he's still working to this day.

Reports of Dylan's most famous teenage performance, Hibbing High School's Jacket Jamboree Talent Festival (which I place in spring 1958), make it clear that Dylan followed the rock and roll muse to a logical conclusion that was in fact quite alien to the music of the day, not just in Hibbing, Minnesota but anywhere in those days, a conclusion that seems startling now in its intuitive understanding of where the music was going (he was an easy eight years ahead of his time): play as loud as possible. Not just wild. Not just raucous. Not even just loud, but AS LOUD AS POSSIBLE, preferably in a context that will allow for maximum outrage. Dylan did exactly that in the Hibbing High Auditorium, with not even his band (and certainly not his friends and contemporaries in the audience) understanding or able to relate to what he was up to. It didn't matter. He was inspired, and he fulfilled his inspiration (until, according to some reports, the principal pulled the plug on him, which lowered the volume but only somewhat—he still had the piano—and certainly didn't stop him). If he'd ended his career right then, he would still have been a rock and roll pioneer and aesthetic hero, not that the world would ever have known.

There were other performances, quiet ones. He met a girl, fell in love, and the first thing he did after they talked and discovered a mutual enthusiasm for rhythm and blues music (outlaw music) was play piano for her (she'd already seen him playing guitar in the street, that was what caught her attention). Echo Helstrom later talked with all of Dylan's biographers, including Toby Thompson who wrote a 1971 book called *Positively Main Street*. The picture that emerges from the interviews with her and Hoikkala and Fabbro and from Shelton's conversations with Dylan's best friend John

Bucklen, is of a guy who from at least fourteen on played music and played with music all the time, constantly writing songs, or improvising words and bits of melody and interesting rhythms, or picking up songs that struck him: rock, pop, hillbilly, blues, re-working them, exploring them from the inside, playing and exper-imenting with them, making them his own.

Hoikkala (to Scaduto): "He'd hear a song and make up his own version of it. He did a lot of copying, but he also did a lot of writing of his own. He would kind of just sit down and make up a song and play it a couple of times and then forget it. I don't know if he ever put any of them down on paper." Helstrom (to Thomp-son): "That Hank Snow song there, 'Prisoner of Love,' Bob used to sing like that, talk-singing. He'd play a couple of verses with John Bucklen, and then go into the talking. He'd make up songs that way, too. Some situation would pop into his head and he'd build on it, going for the longest time. I don't think he ever wrote those songs down, though; they were just fun when he'd make them up on the spur of the moment." Shelton: "Bucklen told me they loved to ad-lib on tape. 'We'd get a guitar and sing verses we made up as we went along. It came out strange and weird. We thought we'd send them in somewhere, but we never did.' "

The private performances were for himself and for the music, and for whoever happened to be listening. Sometimes the marvel-ous comic sense of himself he had while playing could get him through situations where he'd otherwise have been buried by shyness. Echo Helstrom tells a charming story of him coming over, after they'd had a big fight in front of her parents and didn't speak to each other for several days. "I opened the door and there was Bob, decked out in one of those TV gambler's vests he used to wear, beating on his guitar and singing, 'Do you want to dance and hold my hand?'—the Bobby Freeman song that was popular then. He stood there on the doorstep and sang it all the way through once, then pushed past me into the living room and sang it again for my parents. Then he just wouldn't stop, but paraded around the house singing that song 'til all of us were laughing so hard we'd forgotten what the fight was even about."

The public performances were also for himself and for the music, and presumably for that hypothetical person who might be out there somewhere understanding and really digging it. They were never about crowd-pleasing, giving people what they wanted.

If his early childhood performances brought nothing but praise and attention, his teenage performances on stage with his bands brought jeers, laughter, booing, and indifference most of the time, according to most reports, and at times it seemed Dylan went out of his way to provoke those very responses. In June of 1986 in Minneapolis, at a sort of homecoming concert (his mother was there), Dylan joked about this. He said he remembered doing this next song when he was twelve years old (exaggeration; artistic license; the song wasn't on the radio till after he turned fifteen), "which was the first time I was ever booed, a song like this." He sang "Let the Good Times Roll," and afterwards told the crowd, "The times must have changed, though—nobody booed!"

Helstrom: "Bob was sort of oblivious to the whole fact that people were not turned on by his music. He lived in his own world, and it didn't bother him. There was this cat, playing like they were clapping, when they were really booing.8"

Even hearsay is hard to come by regarding Dylan's performances during, and in the summers before and after, his senior year in high school. He and Echo had split up, he was going to St. Paul and Minneapolis fairly often, Scaduto says he had a band in Duluth. Shelton identifies the band as the Satin Tones, and says they played one song on a Wisconsin TV station, one dance at a Hibbing armory, and had a tape played on Hibbing radio.

After graduation, early summer 1959, Dylan worked for a while as a busboy at the Red Apple Cafe in Fargo, North Dakota, where he was given the chance to play piano in Bobby Vee's band. He played on a couple of very small gigs, according to Vee, and then was dropped because Dylan didn't have a piano and Vee, who'd just had his first regional hit, couldn't afford to get him one. When Dylan got to New York a year and a half later he told Izzy Young of the Folklore Center, "I played the piano with Bobby Vee. Would have been a millionaire if I stayed with him."

Shelton also places Dylan in Colorado in the summer of 1959, playing the Gilded Garter, a burlesque house in Central City, and the Exodus Gallery Bar in Denver. Scaduto and others make a convincing case that these gigs, which were apparently "folk-oriented" and during which Dylan met and was influenced by Judy Collins and Jesse Fuller, actually occurred in the summer of 1960. In any case, Dylan left Hibbing for the University of Minnesota in Minneapolis in late August or early September of 1959.

II. Student

"*Do you know what Dylan was when he came to the Village? He was a teenager, and the only thing I can compare him with was blotting paper. He soaked everything up. He had this immense curiosity; he was totally blank, and was ready to suck up everything that came within his range.*"
—Liam Clancy

2.

The phrase next to Robert Zimmerman's name in the Hibbing High Yearbook, 1959, was "To join Little Richard"; but by fall of the same year Bob Dylan was a would-be folksinger, strumming a guitar in a coffeehouse in Dinkytown (a bohemian district near the University in Minneapolis). I doubt that many people catching his act at that time would have guessed that he had been and had wanted to be the screaming, piano-playing leader of a loud rock and roll band. The private Dylan who played blues and hillbilly songs for his girlfriend on an unamplified guitar was now the on-stage Dylan, not necessarily because he'd lost his love for rock and roll performing but because he felt discouraged about the opportunities open to him as a rock and roller. It was a hard scene to break into. And in fact rock and roll had entered a period of decline, both in quality and popularity, by 1959.

Folk music, on the other hand, seemed to be a rising star; and more importantly, the folk/beatnik/coffeehouse scene was the counterculture scene when Dylan got to college, the only place where anything seemed to be happening, and all you had to do to gain entrance as a musician was walk in and ask the coffeehouse manager if you could play.

According to Scaduto, the first place Dylan played in Minneapolis was a coffeehouse called The Ten O'Clock Scholar, starting in October of 1959. "His material was somewhat limited at first. He sang a few traditional folk songs, some country and hillbilly, a couple of Pete Seeger songs, and a lot of material then in vogue because of the popularity of slick, commercial folk interpreters such as Harry Belafonte and the Kingston Trio....He sang in a traditional folk style. He concentrated more on the melody line than he would later....His voice was rather nasal, and most people around thought he was an inept singer."

Scaduto's comments are based on the memories and impressions of people he interviewed, and on some newspaper articles from the mid-'60s about "people who knew Dylan when." Shelton's book offers additional material. Spider John Koerner, who played with Dylan in the Scholar in 1959 and 1960, told Shelton, "Dylan had a very sweet voice, a pretty voice, much different from what it became." Harry Weber, who knew Dylan in the same period, offered a different view: "I was afraid Dylan wasn't going to have any voice left. He obviously knew what he was doing, but he was abusing his voice, shouting out raucous, loud songs." Paul Nelson, also in Shelton's book, provides a clue to the contradictions: "Dylan seemed to learn so incredibly fast. If you didn't see him for two weeks, he made three years' progress....Every few weeks, Bob would become a different person with a different style."

Dylan was in Minneapolis from the fall of 1959 to the end of 1960, playing at the Scholar, at the Purple Onion in St. Paul, at the Bastille, and seemingly at every party he managed to find out about. Several different sources report that he would play whether he was asked to or not, and that he was very difficult to stop once he got started. His first performances at the Scholar were unpaid, but sometime in late 1959 or early 1960 he began earning a few dollars a night—as much as five dollars by May 1960. (He was enrolled at the University for three semesters, through fall 1960, but apparently he attended few or no classes after the fall of 1959.)

He did go off to Colorado sometime in the summer of 1960, played briefly in a burlesque house, and played and hung out at a folk club in Denver. He met Jesse Fuller, and may have learned from him about the harmonica holder (which allows simultaneous

guitar and harmonica playing, an important part of Dylan's subsequent performance style). Shelton says Dylan met another black
singer in Denver, Walt Conley, who taught him a song called "The
Klan." Dylan's friend David Whitaker told Stephen Pickering in an
unpublished interview, "Dylan came back [from Colorado] with a
difference in accent. He spoke differently. He was more sure of
himself really. He had gone to Denver, to the Exodus, and he came
back with one song that he used to play, that was entirely a new
level in show business called 'The Klan.' It was a surrealistic poem."

The earliest performance tape of Bob Dylan is supposedly
from May 1960, recorded in St. Paul; there are questions about its
date and its authenticity, however, and in any case the sound
quality on the tape I've heard is so poor it doesn't much matter if
it's Dylan or not—nothing is revealed. The other tape from before
Dylan's first trip to New York is dated "autumn 1960," and consists
of ten or eleven songs apparently recorded at a friend's house in
Minneapolis.

Like most of Dylan's recorded performances prior to 1962,
the autumn 1960 tape does not in itself suggest the coming of a
major artist; yet it is fascinating to hear how much of the Dylan we
now know was already present even during the years when he was
floundering around, searching for and building a musical identity.

His guitar technique is crude; unlike most young musicians,
he makes no attempt to impress his listeners with what his fingers
have learned to do. Prevailing standards of vocal performance,
such as clarity and beauty, also seem to carry little weight with him.
And yet he is not unconcerned with the quality of his performance—he doesn't give the impression that he's just fooling
around with his friends and doesn't care how it comes out. So
already we're confronted with a riddle that persists throughout
Dylan's career to date: what is it he's reaching for, what are the
musical or performance values that matter to him?

(This question is important because very often it turns out that
Dylan is reaching for something other people haven't thought of, is
responding to a call others haven't heard or acknowledged. To
whatever degree he achieves it he breaks new artistic ground. On
some occasions the whole world has seemed to follow him, excited
to explore the new territory; other times his efforts have been
ridiculed, or simply ignored. In every case he has eventually heard
a new call and has gone off on another creative adventure.)

What strikes me on the autumn 1960 tape is the malleability of his voice, the way it shapes itself to the rhythm and character of each different song. It is as though he's trying to become the song. We know the enthusiasm with which Dylan pursued new material throughout 1960 and 1961—it might not be too much to suppose he was searching for his own identity and that the songs, with their powerful links to real and mysterious feelings and states of awareness, were the best clues he found, the most rewarding places to search. Not his own songs, at this time—because they couldn't tell him anything new, presumably—but the traditional songs, other people's songs, anything he came across that might have that spark, that power.

On this tape he sings "(I Wish I Was A) Red Rosey Bush," "Johnny We Hardly Knew You," Woody Guthrie's "Jesus Christ" (to the tune of "Jesse James," cleverly and accurately portraying Jesus as an outlaw and a radical: "if Jesus preached today what he preached in Galilee, they would lay Jesus Christ in his grave"), "I'm a Gambler," Jimmy Rodgers's "Blue Yodel," and a sequence of talking blues, two by Guthrie, one presumably by Dylan, poking fun at his roommate, and one called "Talking Lobbyist" which doesn't seem to be by Guthrie but probably isn't by Dylan either, judging from the language.

The most powerful performances are the first two. "Red Rosey Bush" is done very slow, with a wonderful sense of timing, mournful and sweet. The beat carries the performance, and the vocal expands and expands within it, unpretentious and somehow very convincing, probably because it was in fact deeply felt at that particular moment. (I can easily imagine the same song being tossed away without feeling twenty minutes later.) "Johnny We Hardly Knew You," a familiar antiwar lament, is also done with surprising conviction and freshness; Dylan affects an Irish accent and it works, partly because of his sensitivity to the dramatic rhythms of the song, and because he clearly loves the melody. Here already is his startling ability to project himself into the character of a song's singer, not in an intellectual way but by riding his own feelings. Later on in the tape, when he complains that if he's going to record a talking blues he wants it to be a Guthrie song, his mind is in charge again; but these first couple of performances are from the heart.

There's an interesting exchange in the latter part of the tape, when a friend named Cynthia is interrupting Dylan's song, teasing him to do the song she requested instead. She's bold and quite clever, at one point apparently singing an impromptu verse herself to get her point across; Dylan on the other hand can think of no response except to giggle and say "Screw you, Cynthia!" three or four times. He's self-absorbed and inarticulate and yet somehow still likable, in fact charming. This charm seems to have been, along with his ambition, the main thing that carried him through his early years of performing—according to many contemporary accounts, particularly of his 1961 performances, his hangdog antics tuning his guitar or trying to put on his harmonica holder were sure crowd-pleasers, even when people weren't particularly excited about the musical part of his show.

Dylan arrived in New York in late January of 1961 (he left Minneapolis in December 1960 with the goal of meeting Woody Guthrie, and spent some time in Chicago and in Madison, Wisconsin on his way to New York). He brought with him two stage props that he'd tried on during his Minneapolis period and that had become as much a part of his identity as his guitar: his cultivated Okie accent and his stage name.

Both of these acquisitions served Dylan's need to be secretive and mysterious, to hide his bourgeois, Jewish, ordinary (in his young eyes) midwestern upbringing; but they did more. They gave him something to work with, an opportunity to shape his perceived image and the very sound of his voice into something that more accurately reflected and made space for who he felt like inside. He was inspired, moved, by a pantheon of American voices, musical heroes, from Johnnie Ray and Jimmie Rodgers and Elvis Presley and Little Richard to Odetta, Ray Charles, Hank Williams, Leadbelly, to Robert Johnson, Buddy Holly, and Woody Guthrie, and a couple of actors, Marlon Brando and James Dean. He intended to join their company, not in terms of success but in terms of greatness, spirit. And nothing would stop him; if his given name and his natural voice and the circumstances of his childhood didn't seem to him appropriate vessels for the spirit that was moving him, he was ready and eager to change them all, to recreate himself in the composite, unfocused but palpable image of everything that was inspiring him and moving inside him.

Robert Shelton's book offers a new and unexpected twist to the old controversy about why Dylan chose the name "Dylan":

Shelton says that the name was chosen in 1958, that it was "Dillon" for at least the next two years, and that it "probably had two sources": a pioneer Hibbing family named Dillion, and Matt Dillon, hero of the popular television western *Gunsmoke*. I find this very believable, if somewhat myth-shattering, and I'd add that the sound of the name was probably at least as important to Dylan as any associations it might suggest. (Note that his first and middle names are Bob Allen.) Similarly, it's easy to imagine that later, when he came across Dylan Thomas's name if not his poetry (there's no evidence other than the presumed evidence of the name that Dylan was ever really interested in Thomas's poetry), he was tickled by the alternate spelling and adopted it because he liked the way it looked (and he may also have realized by that time that it's more hip to identify yourself with a Welsh poet who died young than with a TV sheriff).

As for the accent, Dylan's passionate discovery of Woody Guthrie in the summer of 1960 clearly played a big part in it, although it's possible that he was already starting to experiment with giving himself a more "authentic" folk voice before his Guthrie fascination came along and confirmed him in this course.

The accent gave Dylan something to work with, like an actor with a cane in his hand, and it also gave him freedom. If he had been trying to pass himself off as a person from a particular place who spoke a certain way, then the accent would have been restrictive, a mask that always has to be remembered and maintained in place. But the very ambiguity of the accent, and the fact that in many ways it was just an exaggeration of his natural tendency to mumble and slur words and mess around with where the emphasis goes (in a word or a sentence or a line from a song), meant that the adoption of his "Dylan voice" left him more free to be inventive, to play with his performance from word to word and note to note as well as from song to song.

3.

Legend has it, and it may even be true, that Dylan ended up playing harmonica in the Cafe Wha? in Greenwich Village his first night in New York City. Certainly he insinuated himself into the Village folk scene extremely quickly. Within a few days of his arrival he realized his dream of meeting Woody Guthrie, and was singing and playing guitar for Guthrie at his hospital bedside in New Jersey (Guthrie was slowly dying of Huntington's Disease). Guthrie was spending weekends at the home of Bob and Sid Gleason in East Orange, New Jersey, and Woody's friends would come out from Manhattan to be with him and each other. Dylan successfully invited himself into this scene, and soon became a protege and friend not only of Guthrie but of Pete Seeger, Cisco Houston, and Ramblin' Jack Elliott. Hanging out in Village bars and coffeehouses when he wasn't visiting Guthrie, he also made friends with Dave Van Ronk, Fred Neil, Paul Clayton, Mark Spoelstra, Peter La Farge, the Clancy Brothers—it must have been very heady. The small town kid who wanted to be a folksinger found himself welcomed and accepted at the center of the action in New York.

He performed for free in the coffeehouses between acts or in the afternoons; he also backed other singers with his harmonica playing. The popular Monday night hootenannies at Gerde's Folk City, where new and established performers took turns playing for free to several hundred onlookers, gave him an excellent opportunity to build a following. On April 5, 1961, he gave a paid performance before the New York University Folk Music Society; there was even a flyer announcing the event in advance. On April 11, a major breakthrough: he began a two-week engagement at Gerde's as the opening act for the great Detroit bluesman John Lee Hooker. (Twenty-five years later, Hooker, who is still playing the clubs, made a guest appearance at Dylan's August 1986 concert in Mountain View, California.) On May 6, 1961, Dylan performed at the Indian Neck Folk Festival in Branford, Connecticut, where he met and made friends with musicians from the active folk scene in Cambridge, Mass.; later in the summer he visited Cambridge a number of times, significantly expanding his circle of musical friends, influences, and supporters.

In the summer, probably June, he did his first professional recording, as a harmonica player at a Harry Belafonte recording session. He complained afterward that he couldn't stand playing the same song over and over again. Late in June he wrote and started performing a humorous talking blues based on an incident from a newspaper, "Talking Bear Mountain Picnic Massacre Blues," which along with "Song to Woody" was one of the first songs to bring him some attention as a songwriter.

September/October 1961 completed his transition from amateur to professional status. He got another two-week gig at Gerde's, opening for the Greenbriar Boys, September 26 to October 8. Robert Shelton came to opening night and gave Dylan a rave review in the *New York Times*. Dylan played harmonica at a recording session for Carolyn Hester and met John Hammond of Columbia Records. Before the end of October, Dylan had a recording contract with Columbia, and in late November he went into the studio and recorded his first album. Also in November he played his first scheduled solo concert, at Carnegie Chapter Hall, a smaller auditorium in the Carnegie Hall building.

The album *Bob Dylan* is the official document of the 1961 Bob Dylan, a folksinger/blues singer/comedian (his comic bits, though he could make them appear almost unintentional, were a major

part of his act at the time) who primarily performed traditional
material and songs by other writers, rather than his own songs.

In addition, there are tapes in circulation of Dylan performances from throughout the year: a tape from the Gleasons' home
in East Orange from February or March; three songs from the
Indian Neck Festival in May; twenty-five songs recorded by a
friend on a visit to Minneapolis in late May; the Belafonte session
from June; a live radio broadcast from Riverside Church in July;
six songs from a Gaslight Cafe show in September; the Carolyn
Hester session from late September and another recording session
from October, Dylan playing harmonica with blues singers Big Joe
Williams and Victoria Spivey; seven songs from the Carnegie
Chapter Hall concert in November; part of an interview done with
a publicist at Columbia Records; and home tapes made in November and December by friends in New York (the McKenzie tape) and
Minnesota (the "hotel tape"). Some songs from the Minnesota hotel
tape gained wide circulation when they were included on the 1969
bootleg album called *Great White Wonder*.

There is nothing in these recordings, including the first
album, that in itself justifies the rapid rise of Bob Dylan in the New
York folk scene—major club appearances, a recording contract,
rave reviews and so forth. It seems safe to say given the breadth of
recorded evidence (even keeping in mind how much more went
unrecorded) that Dylan was not performing great or even first-rate
music in this period, and was in fact not as good at what he was
trying to do (sing the blues, sing Woody Guthrie songs) as many of
the musicians around him whose careers were not moving as
quickly (not moving at all, in some cases).

Given that the many people who felt Dylan had enormous
potential turned out to be right, what was it they were noticing? I
don't think it was his latent songwriting talent—he didn't perform
many songs of his own in 1961, and the ones he did perform, with
the possible exception of "Song to Woody," offer little hint of the
songwriting genius that would soon be let loose on the world.

My own conclusion, based on the recordings and on the many
firsthand accounts of Dylan performances quoted in Scaduto's
book, Shelton's book, and Eric von Schmidt and Jim Rooney's
history of the Cambridge folk scene, *Baby Let Me Follow You Down*, is
that people experienced something from being in Dylan's presence
when he performed in 1961 that can't really be heard in the

recordings of those performances (except in bits and pieces, and with the benefit of hindsight).

The evidence is that it wasn't Dylan's skills as a guitar player or the originality of his Guthrie interpretations or even the cleverness of his Chaplin-like stage antics that moved people. They were moved by something else—something about him that communicated itself when he played guitar and sang Guthrie songs and stumbled around the stage. For lack of a better phrase, call it his stage personality. In 1961 the Bob Dylan whose name Robert Zimmerman had found back in high school, and whose weird Okie voice he'd discovered sometime in his college dropout period, was emerging more and more, not through a process of consciously creating an identity but rather a process of giving birth to something already there, something that had been gestating and working its way out for a long time.

As Dylan grew as a performer, and continued his work of absorbing the influences that attracted him and making them his own, a moment arrived when his personality, his presence, could successfully communicate itself not just in person but through his songwriting and his recorded performances as well. At that moment Dylan became a star almost overnight, a focal point of attention in the U.S. and around the world. But that bright Bob Dylan flame was already burning in him in his apprentice days, and if you got close enough to him you could feel it. According to Shelton, John Hammond offered Dylan a recording contract even before he heard him sing!

(Hammond had, however, watched Dylan play harmonica. In other words, he'd seen him perform, and that was enough. If Hammond had gone on to audition Dylan formally, he might have gotten caught up in thinking the kid wasn't ready yet, as other record producers had done around that time. But Hammond—who also discovered Billie Holiday and, later, Bruce Springsteen—had the wisdom to follow his heart.)

On the East Orange tape, Dylan sings uninspired versions of a Jesse Fuller song, a Reverend Gary Davis song, and a number of Woody Guthrie songs. His best performance is of a song that has little to do with the image he's trying to project: a pop/country tune called "Remember Me." Dylan puts some feeling into it, perhaps because he's less self-conscious about how he "should" be singing it, and perhaps also because there actually was a girl back in Minneapolis he wanted to be remembered by.

The brief Indian Neck Folk Festival tape is the earliest recording of Dylan in front of an audience. He's surprisingly self-assured; his confidence is particularly evident in his timing—all the songs on the tape are talking blues (written by Guthrie), a difficult medium in which timing and rapport with the audience are everything. Dylan sings them with the relaxed power of a Pete Seeger; he sings as though the audience were good friends with whom he's been having an ongoing dialog for twenty years. His guitar and harmonica are as full of personality as his voice, and serve as a rhythmic drone that pulls in any portion of anyone's attention that might be straying, so that all the energy of the crowd stays focused on the performer. We know from contemporary accounts (and later performances) that Dylan alternated between stage fright and tremendous poise; here he offers an example of the latter.

Another sort of record besides the tapes is photographs. *Baby Let Me Follow You Down* includes four photos of Dylan from Indian Neck, two performing (he looks intense and a little worried before he opens his mouth, intense and happy when he's actually singing) and two hanging out in the crowd (looks lonely). There's also a very poetic photograph, probably taken in Cambridge a little later that summer, of Dylan alone, looking wistful and deep and waiflike. The Rolling Stone Press volume called *Dylan*, a big coffee-table picture book with text by Jonathan Cott, includes a variety of 1961 photos: a classic folksinger pose, eyes closed, serious look on his face, strumming the guitar, supposedly taken at a Gerde's hoot; a marvelously baby-faced shot of him in action at Indian Neck; a shot of him in the instantly-famous black corduroy cap (one of his most obvious and effective stage props; it contributed to his off-stage image as well) playing harmonica with Karen Dalton and Fred Neil at the Cafe Wha?; a couple of extraordinary shots of Dylan the clown, pulling up his baggy pants and posing with cap, boots, guitar, and harmonica—Cott's caption reads, "part Huck Finn, part Charlie Chaplin, and part Woody Guthrie" (these photos are especially valuable in helping us experience across the years the non-musical, nonverbal aspects of his presence); the photo of him with Victoria Spivey that appears on the back of his 1972 album *New Morning* ("a poor little baby," she called him, "a tiny little thing"); four great shots of Dylan at the sessions for his first album,

Hammond looking avuncular; and a couple of other undated photos that could be from 1961 including a very rare shot of Dylan (with his girlfriend Suze Rotolo) wearing glasses. Another major but invisible aspect of his stage presentation was his choice from early on not to wear glasses despite his myopia. He didn't wear contact lenses either in the early days, and I don't know if he wears them now. So we must assume that he couldn't actually see his audiences very well, and that his experience on stage was shaped by that special fog of uncorrected near-sightedness in which other people's gestures and expressions are lost and the world becomes small and personal and closed. A lonely place, but perhaps also a powerful place for a person who believes very strongly in himself.

Dylan expresses awareness of photographs as a kind of recorded performance on the Minnesota hotel tape, when he enthusiastically says to Tony Glover, "Hey man, you oughta see some pictures of me. I'm not kidding! Mm. I look like Marlon Brando, James Dean or somebody. You oughta see me. I got this blue turtleneck sweater on. All kinds of pictures of me. Without a guitar. Or else you can just see the top of it, you know."

The "Minnesota party tape," from May 1961, contains a large selection of material. At least 10 of the 25 songs are Guthrie songs; probably more, since Dylan learned many of the traditional songs he was doing at this time by listening to tapes of Guthrie performing (the Gleasons had a huge library of such tapes). There are no Dylan-written songs here. For the most part the tape is pleasant but unspirited. One of the few really powerful performances on the tape is Reverend Gary Davis's "Death Don't Have No Mercy," which Dylan plays and sings with real passion. Unfortunately he stops abruptly after two verses, perhaps because (as his comments indicate) his purpose in playing the song is to teach a friend the chords. The contrast between this and most of the other songs makes me think that the blandness of the tape doesn't have to do with Dylan's abilities at the time but with a kind of self-consciousness. He seems to sing more powerfully, certainly with less inhibition, when all he's trying to do is demonstrate chords. (What is he trying to do the rest of the time? I don't know. But I suspect it has to do with making an impression, projecting some sort of image. Dylan was back with his college-town friends, after his first months in New York City. He'd just had his twentieth birthday.)

I do find the version of Guthrie's "Pastures of Plenty" that ends the tape extremely moving. It's not at all dramatic, almost mumbled, and it can take a few listenings to get into the mood of it, but it comes across to me as achingly human, perhaps an indirect expression of Dylan's feelings about Woody, his feelings about spending time with a crippled hero whose spirit is still there but who can no longer sing or speak clearly or even walk around very much, a loved one in constant pain. Dylan starts by boasting about how Woody taught him the song (probably false) and then says, "once he told me I sing it better than anybody." The latter boast is probably true, Woody probably did tell him that, and this seems to humble Dylan, suddenly makes Woody real to him instead of an object, a prize brought back from the big city to show off with. And, humbled, Dylan starts singing and playing from a place deep inside him, almost in a trance.

All of the recordings from this "student" period are of interest to the student of Dylan, to anyone looking for clues as to how he became the performer and songwriter and musical hero he was soon to be. Listening to him play harmonica on the title track of Harry Belafonte's *Midnight Special* album, we get insight into how constraining the world of commercial music was to him, with its careful arrangements and "professional" recording techniques and values. It would have been impossible for him to "sell out" to this world if he'd ever wanted to; he didn't have the patience or the humility, and he valued his own spirit too highly. He could never have fit in.

On the Riverside Church WRVR tape from late July we find Dylan singing and playing guitar with real subtlety and power (particularly on "Handsome Molly"), displaying some of the inventiveness and keen musical awareness that will come to characterize his performances throughout his career. It's also nice to have on tape an extended example of Dylan perversely winning over an audience by acting helpless and spending long minutes between songs trying to fix his coat-hanger harmonica holder with a borrowed knife. His timing is exquisite. "I really ain't no comedian," he mutters, as the crowd howls with laughter and the announcer tells the radio audience, "I wish we had television."

The next tape is a club performance in early September, at the Gaslight, and again there's none of the self-consciousness and resultant flatness of performance that we hear on the various home (and party) tapes. The challenge of a live audience seems to press

Dylan into a more alert, intense state of awareness (not always, of course; but it's striking just how intense that state can be when it does come over him).

On this tape, for the first time, we hear Dylan singing some of his own compositions: "Bear Mountain," "Song to Woody," "Man on the Street." He also does a very affecting version of a traditional song called "He Was a Friend of Mine."

Dylan shifts his vocal and instrumental style for each song on the tape, sometimes in very subtle but significant ways. "Song to Woody" pushes the vocal forward by pulling the guitar back; individual words of the song are stretched or compressed, not just for lyrical effect but as part of the musical arrangement, the unique melody and rhythm of this particular performance of the song. With techniques like these Dylan leaves room for every performance of a song to have a different shape and convey a feeling unique to that moment.

Dylan plays a few notes of harmonica at the start of the Gaslight version of "Song to Woody," then puts the instrument aside until the very end, and those three seconds of mouth harp at the end of the performance tie the whole song together...and offer an early taste of a certain sound Dylan creates with the harmonica, the same sound that pierces the heart of everyone who hears *Bringing It All Back Home* or "Just Like a Woman," the sound that has caused audiences through the years to clap and cheer whenever Dylan starts playing his harmonica on stage.

Other sorts of Dylan harmonica can be heard on three tracks from Carolyn Hester's album *Carolyn Hester* (recorded Sept. 30, 1961) and on four tracks from *Victoria Spivey: Three Kings and a Queen*, Volumes 1 and 2 (recorded Oct. 21, 1961). This is loose, high-spirited music (unlike the Belafonte session); Dylan is free to express himself creatively, and he does, with a vengeance. He blows wild and woolly, darts all over the place, and shows a surprising facility for working with and stimulating other musicians while at the same time pushing forward his own personality boisterously and unflinchingly. (There is, incidentally, a charming duet with Dave Van Ronk on Woody Guthrie's "Car Car" included on the Gaslight tape; Dylan's harmonica work behind Danny Kalb on "Mean Ol' Southern" on the Riverside tape is also a pure delight.)

What is particularly impressive, and revealing, is the unselfconscious blackness of Dylan's harmonica playing with Big Joe

Williams and Victoria Spivey on the Spivey albums. For a white kid to play with black blues singers—at their invitation—was all but unheard of in 1961; for a white kid to play with this much soul and sheer ballsiness is still remarkable. Part of the reason is clearly that Williams really dug Dylan and encouraged him, gave him a lot of space. The rest of the story is that Dylan had a genius for the blues, as these recordings (especially "Wichita" and "Sitting on Top of the World") reveal. It must have given Dylan a lot of confidence in himself as an American musician to be so warmly embraced early in his career by the likes of Woody Guthrie, Victoria Spivey, and Big Joe Williams.

The final tape (that I know of) of Bob Dylan prior to recording his first album is a partial recording of the Carnegie Chapter Hall concert, November 4, 1961. The tape is of good sound quality, Dylan tells some funny stories (accompanied by appropriate guitar doodling), and the performances are energetic and entertaining. But there's a funny kind of distance here, very different from the intimacy of the Gaslight performances. It's very possible that this is something that varied from show to show, depending on his mood and the circumstances around him and the alcohol level of his blood (too much, not enough, just right—Dylan's tendency to drink before performing, in 1961 and subsequently, is well-documented). But it may also have to do with his success (the review, the record contract) and his nervousness about how the other people in his circle might feel about his "good luck." In any case, Dylan's feelings about his audience, and his need to protect himself in some way from their (presumed) love or hatred or both, were to be a major influence on his live performances from this time forward. He learned to take his own discomfort and kind of ride on it, as an artistic force, and to some extent he does that in these Carnegie Chapter Hall performances. He's a man in motion, and it's attractive. And at the same time one gets the impression from this tape that this is a performer who doesn't know who he is right now, or who he really wants to be.

4.

" 'He [John Hammond] asked me what I do,' Bob told a friend a short time later, 'and I said I've got about twenty songs I want to record. Some stuff I've written, some stuff I've discovered, and some stuff I stole, that's about it.' "
—Sy & Barbara Ribakove, in *Folk-Rock: The Bob Dylan Story*

"There was a violent, angry emotion running through me then. I just played the guitar and harmonica and sang those songs and that was it. Mr. Hammond asked me if I wanted to sing any of them over again and I said no. I can't see myself singing the same song twice in a row. That's terrible."
—Bob Dylan, 1962

Bob Dylan recorded his first album in New York City in two days: November 20 and 22, 1961. Two of the thirteen songs are Bob Dylan originals, which meant, in the tradition of Woody Guthrie and folk music in general, that he wrote the lyrics and borrowed the tunes. Seven others are by black singers or have their roots in traditional black music, two are traditional country music songs (rural white

27

American), and two were originally English ballads. Dylan sings and plays guitar and harmonica and is the only performer on the album. John Hammond produced the record; he may have made the decision as to which of the twenty or so songs they recorded actually went on the album. One gets the impression that Hammond encouraged Dylan and tried to help him feel at ease in the studio and warned him not to pop his p's, and otherwise stayed out of his way. Dylan's girlfriend Suze Rotolo, whom he'd met at the Riverside Church broadcast in July, was also at the sessions.

I have said that a performance, whether on stage or in a recording studio, is always "live" from the artist's point of view in that it occurs at a particular moment, and all the variables involved, such as the particular way the fingers hit the guitar strings or the amount of breath used to sing a word or phrase, act to express not only the pre-written song but also the performer's feelings and state of mind at that moment. (Arguably what is expressed is not only the performer's subjective experience but also certain "objective" elements that characterize the moment of performance, from the temperature of the room to the mood of the times.)

I need to add, however, that modern recording studio techniques can take away the "live" quality of a recording session, by building up a recording piece by piece so that musicians are not in each other's presence or singers never actually sing an entire song at one time. When this occurs, as it commonly does in the 1980s, I would not describe the resultant piece of music as a performance in the sense in which I use the word. It seems to me more closely related to a composition.

Of course the act of composing also involves spontaneity and serendipity, just as the act of performing requires a certain amount of calculation and forethought; my point is simply that when I include Dylan's studio recordings under the heading of performances, I do so because by and large he has chosen to perform live or as live as possible in the studio environment. He records his songs, often, in one or two takes, with musicians who usually play at the same time Dylan is singing (and who in many cases have not had a chance to rehearse the song before arriving at the studio). He does relatively little overdubbing and building of recordings in layers (something the Beatles did habitually and very effectively). He seems to prefer to treat the studio as though it were the stage of a coffeehouse, with the people who will eventually buy and listen to the record sitting out there at the tables, challenging him to get and hold their attention right now.

And this brings up the essential and obvious difference between live performance and studio recordings, even for a "primitive" recording artist such as Dylan: on stage the audience is in front of you and their reactions are immediate (albeit open to interpretation: sometimes from the stage fascination is mistaken for stupor, and vice versa). In the recording studio you have to imagine, project, the audience. The audience is there for the performer (else performance is impossible) but it is perceived through some sense other than the five physical ones.

If there is something missing on this debut album, and I think there is, it is probably a strong sense on the musician's part of who his audience is, who he's singing to, who he is in relation to us. Up to now, his ambition has had a strong focus: to be accepted as a folk performer, to get on stage and be noticed, to move people with his performances, and to get to the point where he'll have the chance to make a record. Ten months after arriving in New York, he has achieved all these goals. Now what? He's in an alien environment—alone in a recording studio for the first time—singing to an invisible audience. He does a good job; shows off what he's learned; shares some deep feelings. But beyond the standard young man's ambition to cut a romantic figure, he's not sure what he wants to accomplish here.

The result is an attractive but somehow indistinct album. "Bob Dylan"—the myth, the persona, the larger-than-life figure—has not yet arrived. Hints of what's to come are plentiful, at least in hindsight, but mostly what we hear is an interesting but immature white blues singer (a la Van Ronk or Von Schmidt but with less grittiness, individuality, character). He has a weird and obviously contrived accent. He looks very young and sings a lot of songs about death.

It's interesting, but not really peculiar, that a twenty-year-old singer would fill his first album with songs about dying ("In My Time of Dying," "Fixing to Die," "See That My Grave Is Kept Clean," plus references to the singer's death in "Man of Constant Sorrow," "Highway 51," "House of the Rising Sun," and—humorously—"You're No Good," and to someone else's death in "Pretty Peggy-O"). Teenagers are typically concerned, sometimes obsessed, with death, and not necessarily because of any close experiences with it…often, perhaps, because of a lack of experience with it. (There is no evidence that Dylan was seriously ill as a teenager, as reported on the back of his first album, other than that Dylan told Shelton—who wrote the liner notes under a pseudonym—he had been. Dylan told Shelton a great many things, a number of them demonstrably false.)

A young man wishing to project a romantic image of himself will generally, I think, reach for images of sex, hard travelling, dissipation (alcohol, drugs, nights without sleep), and death. Along with death, we find plenty of hard travelling on this album ("Man of Constant Sorrow," "Highway 51," "Freight Train Blues," "Talking New York," "Song to Woody"), but surprisingly little booze or sex. Both subjects appear in "House of the Rising Sun," but not in a way that makes the singer seem particularly daring or bad-assed. "Baby Let Me Follow You Down" is certainly about sexual desire, but the lyrics are quite respectful and the voice isn't the least bit lascivious (in contrast to Dave Van Ronk's version of the same song, called "Baby Let Me Lay It On You"). About the only sexy line on the album is "when you get a crazy notion [of] jumping all over me" in "You're No Good." Dylan may well have been as much of a womanizer in his Village days as his idol Woody Guthrie had been, but that's not an image he chooses to project on this recording.

It's interesting to note that all of the songs on the album speak in the first person (unlike many folk ballads which tell a story in the third person), and all but two are about the person who is singing ("Gospel Plow" and "Pretty Peggy-O" are the exceptions). Not all of these characters are meant to be Dylan, certainly—"House of the Rising Sun" is even told from a woman's viewpoint (appropriately, but still an unusual thing for a male singer to do). Rather it is as though he feels that what songs like these have to offer is the opportunity to insert yourself, as singer and as listener, into someone else's experience.

In two songs, the ones he wrote himself, Dylan speaks directly of his own experience. The first of these, "Talking New York," is noteworthy for many details of performance: the way he puts a little laugh into his voice, the way harmonica and guitar are used to keep the narrative going, his effectiveness at communicating irony and at engaging the listener's sympathy, and, as always, his timing. But it is the song on the album I find most difficult to listen to again and again, partly of course because it's spoken—proof, if you will, that it isn't just Dylan's words that appeal to me but the way those words sound when he sings them. The real strengths and weaknesses of the song, however, are in what it says and doesn't say about Dylan's experience.

"Talking New York" is appealing because it conjures up events and images very clearly with just a few words, and serves as effective, seemingly modest myth-making: small-town kid comes into the big city, walks through the snow with nowhere to go, ends up in the Village, is rejected by a hypocritical club-owner, gets some work but is underpaid, finally gets a break but decides to leave the big city because people there are too unkind. You can't help but like the guy after you hear him say "I froze right to the bone." With this song, and the youthful, confident, dour, amused, corduroy-capped face on the album cover, the Bob Dylan myth begins to introduce itself to the record-buying public.

What I don't like about the song, I suppose, is its hypocrisy. In effect, Dylan is claiming to have been mistreated in New York, when from what we know the opposite is the case—he was taken in and cared for from the beginning; for Bob Dylan, at least, New York was the most hospitable town there ever could be.

It seems likely, again despite what Dylan told Shelton, that "Talking New York" was written around the time it was recorded, and that it reflects Dylan's paranoia about what people might be saying about his sudden success and, even more specifically, reflects his conflict with his girlfriend's mother. Scaduto reports that Dylan at this time was talking about leaving town and was trying to get Suze to go with him, over her mother's objections. This might explain the ingratitude the song expresses—Dylan isn't really talking about how New York has treated him during the last ten months; he's talking about how he feels *right now*. This seems to be true of Dylan's performances in general—they communicate his immediate feelings, regardless of context or circumstance. He is not a person with a sense of history. He lives inside his own moment.

Two word tricks in this, the very first song in Dylan's book called *Lyrics*, give us insight into how he writes. In the third verse he says, "I swung on to my old guitar/Grabbed hold of a subway car." This has a nice offbeat sound to it. Notice that he's reversed the verbs in these two lines (i.e., I grabbed hold of my old guitar, swung on to a subway car). By doing so he comes up with a fresh image, a line of nonsense actually but appealing nonsense, it sounds like it means something and it has life in it. Given the way Dylan has habitually switched or forgotten song lyrics throughout his career (of course it's amazing he remembers as much as he does, given the size of his repertoire), it's quite possible the lines got jumbled by accident, at least the first time. In any case, it works, and it demonstrates Dylan's poet instincts, his willingness to make free with the language.

A more significant and subtle trick occurs in the next-to-last verse:

> Now a very great man once said
> That some people rob you with a fountain pen
> It didn't take too long to find out
> Just what he was talking about.
> A lot of people don't have much food on their table,
> But they got a lot of forks 'n' knives,
> And they gotta cut somethin'.

What's amazing about this is that Dylan communicates his feelings so well (not necessarily on paper, but when you hear the lyrics performed), that you understand intuitively what he wants to say and therefore you tend to believe that he's said it (and said it well). But in fact, here and in many instances in Dylan songs from throughout his career, a close look at the words shows that what we hear may not be what they say.

The great man is Woody Guthrie and the reference is to his song "Pretty Boy Floyd"; people who rob you with a fountain pen are, for example, dishonest lawyers and bankers who take people's property unjustly (and often by trickery). Dylan uses this to lead into a similar image, "people [who] don't have much food on their table, but they got a lot of forks 'n' knives, and they gotta cut something." What we pick up from this, quite accurately in terms of what I believe Dylan intended, is people who resent you having something they don't have, and attack you (probably verbally—they "cut" you) unjustly as a response. What we don't pick up, at least I never did before, is that Dylan has pulled quite a reversal on Guthrie here. Guthrie's irony was aimed at the haves who take from the have-nots; Dylan's is just the opposite, it addresses the have-nots' resentment of the haves. By any reasonable interpretation of the language, "people [who] don't have much food on their table" are poor people (even if it's metaphorical, and what they're poor in is, say, musical talent). On the face of it, Dylan is criticizing poor people for their resentment of the rich. Quite a different emphasis from what Woody Guthrie and Pretty Boy Floyd had in mind!

I don't suggest that this is intentional on his part. On the contrary, I use it as an example of Dylan being in control of his communication (what we actually hear, what we think he said) but not his words. Throughout Dylan's career we will find that although he has a reputation as a master of words, his mastery is more specifically of performed language—separated from his performance, his words can lose their power and even their meaning.

The irony here is stark because of Dylan's middle lines: "It didn't take too long to find out/Just what he was talking about." No matter how you interpret Dylan's comments about people who don't have much food but gotta cut something, I doubt that a case can be made that this is "just what [Guthrie] was talking about" when he said some people rob you with a fountain pen. The similarity is actually in the type of metaphor, not at all in the content of the metaphors (what they're "about"). Dylan claims a connection that isn't there, and he does it so convincingly (because of his power as a performer, and because he really believes it's so—he hasn't noticed that the words that came out of his mouth don't express the thought that was in his mind) that we the listeners never think to question him.

A different example of this sort of peculiar use of language occurs in the last verse of "Song to Woody." The first lines are, "I'm a-leaving tomorrow but I could leave today/Somewhere down the road someday." What does it mean, that last part? I don't know. I like it when I hear it. It *feels*. It feels like going on down that road, with maybe a hint of meeting you or somebody "somewhere down the road someday." It evokes. This is what poetry and song should do, and it's quite arguable that the radical disconnection here from English as she is spoken helps to open up the imagery and let it speak the singer's heart more freely.

The next two lines give us more of the same (and it's certainly possible that the second line above is meant to attach to this sentence rather than the first, or to either or both ambiguously):

The very last thing that I'd want to do
Is to say I've been hitting some hard travelin' too.

So, does he want to say he's been hitting some hard travelin', or does he want not to say that? Literally, he doesn't want to say it—"the last thing I'd want to do" means, in our idiom, I'd prefer to do anything else, I'd avoid it at all costs. And maybe this is what Dylan means, maybe he's saying that his travelin' doesn't begin to compare with Woody's and he certainly doesn't want to suggest that it does (fair enough). Or on the other hand maybe he intends what it probably sounds like to most listeners most of the time, which is that the last thing he wants to say (in the song, to Woody) is that he identifies with him, he's been going through some of the same stuff, hitting the same roads. A literal examination of the words tells us he didn't say this, but he may have intended to and he just slipped when he said "I'd" instead of "I." Or he meant it colloquially—"I would" for "I do." That's the advantage and disadvantage of making up your own dialect—the words do mean whatever you want 'em to mean, or else (conversely) they're constantly meaning things you don't intend 'em to mean 'cause they're dancing to rules no one else knows.

Maybe Dylan even intends the ambiguity. Maybe he's aware as he sings of both possible interpretations. I doubt it—but it's possible. At any rate I'm fairly certain that, most of the time, given the choice, he'd rather create confusion than clear it up. More space for art, for what satisfies him, for sheer perversity, that way. This is a guy who in performance constantly starts singing a beat or two early or late, forcing his band to scramble to find him. The first few hundred times you might think it was just an accident.

I like what "Song to Woody" says about Dylan's experience. It speaks of a person inspired to walk in someone else's footsteps, and discovering a world of his own—*the* world, the real world that's out there—as a result. It speaks of the longing that Dylan's appreciation of Guthrie sets up in him—a longing to speak to and have something to say to the person who has spoken so powerfully to him. It's a song from the heart, and it communicates humility, true humility not pose—it's a song full of childlike wonder and love. And it's a good example of how the proper setting, in terms of melody and arrangement and vocal and instrumental performance, can transform an adequate set of words into a truly memorable song.

My favorite tracks on *Bob Dylan* are "You're No Good," "In My Time of Dying," and "Man of Constant Sorrow." "You're No Good" is one of several songs that give hints of Dylan's rock and roll sensibilities ("Highway 51" and "Freight Train Blues" are two others, the latter for the sheer raucous joy of its performance). Dylan's rhythmic sense is at the fore here, and it's startling how he manages to spit out all the words at breakneck tempo, giving firm emphasis to every syllable and extra emphasis to many of them, and finding room to play with the words, laugh, weep, tickle, and slide his voice all around them, while he's doing so. It's interesting that his first album starts with a song addressed to "the kind of woman who makes a man insane." The in-out harmonica is marvelous, and Dylan shows what he can do as a vocalist in the middle of and while creating wild cartwheels of instrumental sound.

"In My Time of Dying," learned from a Josh White album, is a moody, penetrating, haunting performance which, with rough vocals and some surprisingly adept blues guitar playing, demonstrates the transcendent power of conviction. Dylan is totally inside the song. When he sings, "Meet me, Jesus, meet me/Meet me in the middle of the air," you know he means it. Which brings up some questions made more pointed by hindsight: Why does this young Jewish beatnik sing about Jesus so much on this record, and how does he come by his seemingly authentic spiritual awareness? My best guess is that he received it like a direct transmission through black music, through the records he'd been listening to. In "Fixing to Die" he again asks Jesus "to make up my bed." In "Gospel Plow" he sings of Jesus's name, and also the enigmatic (accidental?) lyric, "Mary Mark Luke and John." In "Man of Constant Sorrow" he talks of meeting again on "God's golden shore," and finally in "See That My Grave Is Kept Clean" he gasps out, "My heart stop beating and my hands turn cold/Now I believe what the Bible told!" It's easy to say he's just singing these words because they're in the songs, but that begs the question of why he's singing these songs.

Watching Dylan perform on stage, one can see that something about him—his energy, his aura—turns very feminine when he's playing the harmonica. On a good night, it transforms him into a pure receptive spirit, right in the middle of a song. Something of this can be heard in the extremely beautiful, harmonica-dominated performance of "Man of Constant Sorrow" on the first album. Here is the angel-quality visible in some early (and not-so-early) photos of Dylan, translated into sound. The long-held vocal or harmonica note, endless breath of music with or without rhythmic counterpoint, is characteristic of Dylan's music (and, later, his filmmaking; in *Renaldo & Clara* he shows a great affinity for the unmoving camera, the hold shot, a single visual note sustained for minutes at a time, while the entire unseen universe rearranges itself around it).

Shelton believes Dylan changed the lyric in "Man of Constant Sorrow" to "Your mother says that I'm a stranger" (others had performed it "Your friends may think I'm a stranger"; Dylan in May '61 on the Minnesota party tape sang, "now you say I'm a stranger") because he felt Suze Rotolo's mother was trying to break up his relationship with Suze. Scaduto's report about Dylan wanting to leave New York and take Suze with him adds salt to a line from "Pretty Peggy-O": "What will your mother say/To know you're going away/you're never never never coming back-y-o?" And this makes us hear another line from "Pretty Peggy-O" as being addressed to Suze: "...combing back your yellow hair/You're the prettiest darn girl I've ever seen-y-o." Finally, along these lines, we can imagine a personal edge to this verse from "Highway 51": "If I don't get the gal I'm loving/Won't go down that Highway 51 no more."

A comparison of the May and November recordings of "Man of Constant Sorrow" does confirm what we might have guessed anyway, that Dylan is constantly changing the words (as well as the arrangements) of the traditional songs he performs. A nice touch is the shift from "Through this old world I'm a-bound to ramble" to "Through this open world...." The powerful lines at the end of the November recording—"If I'd knowed how bad you'd treat me/Honey I never would have come"—are probably Dylan's own, since they aren't in the May version. Unchanged is the gorgeous line about "I'm bound to ride that morning railroad," an early example of the train imagery that recurs throughout Dylan's work.

The *Bob Dylan* album was officially released four months after these recording sessions, in March of 1962. In the meantime Dylan renounced it as being no longer representative of where he was at, a pattern he would repeat with other albums in the future.

Some tapes of Dylan singing at the home of his friends the McKenzies were recorded right after the first album sessions; however the copies in circulation are too muddy and fragmentary to tell us much.

The Minnesota hotel tape, on the other hand, recorded December 22 in Minneapolis (Dylan did leave New York briefly, but Suze didn't go with him), is a treasure trove—a good quality recording of twenty-six songs, a fascinating and entertaining portrait of Dylan at the end of his "folk sponge" period. The straightforwardness of these performances sheds some backward light on the recording studio performances a month earlier, showing what a lot of effort Dylan put into his studio work, pushing himself to turn out one tour de force after another in an effort to dazzle Hammond and those future record buyers. In the Columbia studios, Dylan was performing for the first time for an audience he couldn't see. In one sense, this inspired him—he seems to put all his energy and everything he's learned into every song. But his uncertainty about what people wanted from him and what he wanted to give them makes the album less personal, less of a coherent whole; trying so hard actually gets in the way of Dylan making the kind of personal connection with his listeners that he was already achieving in his live performances.

The best tracks on the Minnesota hotel tape include a killer version of Big Joe Williams's "Baby Please Don't Go"; "Hard Times in New York Town," a Dylan original reworked from a traditional song; "Dink's Song," a fine heartfelt rendering of an old washerwoman's song, also sung by Dave Van Ronk, who seems to have been the biggest influence on Dylan at this point in terms of choice of material and certain aspects of vocal and guitar styling; and "I Was Young When I Left Home," a Dylan original that reworks "500 Miles" and several other tunes, sung uncharacteristically sweet and slow. Dylan acknowledges in a spoken rap at the beginning of "I Was Young" that the song might not be right for him, but it "must be good for somebody, this kind of song." A hint of things to come can be heard at the end when he sings, "In the wind...Lord, Lord, in the wind...Gonna make me a home out in the wind."

Another sort of performance that Dylan found himself doing during his first year in New York was the interview. Robert Shelton interviewed Dylan at Gerde's Folk City in September for his *New*

York Times article, and Dylan—despite a warning from Shelton, delivered through Suze's sister Carla Rotolo—felt called upon to embellish some of the stories he'd been telling Village friends and audiences about his background: how he recorded with Gene Vincent in Nashville, met Mance Lipscomb in Texas when he was sixteen, started travelling with a carnival when he was thirteen, and so forth.

More interesting than the tall tales Dylan felt compelled to tell is the rhythmic language of his interviews. Sometime in the fall of 1961, probably just before or after he recorded his first album, Dylan did an interview with Billy James, then a publicist at Columbia Records. A few minutes of the interview survive on tape, and it's fascinating that at times he sounds just like Dylan talking on tape more than twenty years later, same voice, same speech patterns. Even on paper, the rhythm comes through—and the context, the informality of the interview, suggests this was no pretense but represented what was or had become for Dylan a natural way of talking: "I played piano. I used to play the piano. I used to play great, great piano. Very great—I used to play the piano like Little Richard style. Only I used to play, you know, an octave higher, and everything came out— When he played, he had a big mistake. His records were great records, but they could have been greater records. His mistake was he played down too low. If he played high, everything would have compensated. You ever heard Little Richard? Ah, Little Richard, he was something else. He's a preacher now. But I played piano in his style. And I played everything high, and it amplified...."

And this revealing segment:

"I'm not a folk singer. I just sing a certain way, that's all."
"Is Woody a folk singer?"
"Woody was a folk singer. Woody was a folk singer."
"Why do you say you're not?"
"Uh, Woody was a folk singer to the point—Woody was a glorified folk singer. Woody was a man that went back—don't print this on the record—but Woody was a man who dwelled on simpleness because he was getting attention for it."

The beginning of 1962 found Dylan back in New York. As a result of recording an album with two of his own songs on it, Dylan began a relationship with a music publishing company, Leeds Music, and early in 1962 he recorded seven songs for them as a songwriting demo (so other people could hear the songs and consider performing them): "Hard Times in New York Town," "Talking Bear Mountain Picnic Massacre Blues," "Man on the Street," "Poor Boy Blues," "Rambling, Gambling Willie," "Ballad for a Friend," and "Standing on the Highway." The songs are mostly pedestrian reworkings of familiar folk and blues themes, sometimes made more appealing by their performances; they don't give the impression that this young man has anything special to say.

But that was to change rather quickly. In late January Dylan wrote a song called "The Death of Emmett Till." In February the first issue of a mimeographed magazine called *Broadside* appeared, devoted to publication and dissemination of new topical songs. Dylan's "Talking John Birch Paranoid Blues" was included in the first issue. Two more topical songs by Dylan, "Ballad of Donald White" and "Let Me Die in My Footsteps," are believed to have been written in February. Then one night in April, Bob Dylan wrote a song called "Blowin' in the Wind." It seems fair to say his apprenticeship, his student period, officially ended that night.

III. Messenger

April 1962 — July 1963

"I wanted just to sing...a song to sing. And there came a point where I couldn't sing anything. I had to write what I wanted to say, because what I wanted to say, nobody else was writing. I couldn't find it anywhere. If I could have, I probably would never have started writing."
—Bob Dylan, 1984

5.

In *Renaldo & Clara* David Blue, who serves as a kind of one-man Greek chorus for the film, rapping into the camera a delightful, endless monolog about early days in the Village while playing pinball intently, tells a story about Dylan asking him to help him write out the words and chords to "Blowin' in the Wind," which he'd either just written or was writing on the spot. They were in a coffeehouse called the Commons or the Fat Black Pussycat and it was a Monday night, so as soon as the song was written down they rushed over to Gerde's and Dylan played the song for Gil Turner, who was the MC for the Monday night hoots. According to Blue, Turner said, "Jesus Christ, I've never heard anything like that in my entire life! That's the most incredible song!" and ran right up on stage and sang it, and the crowd went crazy, and Dylan stood by the bar and grinned.

It's part of being a performer that you learn from and are directed by the audience's response. That doesn't mean you follow them or feel an obligation to give them what they want. But if you do comedy, you notice what gets a laugh—which jokes, what sort of delivery. Timing is critical to good performance, and a certain amount of a performer's sense of timing may be innate, may even be appealing precisely because it's so odd, so off-the-wall, as was the case with Dylan from his earliest performances. But that sense of timing must also be based to a large degree on what the performer has learned by actually being himself, doing his act, in front of audiences.

The other sort of response that shapes a performer's work is his or her own response to the work. This may take the form of ideas about whether I did that well or not or whether that's a good direction to go in, but there are other, non-mental responses. A singer may find himself or herself really able to get into a particular song in a powerful, creatively satisfying way—without necessarily "liking" the song more than his other material. Of course, once he starts finding the song such a fulfilling creative vehicle, he starts liking it more and more, because of the satisfaction it brings to perform it.

When Dylan started writing topical songs in 1962, the universe gave him strong encouragement, both in terms of other people's response—they were enthusiastic, they praised him, they treated him as something special and genuinely wanted to hear his latest work—and in terms of his own response, which took the form of a tremendous energy. Suddenly he found himself writing songs all the time. He was inspired, possessed. It wasn't only the stimulus of other people's attention—clearly it was also that he had found a vehicle, a voice, for letting out thoughts and feelings that had been dammed up inside him, and for letting through, expressing, the energy that he could feel in the air and in the people and the scene around him.

His writing was itself a performance. Poetry is historically a performing art, with roots that go back long before written communication; but in general the image of the modern poet is not of someone who walks out into the street with his latest pages to read them to the world. That, however, is what writing was like for Dylan, particularly in 1962. Some songs were written only to share, not to keep. On a radio show in May 1962 Dylan said to Pete Seeger, "I write a lot of stuff, in fact I wrote five songs last night; but I gave all the papers away, someplace. It was in a place called the Bitter End. Some were just about what was happening on the stage. I would never sing them anyplace, they were just for myself and for some other people. They might say, 'write a song about that,' and I'd do it."

He started writing so he would have something meaningful to perform, but the writing itself became a performance for which he received applause (and payment; in July he signed a contract with a music publisher, Witmark, for $1000, the most money he'd earned from his music to that point). His process of writing was similar to the song-gathering he'd been doing during his folk apprenticeship, in the sense that it was intuitive (he spoke often of feeling that the song was already there and he just let it come through him) and that he put together songs from a great many sources, freely borrowing melodies and lyrics from traditional songs and from his contemporaries,whatever he could find to help him say what he wanted to say.

What made it work was that, just as his earlier enthusiasm for listening had been authentic, a compulsion, an expression of his true self, something he couldn't help but do, so he now found himself almost helpless in the face of his urge and need to write. But in both cases, I believe, his underlying image of himself was not "folk scholar" or "songwriter" but "performer," and the study and the writing both were preoccupations set off by and ultimately in service to his needs as a performer.

In any case Dylan's songwriting was, during this period, not only his most visible and successful public activity to date but also a primary vehicle for his growth as a performer. The recordings from spring 1962 on display a greater relaxation and depth than the recordings of performances from the previous year, and this is so whether Dylan is singing his own songs or singing traditional material. This maturation seems to be an expression of a self-confidence and self-awareness that grew by leaps and bounds as he discovered that he had something to say—something more immediate than "listen to this great song I dug up"—and that people wanted to hear it. It gave him access to a deeper level of himself. The passion in 1961's "Fixing to Die" and "Gospel Plow" is sincere but superficial compared to what Dylan is able to give of himself in such classic 1962 songs and performances as "Don't Think Twice" and "Hard Rain."

The transformation is already evident on the tape of the May 1962 *Broadside* radio program, when Dylan sings his topical song "The Death of Emmett Till." The performances of "Ballad of

Donald White" and "Blowin' in the Wind" on the same tape are rather lackluster, but "Emmett Till" is riveting. Dylan mentions before playing it that it's the first song he's written in a minor key, and possibly that has something to do with his enthusiasm for it—certainly the richness of the vocal performance, and the effectiveness with which melody and rhythm support the dramatic language of the song, are major factors in the performance's power. Sometimes it seems that Dylan's attack on the guitar, like the attack of a classical pianist, expresses his conscious commitment to or bored disinterest in a given song at a given time (the demo recording of "Emmett Till," made in December 1962, sounds flat and lifeless; Dylan's voice is without character and the guitar is strummed listlessly and repetitively).

"The Death of Emmett Till" is about a black teenager from Chicago who was murdered for kicks by white men in a Mississippi town; the murderers were tried and acquitted by a jury some of whose members, according to Dylan, were participants in the crime. The song is written in the form of a story—like "House of the Rising Sun" and "Talking New York" on the first album except this has a much stronger narrative quality and is told in the third person. Dylan follows the narrative with a moral statement: a startlingly direct and vivid exhortation to the listener to "speak out against this kind of thing" (if you can't, he says, "your arms and legs must be in shackles and chains"). He concludes by saying that this song is a reminder of how things are, and how much better they could be if "us folks that thinks alike gave all we could give." Like Guthrie, he appeals for fairness and human rights by appealing to love of nation—"we could make this great land of ours a greater place to live."

With this song, and this performance, Dylan finally assimilates what attracted him about Guthrie: the dignity and commitment of his expression, and his ability to unite the strong feelings evoked by melodic and rhythmic music with the strong feelings evoked by stories of hard times, injustice, and solidarity. I say "assimilates" because this is no longer an attempt to imitate. Dylan is fired up, he cares deeply about what he's saying (at the moment of writing the song, presumably, and certainly at the moment of singing it for this radio show), and he intuitively brings together what he's learned about singing and playing and writing to get his message, his feelings, across. And he has the courage, again reminiscent of

Guthrie, not only to bring the listener right into the tragic event, but then to go beyond identification by connecting the listener with the event: if you can't speak out, you are dead yourself. There is also a hint of the Biblical prophet here, the fiery-tongued preacher.

Dylan, from the *Broadside* radio tape: "The song was there before me, before I came along. I just sort of came down and took it down with a pencil, but it was all there before I came around." Gil Turner, from the same tape: "I feel about Bob Dylan's songs very often that Bob is actually a kind of folk mind, and represents all the people around; all the ideas current just filter down and they come out in poetry."

Dylan's development as a performer and songwriter, and the evolution of his self-image, are hard to trace during 1962. His second album is made up of selections from a year of recording sessions, starting in April 1962 and ending in April 1963. Many outtakes from these sessions are in circulation, but there is confusion about the dates and circumstances of recording. As for live appearances, Shelton says Dylan "did very little stage work" during 1962. The stage recordings that exist are believed to be from the following gigs: Gerde's Folk City, spring 1962; the Finjan Club, Montreal, July 2; a hootenanny at Carnegie Chapter Hall, September 22; and the Gaslight Cafe, fall 1962. (He also did a benefit concert for the Congress on Racial Equality in February, and was part of a "Travelling Hootenanny" that played Town Hall in New York October 5; no tapes are circulating from these concerts.)

There is not much accurate information about when his songs from this period were written. Dylan's own songbooks, *Writings and Drawings* and *Lyrics*, are notoriously unreliable—there are so many errors of chronology that the books are useless as far as indicating when or in what order songs were created. Copyright information has been researched but is also misleading, since songs were often copyrighted long after they were written. Dylan recorded demo versions of many of his 1962-63 songs for his song publisher, Witmark; but the dates of these informal recording sessions (done at the Witmark office?) are unknown, and again it's clear that many songs were recorded long after he'd written them.

It does seem certain that Dylan wrote many songs at this time that were not recorded, not as demos nor in performance nor in the studio; and it's quite likely, given how unpredictable he is in this area, that some of these were major songs. "Tomorrow Is a Long

Time" is an example of an exceptional Dylan song from 1962-63 that as far as we know he never chose to record in any of his Columbia studio sessions, although many lesser songs were recorded, sometimes more than once.

There is ample evidence that, already in the spring of 1962 and increasingly throughout the year, Dylan was very highly regarded by his contemporaries and by followers of the folk music scene for the quantity and quality of his songwriting. Yet it was not until 1963 that Dylan began to focus primarily on his own material in public appearances and in the recording studio. Close to half the songs he made studio recordings of in 1962 were traditional (largely blues) rather than his own songs; far more than half the songs he does on the performance tapes are non-originals. Apparently he was still uncertain about whether people would accept a performer doing mostly his own songs. But it's also clear from his performances that he does the old blues songs (very few Guthrie songs remained in his repertoire at this point) because he loves to sing them. He no longer seems to be so interested in what people think of him (as he was on the first album); instead the emphasis is on free expression of his feelings.

April 25, 1962, the first known *Freewheelin'* session, is noteworthy for "Let Me Die in My Footsteps." This song was taken off the *Freewheelin'* album at the last minute, probably because Dylan and Hammond preferred to make space for some excellent newer songs that had just been recorded, and perhaps also because it was thought that this song, "Hard Rain," and "Talking World War III" all on the same album would be too much (since all three have to do with fear of nuclear war). Nat Hentoff calls it "one of Dylan's more mesmeric songs" in an early draft of his liner notes for the album, and quotes Dylan as saying, "I'd like to say that here is one song I am really glad I made a record of. I don't consider anything that I write political. But even if I couldn't hardly sing a note, or even if I couldn't stand on my feet, this is one song that people won't have to look at me or even listen closely or even like me, to understand."

"Let Me Die in My Footsteps" is Dylan's first anthem, in the sense that "Pastures of Plenty" and "This Land Is Your Land" and "This Train Is Bound for Glory" are anthems—songs people can unite around, that can be sung as an expression of belonging, to a nation or a faith or a cause. The song is a refusal to go into a fallout

shelter or into the fallout shelter mentality ("I will not go down
under the ground/'Cause somebody tells me that death's coming
round"), a fist shaken at the death in the soul that fear brings, in
effect a statement that I would rather risk dying in the flesh than
choose a living death, cut off from what gives life its value. Dylan's
ubiquitous "wind" makes another early appearance:

> There's been rumors of war and wars that have been
> The meaning of life has been lost in the wind
> And some people thinking that the end is close by
> 'Stead of learning to live they are learning to die
> Let me die in my footsteps
> Before I go down under the ground.

After six verses of "I," Dylan turns to his audience and addresses them directly: "Go out in your country where the land
meets the sun"—stating that if you make contact with the beauty of
this natural land, you also will choose to "die in your footsteps
before you go down under the ground." The tune is, as Hentoff
says, mesmeric, and Dylan's understated performance leaves a
lasting impression.

The Gerde's tape (late April or early May) and the Finjan tape
(early July) are valuable windows on Dylan's progress from prodigy
to artist. On the Gerde's tape he does "Blowin' in the Wind,"
"Corrina, Corrina," and "Honey Just Allow Me One More
Chance," all songs that he will soon record in the studio, plus
"Talking New York" from the first album and Big Joe Williams's
"Deep Ellem Blues." In the introduction to "Blowin' in the Wind"
he is already feeling the need to get out of or stay out of any box
someone might want to put him in: "This here is just a—It's a—It
ain't a protest song or anything like that, 'cause I don't write
protest songs...I'm just writing it as something sorta that's something to be said for somebody, by somebody." And then the harmonica starts and blows words and thoughts away, clearing a space
for the song to happen.

"Deep Ellem Blues," like "Times Ain't What They Used to Be"
on the Minnesota party tape a year earlier, is a catchall for fragments and verses from various blues songs. Dylan seems in 1962 to
be living in a musical world similar to that inhabited by the delta
bluesmen, where lines of twelve-bar poetry and guitar runs and (in

Dylan's case) harmonica riffs migrate from song to song, recombining and reforming like molecules of DNA. I hear the "Deep Ellem" harmonica figure in Dylan's October recording of "Going to New Orleans," for example. One verse that must have particularly caught Dylan's fancy shows up here in "Corrina, Corrina" ("You've got a 32 special built on a cross of wood/I've got a 38-20, gal that's twice as good"), again in "Going to New Orleans" in October, and again in "Kind-Hearted Woman" on the Gaslight tape, each time with the pronouns changed. The first verse of Dylan's "Kind-Hearted Woman" is from the Robert Johnson song of the same name, but the Johnson-like guitar intro is from some other song. The last verse ("Sometimes I'm thinking you're too good to die/Other times I'm thinking you oughta be buried alive") is one Dylan also used in "Times Ain't What They Used to Be," and it will show up again in altered form in "Black Crow Blues" in 1964.

This game of tracing bits and pieces can be played endlessly; the point is that Dylan does in fact save lines and riffs and chord sequences like bits of string exactly as certain great blues singers did, not consciously but just strewn around the back room of his musical awareness. When he sits down idly with a guitar, talking to someone and picking (we hear little bits of this in *Renaldo & Clara* and other Dylan films, and on the tapes of some interviews), this is what comes out. It is the music (word music, also) of the back of his mind. It is also the source (not just the blues, now, but all songs, Guthrie, folk, country, rock, gospel, anything or any piece of something that's happened to stick in there) that feeds his writing process, both for music and words. A turn of phrase, or just a fragment of a turn of phrase, is enough. For example, Woody Guthrie's version of "Trail of the Buffalo," which Dylan sang in early 1961, includes the line, "Our trip it was a pleasant one." In 1967 a related phrase, "My trip hasn't been a pleasant one," shows up in Dylan's song "Drifter's Escape." My point is that the language we invent, like the melodies we invent, is most often a transmutation (more often than not unconscious) of language we've already heard, spoken, loved. The richness of Dylan's language and music is partly a reflection of the richness of the music and language he's taken into himself, and partly a function of his unselfconsciousness about using whatever comes to mind—and mostly a gift, a talent, handled with skill and grace, a mystery, a gift of tongues.

Wonderful things turn up in those bits of string the mind

sticks away for future reference. Mostly they happen off-mike, of course, but we get tastes of the process. On the Finjan tape, July 1962, "Muleskinner Blues" starts with a jangly guitar strum that is clearly the opening of "Subterranean Homesick Blues" (1965). "Highway 51" on the Carnegie Hootenanny tape, September 1962, features a guitar riff that has evolved from the version on the first album (which he borrowed from the Everly Brothers' "Wake Up Little Suzie") and is starting to sound a lot like the brilliant, ominous guitar figure that runs through "It's Alright, Ma" (1965).

It's impossible to mention all of the impressive performances on Dylan's tapes and albums (and will become more difficult as we go along). The Finjan tape, similar to the early party tapes in that it's a small group of people, and Dylan's aware of the tape recorder and is trying to think of interesting songs to play, has many delights, particularly an electrifying version of Muddy Waters's "Two Trains Running," a fine loose rendering of "Let Me Die in My Footsteps," and a haunting fragment of Robert Johnson's "Rambling on My Mind." On "Two Trains" Dylan sings, "I'm afraid of everybody/and I can't trust myself." The tape also features one of Dylan's most powerful original blues (if you can draw the line between blues songs he writes and ones he assembles from existing songs; definitely a matter of degree, as is true with most blues singers): "Quit Your Low Down Ways." "Quit Your Low Down Ways" is also one of at least eight songs recorded at Columbia Studios July 9, a week after the Finjan appearance, three of which ended up on the *Freewheelin'* album.

"Quit Your Low Down Ways" is a great vehicle for Dylan:

> Well, you can read out your Bible
> You can fall down on your knees and pray, pretty Mama,
> But it ain't gonna do no good.
> You're gonna need
> You're gonna need my help someday
> If y'all can't quit your sinning
> Please, quit your low down ways.

This verse, which opens and closes the song, is lifted from Kokomo Taylor's recording of "Milk Cow Blues." On the Finjan tape, the other verses are all recognizably from various traditional blues songs. But at the recording session a week later those middle verses have been replaced with new verses that may have been improvised in the studio:

> Now you can run down to the White House
> You can gaze on the Capitol Dome
> You can knock on the President's gate, pretty mama
> But you know it's gonna be too late...

None of the three known recorded performances of this song (the third was a Witmark demo tape, December 1962) has been released to the public. (The song was recorded by Peter, Paul & Mary on one of their hit albums.) All three performances are excellent, and quite different from each other, particularly in the way Dylan handles the vocal (bluesy and raucous, understated and wry, fierce and cheerful). It is easy to imagine Dylan singing "Quit Your Low Down Ways" on a current tour, electric or acoustic, doing it at thirty shows in a row and making it fresh and powerful and subtly different almost every time—something he has shown again and again he can do if a song is good enough, resilient enough, if it can be used as a carrier for all sorts of different energies and moods without losing its essential character. Dylan the songwriter is fortunate to have such a versatile performer to work with—and vice versa.

Dylan and others have pointed out that you can get insight into his songs by taking any particular song and imagining that the person who's singing, the person he's singing to, and/or the person he's singing about, is himself. I find it very possible that Dylan, whose girlfriend had left for Europe a month earlier (an event we hear reference to in many of his songs at this time), was telling himself to quit his low down ways. I don't imagine he heeded the warning, but I can hear how much he enjoyed delivering it.

The version of "Blowin' in the Wind" that eventually appeared on *The Freewheelin' Bob Dylan* was recorded at this July 9 session. Of all the available performances of this song from 1962 and 1963, this "official" recording is my favorite. It has a presence, a magic, as if Dylan took a deep breath and thought, "Okay, this one's for posterity." I don't think Dylan ever put quite as much of himself into the song again. He didn't have to. The song itself was in the wind at that point.

Notice the "you" in the first line, and the "my" in the chorus.

With all its universality, this is a very personal song, sung by one person to another ("my friend," not friends).

"Blowin' in the Wind" is not a natural vehicle for Dylan the performer. It's not very elastic. Dylan has performed it a tremendous amount over the years, as a crowd-pleaser and also as a kind of personal talisman (he's superstitious—the song brought him good luck once); sometimes he has succeeded in stretching it, sometimes he has tried and failed, and most of the time he just does it straight, often as an encore, letting it be there as an anthem without trying to recreate it in the moment.

The performance on the album is intimate; it is sincere and affecting in its earnestness. One can imagine a performer reproducing this intimacy night after night, show after show, when he feels it and when he doesn't feel it, because he's a professional and it's what people pay to hear, and he's learned things to do with his voice that will pretty much always tug heartstrings. Dylan the rebel might sneer at this sort of slickness; Dylan the professional might admire it; but it doesn't matter, because it's not what he does or is able to do. It's not in his nature to be openly naked, or to pretend to be. It's in his nature to hide and dodge and obscure. His songs lay his feelings bare, his performances trumpet exactly what's going on for him as he's performing, he can't help that—but he can certainly wrap it in noise and song and dance and confusion and distraction and playfulness and hostility and simplicity and complexity, and he does, usually changing the formula whenever it feels like people are onto him. And the odd thing is, all this stuff is not the wrapping paper around the intimate jewel inside; it is rather the art itself, the spirit of the jewel, all part of what the creator creates, truth just as audible in the crash of Al Kooper's organ on "Like a Rolling Stone" as it could be in the nuances of Dylan's unembellished voice if he chose to recite the song as a poem over a strummed guitar.

What I'm saying is that the sheer unaffectedness of Dylan's July 9, 1962 performance of "Blowin' in the Wind" makes it special; it is the sound, if you will, of the earnest young person inside all of us, strumming the guitar and blowing into the harmonica and asking idealistic questions and refusing to be trapped into linear, limited, verbal answers.

But you can really only be unaffected once, in any particular arena, especially if you get praised and loved for it. The second time you'll be doing your "unaffected" act, and nothing's more affected than that. Dylan's real achievement is that he not only wrote and recorded "Blowin' in the Wind," he also didn't get buried by it. He was strong enough to move on to the next thing.

6.

Two of the eight songs recorded in July were topical, related to current or worldly issues ("Blowin' in the Wind" and "The Death of Emmett Till"). The other six are all love songs of one sort or another, and they all reflect Dylan's fascination with the many aspects of that quintessentially American form, the blues song. (The second album was originally going to be called *Bob Dylan's Blues*.) And despite the emotional connotation usually ascribed to "the blues," only one of these songs expresses real distress ("Down the Highway"—the precise emotion is loneliness). The others are sweet ("Corrina, Corrina," "Rocks and Gravel"), funny ("Quit Your Low Down Ways," "Baby I'm in the Mood for You," "Honey Just Allow Me One More Chance"), and happy (all five). "I ain't got Corrina/Life don't mean a thing" doesn't seem a happy lyric when you look at the words, but Dylan's July performance overridingly communicates his pleasure at being in love and being able to sing such pretty words, such a sad and lovely tune.

"Honey Just Allow Me One More Chance" and "Down the Highway" are on the *Freewheelin'* album. "Corrina, Corrina" was

55

recorded again in October. "Baby I'm in the Mood for You," a sexy song just filled with exuberance for life, is included on the *Biograph* compilation (1985). The other July performances are still unreleased.

It was a productive time for Bob Dylan, songwriter. The Carnegie hootenanny tape from September includes early performances of "Ballad of Hollis Brown" and "A Hard Rain's A-Gonna Fall" (this would seem to contradict the claim on *Freewheelin'* that "Hard Rain" was written during the Cuban Missile Crisis, unless this recording is actually from the October 5 Town Hall appearance). The new songs Dylan brought into the recording studio for his October-December sessions included "Bob Dylan's Blues," "Oxford Town," and "Don't Think Twice, It's All Right."

"Don't Think Twice, It's All Right" is a masterpiece. So is "A Hard Rain's A-Gonna Fall." Dylan's other masterpieces so far are "Mr. Tambourine Man," "Like a Rolling Stone," the movie *Renaldo & Clara*, and "Blind Willie McTell," an unreleased song from 1983.

"Don't Think Twice" is a song about death, the death of a relationship. Dylan is quoted by Nat Hentoff on the back of *Freewheelin'*: "It isn't a love song. It's a statement that maybe you can say to make yourself feel better. It's as if you were talking to yourself." (Shall we take this figuratively—you sing it to yourself to help you feel better about letting go of this person who's rejected you—or literally—you are singing the song, saying goodbye, to a part of yourself?)

Dylan goes on, making a subtle and fascinating link between "Don't Think Twice" and his experience of himself as a musician, an artist: "It's a hard song to sing. I can sing it sometimes, but I ain't that good yet. I don't carry myself yet the way that Big Joe Williams, Woody Guthrie, Leadbelly and Lightnin' Hopkins have carried themselves. I hope to be able to someday, but they're older people. I sometimes am able to do it, but it happens, when it happens, unconsciously."

This is an extraordinary quote. It shows that Dylan was aware, at age 21, of the unconscious element in his creative process, and that he had a sense, from observing other musical creators, that this would change, could evolve towards conscious creativity, with age. And he mentions this not in relation to writing, where issues of conscious versus unconscious creation are more commonly recognized, but in relation to his singing.

He goes on to speak of his art as something whose real purpose is extremely personal: "You see, with those older singers, music was a tool—a way to live more, a way to make themselves feel better at certain points. As for me, I can make myself feel better sometimes, but at other times it's still hard to go to sleep at night."

"I ain't that good yet." With this Dylan acknowledges that the songs, which he started writing because he was feeling restricted as a performer, are now forcing him to grow as a performer. The writer is pressed and inspired by the need of the singer on stage; and then the singer is forced to grow to be big enough for the greatness of the writer's song.

The greatness of the song has to do with its beauty and its universality. My understanding of art is that it occurs when a human has some success in communicating with other humans in a realm that is apart from and deeper than rational, intellectual communication. To say that this realm is emotional is inadequate; to identify it as the realm where beauty is perceived seems helpful. I believe all artistic achievement is ultimately mysterious. And as Dylan's comments about "Don't Think Twice" suggest, the purpose of even the most distressing and painful art is in some sense to make the artist, and the person who receives the art, feel better. At its simplest, this involves relieving a fullness, or filling an emptiness, or both. The singer and the listener are incomplete and uncomfortable as they are, and so they grope towards each other in the dark.

"Don't Think Twice" is about the transmuting of pain into something not only bearable but actually attractive. We could call it "cool" but it's a lot deeper than that. The singer of the song conveys a tremendous dignity, and an authentic lightness, even while also communicating pain, bitterness, confusion, and more than a hint that he would get down on his knees and beg if he thought it'd do any good. He also communicates love. There is no "way" to put all this into a simple song, four verses, that can be understood and sung by anyone. Dylan has done it through a combination of luck (you hit on a clever phrase, just like a country music songwriter, and all of a sudden a whole song drops into your lap), mastery, and conviction. The conviction is evident in the writing and, particularly, in the performance; Scaduto and Shelton fill in the personal details, making it clear that the song addresses Dylan's feelings about Suze when she left for Italy and chose not to hurry back to him—the feelings, not the specifics of the situation. There is a special talent in being able to create a fictional story ("look out your window...") and have it perfectly express feelings that you're experiencing in an entirely different set of circumstances.

I want to stress that there is no mystery about what this song "means." The popularity of Dylan's songs has never been some kind of worship of obscurity; on the contrary, people respond to the songs (including people who have no ideas about Bob Dylan, people who've never heard of him) because the songs speak so directly to and for them. "Don't Think Twice" speaks to and for anyone who's ever come to the end of a love affair, or has let go of a would-be love relationship that isn't working out, or has even imagined themselves in such a situation. It means exactly what the person who's listening to it hears and feels in it.

Difficulties arise when we attempt to express, as in criticism, what we think we heard and felt. A very simple and direct message that is easy to feel may be very hard to re-state (particularly when one is taking something like a song or a painting and trying to convey its impact in words). By way of example, Jon Landau, in a well-considered 1968 survey of Dylan's work, says "Don't Think Twice" is an example of Dylan putting himself above his subjects. He adds, "his lack of sympathy for the girl, the totalness of the putdown...the lack of subtlety are all characteristic of Dylan's one-dimensional myth-making." Now, when I listen to this song, or even read the words, I can find no putdown of the woman he's singing to, just dissatisfaction with her actions towards him. I also believe Landau is mistaken in perceiving "the girl" as the subject of the song; she is being sung to, but the song is clearly about the singer and his feelings. And I'm surprised that someone could apply the term "one-dimensional" in any context to a song that so richly explores layers within layers of human feeling. But Landau goes on to say, "It's just that in 'Don't Think Twice' the beauty of Dylan's vocal-guitar-harmonica performance...transforms verbal meaning of the song into something much deeper and much less coarse." These words tell me that he is in fact hearing and feeling the same song I'm hearing, and that it probably "means" to him something not too different from what it means to me. And I agree with him that the beauty of the song's performance is of primary importance in its success as a work of art and communication. He only gets into trouble (with me) when he tries to put into words

some of what he thinks the words of the song mean. His complaint
about Dylan's "lack of sympathy for the girl" actually sounds like an
attempt to reject or criticize politically the feeling the song expresses (the feeling of being a rejected lover)—an attempt to tell
Dylan (and, presumably, all the people who identify with the song),
"you should have felt something different."

I mention this because there has always been confusion about
"what Dylan's songs mean." I suspect this happens because, being
so moved by the songs, we wish to repeat in some way the "message" we've received, and either we find it impossible, or else we
end up defending a linear description of a multi-dimensional experience. Being unable to say what the songs mean (or to get agreement from others about what we say), we may jump to the
conclusion that we don't know what they mean (or that others don't
know). In fact, we have confused our receipt of the message with
our ability to repeat it. Dylan's songs, most of them, mean exactly
what they say, what we hear. But they are so powerful, and so much
is said in such a short space, that it is almost impossible to re-state
it, except, perhaps, by singing the song yourself.

"Don't Think Twice" was recorded November 14, 1962. "A
Hard Rain's A-Gonna Fall," recorded December 6, 1962, is another
song whose genius and power are so great that our analytical
minds (not our hearts) may have difficulty accepting and recogniz-
ing its simplicity. Yet the "message" of the song is extremely simple;
in fact it is spelled out, and repeated, in a form similar to a nursery
rhyme or a recital in school. In response to the questions asked by
a neutral and loving parent-figure, the song's singer:

> reports on where he's been
> tells what he's seen
> tells what he's heard
> tells who he's met
> and declares what he will do now.

That is all there is in the song. It's a catalog, a "chain of
flashing images." Each listener finds something different in the
catalog, has a unique and private experience which is however
given direction by the juxtaposition of images, by the rhythmic and
dramatic structure of the song, by the chord sequence, and by the
tone and inflection of voice and guitar.

I believe the individual lines in "Hard Rain" were for the most part written spontaneously: what we hear is what came up for Dylan when he asked himself these questions. I doubt that he sat there trying to select images that would have a particular effect on the listener. That is, I don't think he wrote it with a conscious idea about what the song should "mean."

Certainly a performer, however intuitive and spontaneous his performance may be, always works from an awareness of the listener and is sensitive to the effect his words and gestures will have. This is the state of mind that makes performance possible. But it is not a matter of calculation, "I want them to think this, to feel that." The creative process here is one of working with spirit, pressing and extending oneself into an extraordinarily intense, receptive, creative state and applying one's personal power and all available resources to the task of capturing feelings and images in words, allowing the truth to come through.

The poet, in other words, does not premeditate, and in a real sense is inspired, and yet at the same time must work very very hard and have a talent that is uniquely his own, in order to seize the moment and be the voice of his times, his generation. He must also be able to wait for his moment (of revelation), and always be ready for it; and at the same time he can never be certain that it will happen, or happen again. And eventually his power to be the unconscious transceiver will dry up, with age, and he will have to find a way to do his work "consciously" if he wishes to go on. Then everything may depend on how he "carries himself." But that is for a later part of our story.

Dylan told Nat Hentoff, for the liner notes of *Freewheelin'*, that "every line in it ('Hard Rain') is actually the start of a whole song. But when I wrote it, I thought I wouldn't have enough time alive to write all those songs, so I put all I could into this one." This is a good example of using death as an ally (as in Carlos Castaneda's books), letting awareness of mortality (fear of death) serve as an inspiration and an incentive to give more of oneself to this moment. It is also worth noting that "every line is the start of a song" means every image is a jumping-off place, not a summation. Although written in the shadow of (possible) imminent death, this song is not an old man's last will and testament, places arrived at in a lifetime, but rather a young man's collection of first lines, places to begin from.

Dylan's images throughout the song seem intentionally universal—what do I see, hear, etc. as a person alive in this place and
time? They do not seem to include any particulars of his own
biography...until the last verse, where his declarations become
specifically those of a poet-performer-prophet, and unquestionably
are an expression of Dylan's own (heroic) self-image as of fall
1962. He tells us—promises us—that he's going back out (into life,
as opposed to this place away from the storm where he's been
visiting the person who asked him where he'd been and what he'd
seen) " 'fore the rain starts a-fallin' " (again, pressed by the oncom-
ing apocalypse to participate fully in the world while it lasts), and
that he'll "walk to the depths of the deepest black forest, where the
people are many and their hands are all empty." He goes on to
describe the plight of the needy of the earth in another five lines of
flashing images, and swears he will respond by singing about the
situation so the world will hear and know.

These last lines are particularly moving—"And I'll tell it and
think it and speak it and breathe it" as performed by Dylan is
extraordinary poetry. These simple, repetitive, seemingly out-of-
sequence words become a vessel teeming with life that conveys not
only the singer's will but all the richness and flavor of a lifetime
spent expressing and experiencing that will. If we wish to examine
poetic technique, we'll have to assume that the simplicity, the
repetition, the unusual sequence are the very tools with which this
miracle of communication is accomplished. In the next line Dylan
aptly sums up his entire (present and future) career, promising to
"reflect from the mountain so all souls can see it." What an image!

Had "A Hard Rain's A-Gonna Fall" been published as a poem
and never sung, it would have attracted little attention, not only
because the public is not interested in poetry as such (we weren't
much interested in this sort of folk song, either, until Dylan came
along) but because so much of the art, the true poetry and power
of the song, is in the combination of words and music, particularly
the hook, the pop song/rock and roll hook of the building tension
and gorgeous release in the chorus: "It's a hard, it's a hard, it's a
hard, it's a *hard*, it's a *hard rain*'s a-gonna fall!" Take that away, take
away the sound of Dylan's voice as he sings the verses supported
and shadowed and colored and commented on by the insistent
strumming of his guitar, take away the melody that gives flesh and
substance to the spoken images, take away the cadence of per-

formed language, and you might possibly still have a sketch for a masterpiece...but nothing like the real thing. Those who think of song as a simplified form of poetry might find, if they could survey the true history of human literature, that the converse is closer to the truth.

In October 1962, according to current guesses about which tracks come from which sessions, Dylan recorded eight songs, including a couple of songs he'd written at the beginning of the year (centuries ago, in terms of what was happening with his writing), several of his recombinations of old blues songs, and some straight covers (a Guthrie song, a Hank Williams song). These were the first sessions at which he attempted to work with other musicians. The only track that ended up on the *Freewheelin'* album is the October version of "Corrina, Corrina," which turned out to be the only song on that album that features musicians other than Dylan (two guitar players, a bass player, and a drummer—one of the guitar players was Bruce Langhorne, known for his work with Odetta; he had played with Dylan at the Carolyn Hester sessions, and later played on Dylan's 1965 album *Bringing It All Back Home*).

The November 14 session that produced Dylan's exquisite performance of "Don't Think Twice" is supposedly the same session at which Dylan's first rock and roll recording took place—a song called "Mixed Up Confusion," which was released as a single and can be heard on *Biograph*. Dylan says in the notes for *Biograph* that the session wasn't his idea, and Scaduto's research suggests that Dylan's managers were trying to impose on Dylan their ideas of what he should be doing in the studio. Dylan told a friend he walked out in disgust after the third take of "Confusion." The second take, which ended up on *Biograph*, is a good rock and roll shuffle with some evidence of Elvis Presley's influence and this great line (borrowed from "Times Ain't What They Used to Be"): "There's too many people/and they're all too hard to please." A tape of Dylan singing Elvis's "That's All Right Mama" has recently surfaced, probably from this same session judging from the piano/guitar/bass/drums accompaniment. There's no question this all could have developed into something—and did, in time—but Dylan had other roads to walk down first.

The December 6 session that produced "Hard Rain" is also responsible for three other tracks that were included on *Freewheelin'*: "Bob Dylan's Blues," "I Shall Be Free," and "Oxford

Town." The first two are entirely frivolous, presumably included on the album for comic relief and to give a more balanced or at least different picture of Dylan than if he'd put out a record of all his earnest, intense songs. You could say they're not really songs at all, just recorded performances, singing improvisational comedy. (A possibly revealing comment in "I Shall Be Free": "You ask me why I'm drunk all the time/It levels my head and eases my mind.")

"Oxford Town" is something else, a deceptively pretty "talking" song about the confrontation at Oxford, Mississippi over the admission of a black man to the university. The simplicity of Dylan's "banjo tune played on a guitar" fits his lyrics perfectly; the whole song is a testimony to the power of understatement:

> Oxford Town around the bend
> Come to the door, 'n' couldn't get in
> All because of the color of his skin
> What do you think about that, my friend?

7.

Staring close at a Picasso painting in a museum, one marvels at the simplicity and roughness of the brushstrokes that construct, say, a person's face in one section of the canvas—a few quick strokes with drops of paints spattered around, not neat or accurate or impressive in any technical sense, childlike actually—and at the after-the-fact seeming perfection of this hasty, impulsive sketch, the extraordinary expressiveness of what's been left on canvas by a few quick movements of arm and wrist.

The burst of Dylan's fingers against the guitar strings at the start of "No More Auction Block" on the Gaslight tape (fall 1962), the emergence of a few powerful melody notes from the confusion, the astonishing authority these notes take on (highlighted somehow by the light strumming that surrounds them), the deep soulful pain and beauty and the sense of history they convey in the few moments before the singing starts and then the strength and vulnerability in the voice and the incredible awareness the guitar has of when and how to echo and underline and complete what the voice is saying, all of this is an artistry that defies normal concepts of technique and of vocal and instrumental ability. There may be people who think technique such as Picasso's or Dylan's can be analyzed and re-created, imitated, learned, but I doubt that this sort of expressiveness can ever be arrived at except through what seems to be an innate, unreasonable need to follow one's own path and believe in the power of one's own hand and voice and vision.

The 1962 Gaslight tape is quite amazing. Given the stylistic and emotional consistency of the performances, they're probably all from a single evening, maybe even from the same set, but there's no way to know for sure. Out of seventeen songs, the only originals are "Hard Rain," "Don't Think Twice," "John Brown" (a story song in which a mother sends her son off to war to satisfy her own vanity; he comes back blinded and maimed), and "Ballad of Hollis Brown." The other songs include some we've heard before: a superb performance of "Black Cross," Lord Buckley's sardonic story about the hanging of an "ignorant nigger" because he read books and "didn't have no religion" (this was also performed on the Minnesota hotel tape), "Handsome Molly," "Cocaine," "See That My Grave Is Kept Clean," and "Rocks and Gravel" (a Dylan blues adapted from songs by Brownie McGhee and Leroy Carr; he recorded several versions of it at his 1962 studio sessions and it was almost included on *Freewheelin'*). "Moonshine Blues" is a beautiful tune, beautifully performed, which Dylan later recorded in the studio, possibly at the sessions for his third album. And then there are seven songs that are unique to this tape, classics from across the spectrum of folk and blues: "Barbara Allen" (not quite unique; Dylan performed it next in London in 1981), "No More Auction Block" (which provided the inspiration for part of the melody of "Blowin' in the Wind"), Leadbelly's "Ain't No More Cane," Robert Johnson's "Kind-Hearted Woman," plus "The Cuckoo," "Motherless Children," and "West Texas." (The latter another example of Dylan living in a world of his own, linguistically and geographically, when he sings, "I'm going down to West Texas, behind the Louisiana line." The next line gives us an idea what it takes to live or perform with Dylan: "Get me a fortune-telling woman, one that's gonna read my mind.")

Dylan conveys on this tape a great respect for and sensitivity to the material he's performing. In hindsight it seems a kind of farewell salute to his sources, to the blues songs and ballads that have given him so much, because on the evidence of surviving recordings this was his last significant public performance of non-original material for many years.

The richness of Dylan's voice on the Gaslight tape is striking. In a way the entire performance seems a celebration of the songs themselves as musical entities (not for what their words say, but for how deep and full of mystery words and music are, the way they work together structurally, rhythmically, and as conveyors of feeling, mood, sense of place). There is no harmonica on the tape—it's as if there's no room for it, this particular evening is so dedicated to exploring the intensity of the relationship between voice and guitar. At a time when people were becoming excited about Dylan because of the messages and ideas in his songs, he appears more interested in the ways music expresses feelings.

A subtheme that I hear running through some of these performances has to do with difficulty in communicating. Dylan's magnificent interpretation of "Barbara Allen" seems to turn on this point. In "The Cuckoo" he sings, "I wish I was a poet, and could write a fine hand/I'd send my love a letter, Lord, she would understand." The version of "Don't Think Twice" he performs here is different from the studio version—strummed not fingerpicked, some changes of lyric, and a subtly different mood. The thrust of it seems to be, "That's okay, we don't have to talk about it."

"Rocks and Gravel" and "No More Auction Block" on the Gaslight tape are two of Dylan's finest early performances. On both songs there is a magnetic force in the voice that just draws me in, and a hypnotic quality in the guitar playing that holds me fast. Dylan sings about slavery in "Auction Block," not with the fire of one who's been there but with great dignity, as if he wants to acknowledge the power of what he's felt and learned (about freedom) from songs like this one. "Rocks and Gravel" is about the pains and rewards of love, a lyrical and emotional forerunner of Dylan's 1965 classic "It Takes a Lot to Laugh, It Takes a Train to Cry." Driving, steadily building locomotive rhythms on the guitar thrust up against exquisitely sustained train whistle vocalizations, long lonely notes constantly dispersed by the very energy of love and constantly reforming out of the very hopelessness of it all. "It take some rocks and gravel, baby, to make a solid road..."

Biographical data, fall 1962-winter 1963: Suze left for Italy in June, extended her visit, ultimately didn't come back till January. Dylan wrote a lot of songs, looked "lost" according to Village friends, but we have the evidence of his songs and performances that on some level he was finding himself more and more. His reputation as a songwriter was growing as more and more singers started performing his songs: "Don't Think Twice" and "Blowin' in the Wind" were particularly popular, but the average folk song fan had the opportunity to hear dozens of Dylan songs without necessarily ever hearing Dylan himself. According to Dylan, people were stopping him on the street and asking him to explain "Hard Rain" or "Blowin' in the Wind," which made him quite uncomfortable.

In December 1962 Dylan got the opportunity to go to England to act and sing in a BBC-TV drama called "Madhouse on Castle Street." He told his friends excitedly that he was going to go to Italy and find Suze, but it turned out that while he was going to Europe, she was heading back to New York. They reunited in January and began living together again.

The recordings of Dylan made in January 1963 at the *Broadside* office and at Gil Turner's apartment are not very interesting in terms of quality of performance, but they tell us that by January Dylan had written "Masters of War," "Farewell," "Bob Dylan's Dream," "All Over You," "Playboys and Playgirls," and "Walking Down the Line." Dylan had been exceptionally productive as a songwriter during the seven months he and Suze were separated. One of his strengths was that he didn't seem to have a fixed idea of what a song should be. He might use blues structure, ballad structure, talking blues narrative structure, or come up with something that either combined forms or headed off in some unfamiliar, offhandedly experimental direction. He could be serious, angry, intensely poetic in one song, and frivolous and flippant in another. A song might be inspired by the impulse to tell a particular story or communicate a feeling, or Dylan might just find himself with an interesting sentence or phrase and go from there, see where it takes him. Sometimes, I'm sure, he didn't know what the song was about until it was finished, if then.

Quite a few of the demo tapes Dylan did for his song publisher, Witmark, were apparently recorded early in 1963—in some cases the songs were recently written, other times he's "catching up" with songs written many months ago. Dylan's occasional comments on these tapes suggest he had no particular system for informing his publisher (or, one suspects, his record producer or his manager or anyone else) about songs he'd written. When he felt like it, he'd share with them those songs he could remember or the ones he thought would be of interest or whatever came to mind. The Witmark recording of "Let Me Die in My Footsteps" ends in the middle of the third verse (of seven), when Dylan suddenly says, "Do you want this? You wanna put this on? It's awful long. I mean, it's not that long, but it's just that it's a drag [laughs self-consciously], y'know? I sung it so many times." From the beginning, Dylan controlled (by whim) what he performed, what he recorded, what songs he gave his publishers. Very rarely in his career has he given anyone the chance to look over his shoulder and say, "This is a great song, why don't you record (or perform, or publish) this one?" Instead of getting involved in struggles or explanations, he (most of the time) creates a space around himself where the issue can't come up in the first place. He's a master of evasion, and one of the benefits he gets is freedom, the freedom to be whatever kind of singer or songwriter or performer he happens to be today.

The performances on the Witmark demo tapes are often rather flat, "here it is," but there are exceptions. "All Over You," a demo from early 1963, is a particular delight. Dylan says, "Let's put this one down just for kicks," and then rips into a ragtimey jug band number that strikes me as an early and quite successful example of the magic flow of language that served him so well in his *Highway 61/Blonde on Blonde* period. Here is a humor that is both more sophisticated and more zany than "I Shall Be Free" and "Honey Just Allow Me One More Chance." What Dylan is getting into here, which later came to be a primary aspect of his songwriting and performance, is a kind of percussive lyricism, as if every word were a pulse in a rhythmic flow ("my songs're written with the kettledrum in mind," he wrote in 1965). The words to "All Over You" don't say much until you hear him sing them—that changes everything, because now you read the words and hear the emphasis his voice puts on them, you hear the interplay of rhythm and melody, and as in some of the works of T. S. Eliot a kind of crazy intelligence emerges from the nonsensical or singsong language, and won't shake loose.

"Long Time Gone" from the demo tapes is interesting because both the lyrics and the voice Dylan sings it in suggest it's the life story of the mythical wanderer Dylan was pretending to be in his interviews; but ultimately the song doesn't go anywhere. It does have a moment of fire when he sings "So you can have your beauty/It's skin deep and it only lies." This is the Dylan we'll get to know better on *Blood on the Tracks* (1975), a singer who can create a person and communicate his entire character in the way he speaks two or three words.

"Long Ago, Far Away" is another early song from the demo tapes, sung with appealing energy, an ironic list of injustices that happened "Long ago, far away/Things like that don't happen no more nowadays." The song opens with "To preach of peace and brotherhood/Oh, what might be the cost!/A man he did it long ago/And they hung him on a cross." "Masters of War" and "With God on Our Side," both written a few months after "Long Ago, Far Away," also find Dylan thinking about Jesus (and Judas)—not the spiritual Jesus, who shows up in some of the songs on the first album, but Jesus as a mythical figure, the persecuted teacher or truth-teller.

Bert Cartwright, in his excellent pamphlet *The Bible in the Lyrics of Bob Dylan*, goes beyond these references to biblical myths that are familiar to everyone in our culture and finds some lines in Dylan's early songs that strongly suggest a deeper familiarity with the Bible. He points out that "I know I ain't no prophet/And I ain't no prophet's son" in "Long Time Gone" echoes the prophet Amos (Amos 7:14): "I was no prophet, neither was I a prophet's son." And "Let Me Die in My Footsteps" says, "There's been rumors of war and wars that have been," echoing Jesus's words in Matthew (24:6), "And you will hear of wars and rumors of wars." Cartwright suggests that in the period 1961-66 "Dylan saw the Bible as a part of the poor white and black cultures of America with which he sought to identify." I agree. And whether Dylan's biblical allusions came straight from the source or indirectly through blues and gospel songs, conversation, movies and so forth, the amount of biblical reference in his early songs is striking and significant.

On April 12, 1963 Dylan appeared in concert at Town Hall in New York City. It was a big event, his first solo appearance in many months, arguably his first major concert. Columbia Records was taping it for a possible live album. He'd become a very well-known person—Peter, Paul & Mary and Pete Seeger, among others, were travelling from college to college singing his songs and describing him as the most important songwriter in the country. He was important not simply because of his talent but because he was saying something. People, especially young people, heard a message in Bob Dylan's songs, or a set of messages. Something was happening, the civil rights movement was in full swing, the antiwar movement was beginning again, a new generation and a new attitude were starting to express themselves, and Dylan's songs addressed these issues and, more importantly, conveyed a feeling that the singer and his listeners were at the center of the action.

Dylan was perceived as a messenger, a truth-teller, and for a while at least he seemed willing to play the role. The first words he sang at Town Hall were, "Well, I'm just one of those ramblin' boys, ramblin' around and making noise," and he proceeded to play fifteen songs, all Bob Dylan originals, at least half of them "message" songs expressing concern about social issues. He charmed the audience with his stage presence and humor, and quickly established his casual, unpredictable, unprofessional performing style as an asset rather than a liability. He was confident enough to do only one of the songs he was known for ("Hard Rain"), dedicating most of his show to new songs that hadn't been performed publicly before. And he closed the show by doing something he's never done before or since: he read a poem he'd just written, without musical accompaniment. The audience, about 900 people, responded with a standing ovation.

New songs included "Who Killed Davey Moore?", a look at the morality of professional boxing (and an extension of the "Blowin' in the Wind" theme that failing to speak out equals collaboration with evil); "Bob Dylan's New Orleans Rag," a humorous tall tale about a terrifying female; "Hero Blues," a protest against a girl who "wants me to be a hero so she can tell all her friends"; "Dusty Old Fairgrounds," a forgotten, underrated tour de force of cascading language that captures the essence of carnival life; and "With God on Our Side," Dylan's classic about the American illusion (and lie) that our wars are holy wars and divine right is on our side. He also performed "Masters of War," "John Brown" (an antiwar song, but also another song about how dangerous women can be), "All Over You," "Walls of Red Wing," "Tomorrow Is a Long Time," "Ramblin' Down through the World," "Bob Dylan's Dream," "Hard Rain," and "Ballad of Hollis Brown."

The live recording of "Tomorrow Is a Long Time" from this Town Hall concert was included, eight years later, on the album *Bob Dylan's Greatest Hits, Volume II*. This was the only real love song he did that evening, and it more than balances out all the misogyny.

It's a great performance, naked and heartfelt, with a vocal texture that sends shivers down the spine. Here is another fine example of Dylan's power as a performer, his ability to express his deepest personal feelings through his art, using as his primary instrument the relationship between voice and guitar, the silences and resonance and tension created in the musical space between the two mediums. The sound of the song is the sound of a heart beating in a lonely room. And the words are as powerful as the tune and the performance. "I can't see my reflection in the water/I can't speak the sounds to show no pain" and "If today was not an endless highway/If tonight was not a crooked trail/If tomorrow wasn't such a long time" are enormously evocative lines, with the ability to cut right through the listener's defenses and lance the boil of his or her own loneliness and pain.

Someone wishing to study Bob Dylan's skill with words, and the way his sense of himself as a performer affects his writing, could profitably spend a long time contemplating Dylan's other great performance of the evening, his poem "Last Thoughts on Woody Guthrie." In 1965 Dylan told Ralph Gleason, "I always sing when I write, even prose." In "Last Thoughts" Dylan is clearly talking on paper (and then reading what he wrote down), and it's fascinating how this talking resembles his songwriting. He feels comfortable, in fact inspired, by limits: the poem is metrical (occasionally breaking meter appropriately and imaginatively for dramatic effect), and is mostly in rhymed couplets, with occasional brief variations in the rhyme scheme and some non-rhyming lines, again employed consciously and cleverly for maximum impact.

But he doesn't stop there. The poem (which is included in Dylan's book *Lyrics*) takes its shape and personality from a further formalization of spoken English (in addition to rhyme and meter), a kind of chanting—similar perhaps to Buddhist sutras. The first line is an uncompleted "when" clause, followed by two lines that mirror it structurally, followed by three "if" clauses (the first one, cleverly, has the "if" in the middle of the line instead of at the start), followed by a page [!] of "and" clauses (notice the original clause has not been completed, only added to—we're still caught in the tension of waiting for the other half of the sentence). The last "and" clause introduces a whole further parenthesis as the "you" the song is addressed to is in effect quoted talking to himself/herself: "and you say to yourself just what am I doin'/On this road I'm walkin', on this trail I'm turnin'" and so forth, a series of prepositional phrases with participles, and parallel questions asked of the self, then back to the singer telling you what you fear and what you know and what you need, and at this point, halfway through the poem, the "when" clause has been fulfilled ("When yer head gets twisted and yer mind grows numb" dot dot dot "you need something") but we're still not at the end of that first sentence. Eventually Dylan moves on to a follow-up sentence that has to do with looking for that something and features a long list of all the places "it ain't," ultimately acknowledging that "you gotta look some other place" and concluding brilliantly with a suggestion about where you can look and find.

And all this mad Buddhist neo-hip-hop Whitman street rapping/chanting with its elegant comic insane structure is further embellished with internal rhymes and mirror phrases and other spontaneous formal experiments, along with the usual flashing Dylan images and gems of rhythmic language:

> And yer sky cries water and yer drainpipe's a-pourin'
> And the lightnin's a-flashin' and the thunder's a-crashin'
> And the windows are rattlin' and breakin' and the roof
>   tops a shakin'
> And yer whole world's a-slammin' and bangin'
> And yer minutes of sun turn to hours of storm
> And to yourself you sometimes say
> "I never knew it was gonna be this way
> Why didn't they tell me the day I was born?"

The man's a genius, no question about it. But the point is, when he says he sings when he writes, what he means is he hears the music of the words. Not the melody that may be put with the words, if it's a song—he may hear that, he may not, while he's writing words, but that's not what I'm talking about—I'm talking about the music that's in the words. It's closer to a rhythm than a melody, but it's a musical rhythm, like if someone were playing chords or tapping on a snare drum in the back of your mind while these words roll and flow and stop and get stuck and flow some more through the front part.

Dylan's spoken introduction to his Town Hall experiment in poetry reading is unusually sincere, modest, unaffected, and serves as an example of him actually talking, as opposed to the sing-talking (poem-performing) that follows.

Dylan doesn't talk the way he talks in this poem when he's actually talking (he uses incomplete sentences, yes, but they're shorter, have far less content, and are much less likely to actually be completed at the end of the communication). This is a different state of mind—the songwriting state of mind. It's like being on stage. It's performance. He can feel the audience, he's putting on a show for them as he writes. "Last Thoughts on Woody Guthrie" is an incredible show, and would be even if we could only read it on paper. But the fact that he did read it out loud and a recording exists makes it easier for us to connect with his other non-song prose poems, it's a kind of Rosetta stone, a bridge between the public performance on stage and the private performance alone with typewriter or pen.

"Last Thoughts on Woody Guthrie" in performance opens a door to another Dylan, a poet likely to be misunderstood if he's thought of in relation to most other poets, so think of him instead as a musician/songster who occasionally sings without melody, without chords, with nothing but percussive accompaniment (like rap music)—and we the readers supply that accompaniment, imagine it, hear it in the words. Not so different from Whitman, but if Whitman were starting today he'd probably do better to look for a recording contract than to hope for acceptance in the modern poetry world. ('Course Whitman was self-published in his own time anyway; like Dylan or Picasso, an egotist irrationally convinced of the value of his own off-the-wall approach.)

Dylan wrote another prose piece, an autobiography called "My Life in a Stolen Moment," to be included in the printed program for his Town Hall concert. In it he tells a few lies and a surprising amount of truth. This piece is blank verse—no rhymes—the meter is irregular and subtle but there is a meter, and it contributes a lot, when you read the essay you can hear Dylan talking to you, hear the pauses, see him rocking back and forth on his feet as he talks. This is the 1963 version of Bob Dylan's childhood and apprenticeship, his (fairly successful) attempt to rewrite his biography so there's room in it for both the tall tales he's told and the real events of his personal history.

Two weeks after the Town Hall concert Dylan went back to the studio for the first time since December and recorded four more songs: "Masters of War," "Bob Dylan's Dream," "Girl from the North Country," and "Talking World War III Blues." All of these ended up on the *Freewheelin'* album when it was released at the end of May, even though the promotional version of the album was already circulating to radio stations in April. Four songs on the promotional version were bumped to make way for the new stuff: "Rocks and Gravel," "Rambling, Gambling Willie," "Let Me Die in My Footsteps," and "Talking John Birch Paranoid Blues."

The four songs from the April 24, 1963 session are a powerful addition to *Freewheelin'*. They vary from each other significantly in song structure, subject matter, and mood, and by comparing these tracks you can hear the way Dylan's voice changes to fit the song he's singing. Some commonality can be found between "Girl from the North Country" and "Bob Dylan's Dream"—they share a nostalgic quality, a sense of loss, looking back at the good old days with former friends and lovers. (The girl from the north country has been widely assumed to be Echo Helstrom, Dylan's high school girlfriend, but Shelton believes Dylan was thinking about Bonny Jean Beecher, whom he'd known in Minneapolis. In any case the character in the song takes on a life of her own, regardless of who the model was. The song was written in early January, while Dylan was in Italy searching unsuccessfully for Suze.)

On Dylan's first album he expressed an old man's preoccupation with impending death. Here he reverts to middle age, pining for his lost youth. "Bob Dylan's Dream," written in January 1963, shows Dylan reacting early to the loss of freedom success brings. He speaks of "ten thousand dollars at the drop of a hat"—and how glad he'd be to give it up if he could have the simplicity and warmth of youthful days again—long before he was actually earning that kind of money. The song is moving and sincere, and easily evokes old memories of all different sorts for its listeners. It's striking how sentimental Dylan is in certain ways, how readily he romanticizes his past and believes his own romanticization. There is no biographical evidence of a Dylan who "longed for nothing"— he seems rather to have been consumed by ambition since the age of fourteen at least. But then, there is no real reason to assume the "I" in this song is Dylan any more than "Walls of Red Wing" should be taken as an indication that Dylan went to reform school or wants us to think he did. He has a gift for stepping into other people's skin, as a singer and as a songwriter. "Bob Dylan's Dream" on

Freewheelin' is an exceptional performance, dreamy, otherworldly, evocative; the tune he borrows is perfectly matched to the story he tells, and his harmonica playing, voice and guitar testify to how sophisticated he has become at creating an atmosphere of simplicity.

"Girl from the North Country" also displays Dylan's maturity as a performer. If anything, this performance is a little on the slick side; it is impressive but, for my tastes, too controlled. Here he actually is that singer who has learned the tricks that can provoke a feeling of intimacy in the listener whether the singer is feeling it or not. I prefer the nakedness of Town Hall's "Tomorrow Is a Long Time." The good thing about Dylan is he can be counted on to get bored with a song or a way of performing a song as soon as he's on top of it; the next time he sings it, if he does, it will be totally different, he'll have turned it into a challenge, a risk, again.

"Masters of War" seems to contradict everyone who praises Dylan for the understated quality of his political songs; it shouts, it is openly angry, it points a finger, it even rejects forgiveness and calls for the antagonist's death. I was uncomfortable with it in 1963. But 23 years later it has weathered very well—unfortunately. The issue is as real today as it ever was: those who consciously and manipulatively participate in war profiteering still hide behind walls and desks and they more than ever encourage and enable the young of faraway nations to slaughter each other.

Critics complained in the Sixties that "Masters of War" was overstated and one-dimensional; today it seems to me we need more Old Testament prophets as brash and angry as young Dylan, who will talk straight and shout in appropriate anger and point some fingers where they need to be pointed, not with smugness or righteousness but with the humility and candor of the speaker in this song. Brashness is sometimes an expression of clarity and courage, and all three are required if we are to break down the "good family man, goes to church, friends in high places" safe houses in which the real mass murderers of our age hide, even from themselves. I still am made uncomfortable by the claim that Jesus wouldn't forgive their deeds, and the line "I hope that you die"—but it is a creative discomfort, that stimulates and forces tough questions. Dylan wrote this one and moved on, as he always moves on, but the songs stay around, and some of them get more relevant as time goes by.

"Talking World War III Blues" is wonderfully clever. There aren't many comedy routines, even socially relevant comedy routines, that are fun to hear over and over again. This one makes it. The harmonica helps a lot.

After completing the album, Dylan began travelling more and performing more frequently. At the end of April he went to Chicago and played in a club called the Bear; he also spent an hour on Studs Terkel's radio show, talking with Terkel and playing songs. It's a good conversation—Dylan actually talks about what "Hard Rain" means to him—and towards the end of the show Dylan mentions that he's writing a book now, "about my first week in New York. It's about somebody that's come to the end of one road, and knows it's the end of one road, and knows there's another road there, but doesn't exactly know what it is."

Early May: Dylan played at the Brandeis Folk Festival, near Boston, then came back to New York to tape the Ed Sullivan Show. At the last moment the CBS-TV censor decided Dylan couldn't sing "Talking John Birch Paranoid Blues." Dylan in turn refused to appear on the program; there was a considerable fuss, write-ups in the newspapers and so forth. It's been widely reported that Columbia Records, which is owned by CBS, then insisted that the song be taken off the forthcoming album, and that this led to the inclusion of the April 24 recordings on *Freewheelin'*. If so, it must be said that the album came out better as a result. In any case, Dylan came out of the television flap looking like a hero.

In mid-May he flew to California to appear at the Monterey Folk Festival. After the festival he spent several weeks with Joan Baez at her home; they had met before, but their close relationship began at this time. From the beginning there was a show business aspect to the love affair—not that it was insincere, but that it meant so much to other people: the folk queen chooses a king.

The pressure of being a public figure was becoming intense. In late May *Freewheelin'* was released; the first album had sold poorly, but the second one was a hit right from the start. *Time* ran a story on Dylan at the end of May; Nat Hentoff gave him a lot of attention in an article about folk music in *Playboy* in June. And then on June 18, Peter, Paul & Mary's recording of "Blowin' in the Wind" was released as a single. It was an immediate success, eventually becoming the number two record in the country.

Dylan had wanted to be famous, and now he was. It was

exhilarating and scary. The roller coaster had started moving. Nothing to do now but hold on tight, and pray, and enjoy the thrills.

In June or early July he wrote another prose-poem, to be published in the program book of the Newport Folk Festival, called "For Dave Glover." It was a letter to Tony (Dave) Glover, Dylan's friend from Minneapolis days, again an inspired performance on paper (not included in *Lyrics*, unfortunately):

> Yuh ask in the last letter how come I ain't wrote lately—
> Yuh say that writin' t me's like blowin words at a stone
>   wall—

and so forth, an inspired rap that salutes Glover by starting six lines with his name, goes on to remember old days and "the songs we used t sing an play," talks about Woody's songs and times and how things have changed since then, which leads to a rap on the world today and what's been done to it ("They robbed the Constitution of the land an snuck in the censors of the mind")—classic Bob Dylan 1962-65 group mind stuff, all leading up to the personal part of the letter, which is also of course Dylan's proclamation, statement of purpose, to everyone who'll be at Newport—he's writing to an old friend as a way of writing to his (new) audience.

> Yuh ask how I'm doin Dave
> I'm still singin—I'm still writin
> I'm still doin all a things I used to do I guess
> But the difference is probably that now I really ain't
>   thinkin about what I'm doing no more
> I'm singin an writin what's on my own mind now—
> What's in my own head and what's in my own heart—
> I'm singin for me an a million other me's that've been
>   forced t'gether by the same feelin—

and goes on to say "I can't sing 'Red Apple Juice' no more/I gotta sing 'Masters a War'," acknowledging that the folk songs showed him the way and brought him to this point, and now "I gotta make my own statement bout this day/I gotta write my own feelings down the same way they did it before me in that used t be day."

The first week in July, Dylan joined Theodore Bikel and Pete

Seeger in Greenwood, Mississippi, to play a concert supporting the
voter registration drive. There's some marvelous footage of this
event included in the film *Don't Look Back*, Dylan singing his new
song about how poor whites are set against blacks through the
manipulations of the politicians (typical of Dylan, a whole new
angle on the issue, a new kind of "freedom song"), "Only a Pawn in
Their Game." In Cott's book *Dylan* there are photos of Dylan in
Greenwood. The image of him sitting on the steps of a Mississippi
shack, playing guitar, surrounded by young freedom workers,
momentarily part of the family, is a moving one. Of course, the
image of Dylan that is most associated with this time is the cover of
Freewheelin', a photo taken the previous winter, walking with Suze
on a New York street in the snow, she's grinning and clutching his
arm, he's hunched against the cold, hands in pockets, watching his
feet, looking vulnerable.

Mid-July, Dylan and Suze, her sister Carla, and Dylan's manager Albert Grossman flew to Puerto Rico for a Columbia Records
sales convention where Dylan performed for the salesmen, pro-
moting his album. And then suddenly it was the end of July, time
for the Newport Folk Festival. Dylan performed solo the first night,
July 26, singing "With God on Our Side" and "Bob Dylan's Dream"
and "Hard Rain" for 13,000 people. Peter, Paul & Mary were at the
Festival, and Joan Baez, and Pete Seeger, and they all performed
Dylan songs, and asked him to sing with them, and the crowd grew
excited every time his name was mentioned. Bob Dylan was the
man of the moment. The messenger had become a star.

IV. Folk Star

July 1963 — June 1965

"People ask why do I write the way I do
how foolish
how monsterish
a question like that hits me...
it makes me think that I'm doin nothin
it makes me think that I'm not bein heard"
—Bob Dylan, 1963

8.

Jonathan's Cott's book *Dylan* contains a dozen photographs of Bob Dylan at the Newport Folk Festival, July 1963. One of them, by David Gahr, shows Dylan with a cigarette in his mouth, standing in front of a brick wall and cracking a twenty-foot bullwhip. He has a look of intense concentration on his face, body taut, one leg back and the other forward, carefully keeping his balance. One biographer says Dylan walked around most of the weekend with the whip "wrapped tightly around one shoulder." Another reports that backstage, and at the performers' motel, Dylan "strutted" with the whip, "lashing with it, over and over again." Someone asked what he did with it, and Dylan answered, "I flip people's cigarettes out of their mouths. That's what I do with it, man."

Suze and Dylan were still living together, and she was at Newport with him. Joan Baez was also there, and there are many photos of her and Dylan together. And Dylan's new audience was there. They were young, and didn't necessarily know anything about folk music. But they recognized Bob Dylan the way Dylan and his contemporaries had recognized James Dean a few years earlier: instantly, intuitively. And fell in love.

There are photos of Dylan at Newport pacing alone backstage with his guitar, pictures of him laughing with friends, diving into the motel pool, singing into a microphone with such joyous power that you can hear his song with your eyes, and standing linking hands with Baez, Seeger, Bikel, the Freedom Singers, and Peter, Paul & Mary, on the festival stage, singing "We Shall Overcome." There's a photo of vulnerable Dylan with Suze, "you and me against the world," and photos of Dylan with Baez, furrowed brow, serious young artist. The available recordings of Dylan at Newport 1963 are moving: he sings "Blowin' in the Wind" with Baez, Peter, Paul & Mary, and the Freedom Singers, "Playboys and Playgirls" with Seeger at a workshop on topical songs, and "With God on Our Side" with Baez during her solo appearance the last night of the festival. Dylan's musical energy and spirit come through in these collaborations; the excitement and specialness of the moment are communicated. But the photographs speak louder than even the music can of all the people he was at that moment, all the feelings and forces that were moving in his life.

Things were happening fast. "Blowin' in the Wind" was a top ten record, and by early August was number one in many parts of the country. Two days after Newport Dylan taped two songs ("Wind" and "Pawn") for a television special called "Songs of Freedom." Less than a week after Newport he was again performing before crowds much larger than anything he'd experienced before the festival: Joan Baez was on tour, and she brought Dylan along as a surprise guest. She would sing some of his songs in the first half of her show, and then bring him on in the second half; they'd sing together, and he'd do some songs alone. They did ten concerts in the northeast in the month of August.

The first Baez/Dylan concert was August 3. On August 6, Dylan went into Columbia Studios in New York and began recording his third album, *The Times They Are A-Changin'*. There were sessions on August 6, 7, and 12. Sometime in August Suze Rotolo moved out of Dylan's apartment. Dylan began spending time at Albert Grossman's country home in Woodstock, New York, a small town several hours from New York City. On August 17 Dylan and Baez performed at Forest Hills, New York in front of 14,000 people, and Dylan sang a new song called "I'm Troubled and I Don't

Know Why." On August 28 they performed for 200,000 people at the March on Washington, a mass rally for civil rights. Dylan sang "Only a Pawn in Their Game." Martin Luther King, Jr. gave his "I Have a Dream" speech that day from the same podium.

In September Dylan stayed with Joan Baez at her home in Carmel, on the California coast. He got some rest and did some writing. In mid-October he appeared at a Baez concert at the Hollywood Bowl; he sang the same song for half an hour and the audience booed. Baez describes him as "drunk and scared...terrified" at many of these concerts.

The rest of the third album was recorded in late October. Three songs were recorded October 23 and 24; the last, "Restless Farewell," was recorded October 31, after two major events—a triumphant Dylan solo concert at Carnegie Hall, October 26, and a very nasty article about Dylan in *Newsweek* (the November 4, 1963 issue, which went on sale a day or two after the concert).

Dylan's third album reflects his mood in August-October 1963. It is also the product of his need to live up to and expand on the role he found himself in, topical poet, the restless young man with something to say, singing to and for a new generation. Where *Freewheelin'* was a mosaic, the diary of a phenomenal year of growing and writing and recording, *The Times They Are A-Changin'* is a more unitary work, a portfolio or song cycle consciously worked on over a period of three months with a specific end in mind.

The process as I imagine it probably began right after Newport with Dylan getting a feeling for what he wanted the next album to be, based on what was happening inside and around him, and the songs he had and the songs then in progress—a taste of what was possible, how it might all add up. What's exciting in the creative process is the sensation that something bigger than the sum of the parts is lurking just ahead. A fellow named Karl Gauss once said, "I have had my solutions for a long time; I do not yet know how I am to arrive at them." The task of arriving is the great challenge and satisfaction in creative work; any real inspiration requires an artist to reach beyond his or her present abilities, beyond what he's sure he can do, and into the unknown.

So Dylan went into the studio in early August and recorded "Ballad of Hollis Brown," "Boots of Spanish Leather," "With God on Our Side," and "Only a Pawn in Their Game," songs in his current repertoire that he believed belonged on the album. He also recorded two new songs that were ultimately included on the record: "North Country Blues" and "One Too Many Mornings." The latter is the only song known to have come from the August 12 session; he probably wrote it sometime in the five days since the previous session, a spontaneous expression of what was happening in his relationship with Suze.

Dylan was working with a new producer, Tom Wilson—apparently their relationship began with the last four songs Dylan recorded for *Freewheelin'*. Wilson was young, black, interested in Dylan but not in folk music as such, and in any case inclined to let Dylan take the lead and make the decisions about what he'd record and how he'd record it. (Nat Hentoff quotes Wilson as saying, "With Dylan you have to take what you can get.") With support from Wilson and John Hammond, and with his image as an independent voice and the strength of his belief in himself also going for him, Dylan enjoyed an unprecedented degree of artistic freedom for a young musician under contract to a large record company.

It was Dylan's belief in himself that allowed him, even forced him (given the rate at which he was growing and changing), to make each new album a complete departure from what he had done before. *The Times They Are A-Changin'* has a very different sound and style from *Freewheelin'*. In many ways it is a regression—there's very little humor, the guitar playing and the singing are often monotonous and lacking in subtlety, certainly none of the performances reaches the heights achieved on some tracks of *Freewheelin'*, and the album as a whole is narrower and not quite as rewarding (musically or poetically) as its predecessor.

And yet the album represents an important step forward for Dylan as an artist, because he sets out to catch a certain sound, a certain perspective, in the album as a whole, and he succeeds. He fulfills his original inspiration, and in doing so not only produces a significant work of art but also asserts (to himself) his power to create, to tackle the unknown and to take on whatever challenges his need to communicate may present to him.

On future albums we'll see him do this in the face of opposition from audiences who want him to stick to the approach(es) they've come to expect from him. In this case, however, I believe he consciously is responding to and cooperating with the expectations of his audience (his topical songs have brought him the most attention, so he offers further work of that sort). The irony is that even so, he produces an album and a "Bob Dylan sound" quite different from anything he's done before. Even when his wish is to satisfy his audience, he does it not by giving them more of the same but by moving forward to produce the next installment of "singin and writin what's on my own mind now...for me an a million other me's that've been forced together by the same feelin." He truly believes that he can best speak for his listeners by being true to himself.

As has been pointed out elsewhere, the monochrome photograph on the album cover, head and shoulders Dylan looking solemn and disdainful (stare at him as long as you like; he'll never meet your eyes), all foreground and no background, aptly mirrors the record inside.

"North Country Blues" was apparently the first of these songs Dylan recorded. Like many of the songs on this record, it affects a curious combination of distance and intimacy. The character is a woman who grew up in an iron ore mining town; she tells about the people in her life as if they are no more than extensions of the mine itself, regulated by its success and failure. This has been referred to as a "protest song" but any anger or even any moral must be supplied by the listener; the song itself offers only the sad, believable blankness of the narrator's experience. As much as anything else, the song conveys the mood of the northern midwest plains as fall turns to winter. The contradictory lines in the first verse ("The cardboard-filled windows/And old men on the benches/Tell you now that the whole town is empty") are appropriate—Dylan's voice here has a resonant flatness, a chill of approaching winter, that makes it easy to believe in a town that seems empty not in spite of but because of the people you see in it.

It is tempting—and probably not far from the truth, or part of the truth—to say that the whole album is about emptiness, the emptiness that haunted Dylan's inner world and his experience of the outer world at this time. "Ballad of Hollis Brown" is about a man who kills himself and his family because of what they don't have. It starts and ends in the third person; most of the song, eight verses, is in the second person, a litany of poverty and rising pressure with no balancing hope ("your empty pockets tell you that you ain't got no friend"). Again, any hint of protest must be added by the listener—the anger in the song is in its structure, the unrelieved tension of the performance, there's never any anger in Dylan's voice (if there were, it would provide release, might break the tension, let the listener off the hook). And no moral is offered, except the ambiguous observation that "somewhere in the distance there's seven new people born." Is that good or bad? Neither, apparently; like the destruction of the north country family and town, it's just the way it is.

The emptiness in "With God on Our Side" is provided again by the performance: the singing and the guitar/harmonica accompaniment evoke a clear picture of a young man alone in a room with nothing to believe in. My name: nothing. My age: means less. What I've been taught: all lies. Heroes: names to memorize. Pride, bravery: empty emotions, incentives to accept the unacceptable. Dylan's performance goes too far—the album track becomes tedious to listen to—but the power of the song cannot be denied. In relatively few words it spells out the dilemma specifically of Americans and generally of any individual in any nation-state: that lies and propaganda continue to be so effective in provoking us to hate, fear, and kill our neighbors, and the name of God, which should be our protection against evil thoughts, instead becomes our justification for them. The singer concludes first by expressing his weariness and confusion, and then, unexpectedly and movingly, by offering a prayer:

> The words fill my head
> And they fall to the floor
> That if God's on our side
> He'll stop the next war.

Weariness, emptiness, confusion are the themes of most of the third album songs that were recorded in August (although, paradoxically, Dylan performs them with energy, presence, and clarity—a laconic energy, carefully measured, but it's there—only on "With God on Our Side" does he actually drag). "Only a Pawn in Their Game" is something of an exception—there's confusion here ("he never thinks straight"), and an implicit emptiness in a person who's so manipulated that he "can't be blamed" even for an act of murder. But the focus is elsewhere, perhaps because this is the only song on the album that's sung entirely in the third person. It's also the only out-and-out "finger pointing" song on the album; "With

God on Our Side" comes close, but it never names the source of the evil. "Pawn" does: "the south Politician." As in "God," much of the dirty work is done in school, by or through teachers. "Only a Pawn in Their Game," like many of the third album songs, manages to communicate intellectual insights (regarding the American social structure) in a visceral way, so convincingly that we can be sure the analysis arose spontaneously from observation and feelings, rather than vice versa. In other words, Dylan was moved by Medgar Evers's death, asked why, put himself in the shoes of the presumed perpetrator, and came up with an unusual and powerful insight into the whole situation by doing so. Dylan's empathy for the person he's singing about, and quite possibly his pleasure in twitting the northern liberal's knee-jerk condemnation of the poor white, inspire him to masterful use of imagery, meter, and rhyme, each verse building on itself in a crescendo of language that communicates by sound even when the content of the words is questionable (does a dog on a chain, or a Ku Klux Klan assassin, really "kill with no pain"?). Dylan's singing is compelling (notice how he makes "pawn" a four-syllable word); his guitar-playing couldn't be more simplistic, or more effective.

"Boots of Spanish Leather" is beautiful, the best performance on the album, similar in dynamic effect (and guitar part) to the Town Hall recording of "Tomorrow Is a Long Time." Dylan's voice is so rich here. Again, he plays with form: a dialogue between lovers, the singer taking both parts until the seventh verse, in which he suddenly establishes himself as the male (retroactively casting the first six verses as his recollection of their dialogue) and addresses a third party: "I got a letter on a lonesome day/It was from her ship a-sailin'." In the last two verses he is speaking to his lover again, but it's clear she's not present as he speaks. The last verse is a heartbreaker: still in love ("take heed, take heed of the western wind"), he bitterly resigns himself to her disinterest, by acceding to her request that he name a gift, a material object she can send instead of returning herself. The understatement here, the successful marriage of romanticism (in both the language and the music) and spare, stark realism (in the performance, and in the very simplicity and clarity of the situation portrayed), connects this track to the rest of the album. It's a love song, but it offers a perspective and a style of expression similar to the "social realism" of the other songs on the record. And when this song, with all its sweetness and fullness of voice and guitar and language, also turns out to be about emptiness, the effect is devastating.

The five songs just described were the first ones recorded, and make up half the album. We don't know when the outtakes, the unused songs, were recorded; certainly some of them are from the August 6 and 7 sessions. Some of them Dylan must have known right away wouldn't fit on this record—"Farewell" is sweet but less than half the length of other versions, he either couldn't remember the other verses or just didn't care. Others were probably only eliminated when the final choices were made (I assume in November). "Seven Curses" is a great performance of a powerful song, quite probably from the August sessions, and maybe left off the album in the end because all of the songs on the album are contemporary in setting, and "Seven Curses," though appropriate stylistically and thematically, seems a story of an earlier era.

"One Too Many Mornings," a love song and clearly one of Dylan's favorites (it shows up again and again, in many different forms, in his live performances through the years), is transitional in terms of the development of the album: it deals with weariness and emptiness, certainly, but its mood is light, forgiving, almost relieved. The harmonica solos are wonderful.

More than two months passed before Dylan went back to the studio to complete his third album. The album needed something—both aesthetically and commercially it needed an anthem, something that would speak of the common moment Dylan felt himself and his listeners to be in. Every performance on the record reflects that moment, but Dylan needed something more overt, aesthetically to tie the threads together, to help us feel the connectedness of these song-stories (to each other and to our new sense of common purpose), and commercially because Dylan had come to public attention through "Blowin' in the Wind" and he needed to come up with another very powerful message of the times or risk being bumped from his perch by the writer of the next hit anthem.

He worked hard on "The Times They Are A-Changin'," and although conscious craft is not always his strongest suit, it served him well in this case. In his notes for *Biograph* Dylan says of "Times," "This was definitely a song with a purpose. I knew exactly what I wanted to say and for whom I wanted to say it. I wanted to write a big song, some kind of theme song, ya know, with short concise verses that piled up on each other in a hypnotic way."

He succeeded. "The Times They Are A-Changin' " expresses a feeling that was in the air but had not yet been put into words (not in a popular, accessible medium), that all these political and cultural (and personal) changes going on were part of one large Movement, a sea change, something of historical proportions, the sort of thing spoken of in biblical prophecy. This song may have been the decade's first public identification of what later came to be called the "generation gap"—the new road of the children against the old road of their parents. Dylan took his own advice, seized the chance and wrote a hymn that would continue to be relevant throughout the changes of the next six years (at least). Naming the album after the song was a natural move, and served to heighten the dramatic impact of both album and song.

"The Times They Are A-Changin' " is notable for its words and what the words communicate to people; but as with other Dylan songs the words cannot be separated from their performance. If they are read on paper as they would be read by someone who had not already heard them performed, they seem artless and communicate little. In the first verse, for example, taken as written word/poem rather than performed-musical-word/song, the imagery is awkward: "drenched" is a word that evokes rain, particularly the condition after coming in from being exposed to heavy rain, and seems out of place with the "rising tide" imagery of the other lines. And in my reading the written words convey little sense of connection between rising waters and changing times. Why "sink like a stone" from not swimming? It makes no real sense—drowned bodies float—and there's nothing in the language alone to make us want to take the poet's word for it.

The same words received as song—combined with music, performed by a singer with rhythmic accompaniment, heard rather than read—have an entirely different impact. Now the verse resolves into a rhythmic, musical oration, with the emphasis not on the imagery but on the exhortative verbs: gather, admit, accept, start swimming—and a secondary emphasis on the rhyming words: roam, grown, bone, stone. The use of near-rhyme is effective here, especially on the alternate rhyme: savin' and changin' (doesn't work at all on paper, works brilliantly in the performed song). Dylan's words on paper lack elegance and trip over each other; but they function in song structure like the elements of a Swiss watch, so perfectly fitted to each other that they seem inseparable, divinely inspired, even when we can see the evidence of human effort and handiwork. "Sink like a stone" clearly communicates the choice between rising and falling, and "swimming" means participating as opposed to resisting or denying. Everything about the sound of the words as performed makes us want to take the singer's word for it.

"When the Ship Comes In" is another anthem. In "Times" Dylan states that "the wheel's still in spin/And there's no telling who/That it's namin' "; but implicit in the song is a contradictory message: it's us, our time has come. This becomes explicit in the last verses of "Ship," a song about the triumph of the chosen people.

The first five verses of "When the Ship Comes In" are told in the third person, switching to the second person ("your weary toes") for the sixth verse. The seventh verse is in the third person again, but the eighth and last is in the first person plural ("we'll shout from the bow"), suddenly transforming the whole song into a rather bloody vision of "our side" vengefully triumphing over "the foes." Unlike the mightily-provoked, heartfelt rage of "Masters of War," the murderousness in this song is pure righteousness and essentially ugly; it could be said that here is Dylan already trying to suggest (with no trace of irony) that his crew has God on their side.

Joan Baez has said that Dylan wrote the song one night when they were on tour together (August or September) and Dylan was treated rudely by the motel desk clerk. "He was so pissed...he went to his room and wrote 'When the Ship Comes In'...to get back at those idiots." We can imagine him opening the Gideon Bible to the Book of Revelation, Chapter Seven, reading about the stopping of the winds before the rising of the saved and the torture of everyone else, combining that with the image of "The Black Freighter" from Brecht and Weill's song (Pirate Jenny's fantasy of vengeance— Dylan has acknowledged the influence of Brecht, and this song in particular, on his writing at the time), and just ripping into it. A year or two earlier he'd treated the same material (the last trump as a vehicle of personal revenge) humorously in a song called "I'd Hate to Be You on That Dreadful Day," but now he was a new and rapidly-rising star, and his people were on the march and changing the world—it was a heady time, a time when one could easily lose one's sense of balance and sense of humor.

In "Times" Dylan appeals to all who will listen, to save themselves by swimming with the changing times; in "Ship" he simply declares that the righteous will be saved and the foes, even if they capitulate, will be drowned. Dylan was born under the astrological sign of Gemini, the twins, and has acknowledged in interviews and songs his occasional sense of being two people, holding and expressing two contradictory views at once or in close succession. These two songs, similar in so many ways and written and recorded in the same time period, express two sides of Dylan: one is generous, evangelical, eager to share the truth with the whole world; the other is spiteful, a zealot, waiting for the day when God's justice will fall on those who've dared to cross him. I make the latter sound like an unpleasant fellow; but in fact he's responsible for many of Dylan's finest songs and performances.

"The Lonesome Death of Hattie Carroll" is an extremely moving song that has stood the test of time better than any of Dylan's other early topical songs of this sort (retellings of real events, usually tragedies, usually with a moral attached or implicit). Dylan sings it from the heart; he really cares about the woman who died—her dignity and the value of her life come through in the song, it is a memorial to her and a tribute to people like her as much as it is an attack on her killer and people like him and the system that coddles them.

There is something very special about the structure of this song—it resembles "Hard Rain" in the rhythms of its performance, and like "Hard Rain" the music seems to come to completion at the end of each line, only to start again, building on itself, becoming more intense with each new musical and lyrical phrase. One result is that every word and every note is heard, sinks in, communicates its content to both mind and heart. The verse without words— Dylan playing the melody on the harmonica—is equally deliberate, extending and deepening the feelings already evoked.

Because the song is so clear, and so deeply felt, I am not satisfied with the usual interpretation of the chorus "message."

Most people seem to hear it as saying that the real tragedy is not the murder but the fact that the murderer got off with a six-month sentence. This to me is not consistent with the sarcasm I hear in the singing. "You who philosophize disgrace/And criticize all fears"—who is Dylan singing these words to? I don't think it's anyone he likes. A person who "criticizes all fears" seems to me closer to a William Zanzinger than a Hattie Carroll; lacking any other ideas, I hear the chorus as being addressed to cause-chasing liberals who concern themselves with the issues and have no real empathy for people. Dylan, I imagine, sees himself (and expresses himself, in this song) as someone who is apt to cry over Hattie Carroll's death at least as much as over the failings of the Maryland judicial system. So he uses the song in a variety of ways: to talk about Hattie Carroll, to talk about Zanzinger's arrogance, to talk about the court's hypocrisy, and finally to express his dislike of people who are on the right side of the issues but don't care about the human beings involved—hypocrites crying crocodile tears.

The last song on the album, "Restless Farewell," sounds like a coda, and in fact was recorded a week after the other October sessions—on Halloween, after Dylan had debuted his new songs in a prestigious and well-received Carnegie Hall concert, and after his paranoia about being famous justified itself when *Newsweek* published a "rumor tale" on him, a bit of character assassination in response to his refusal to cooperate with their interviewer. (They catch him in a lie about his parents—he says he's lost contact with them, whereas in fact he'd brought them to New York to see his Carnegie Hall concert, a bit of filial devotion that didn't fit with the rebel image Dylan wanted to project—slant their language to make him seem a phony, and irresponsibly repeat a rumor about Dylan having stolen the song "Blowin' in the Wind" from a New Jersey high school student. The rumor has been proven quite untrue, but it persists to this day in some places, a testimony to the power of a bit of false press, and the consequences of not playing ball with the power brokers.)

"Restless Farewell" signals Dylan's awareness that he has achieved what he set out to do in this album, this period in his artistic life, by announcing, directly and indirectly, that he is ready to move on. There is nothing else that needs to be said, and so the artist pulls back the veil a little and discusses his own situation, as an artist, as a private person, and as a public figure. The title harks back to "One Too Many Mornings": "it's a restless hungry feeling that don't mean no one no good." The directness with which he has portrayed other characters on the album he now turns on himself: he's self-conscious about the money he's making so he gives it to his friends, they drink it up together but there comes a moment when all the bottles are empty and the hanging out has gone as far as it can go (I see this picture of everyone passed out except restless

Dylan) so he has to move on to something else. He says farewell, first to his friends, then to his girl ("since my feet are now fast/and point away from the past," he explains, frankly if unromantically), then to any causes he's espoused (not ruling out that there may be more causes, more girls, more friends around the corner), next perhaps to his songs in their present form ("till we meet again"), and finally to whatever image anyone may have of him. This last verse makes reference to the *Newsweek* story ("the dust of rumors") and states his awareness that he is being measured. His response is more of the sort of noble (and sincere) posing that we find throughout the song, but significant because his convictions ring through and we know that he did in fact live up to them, in the face of intense pressure: "If the arrow is straight/and the point is slick/It can pierce through dust/No matter how thick." Many have believed this, but few artists have succeeded in living up to the lines that follow: "So I'll make my stand/And remain as I am." Dylan has, because he has been more deeply committed to staying straight (being true to himself) and to keeping his point sharp (renewing his piercing vision). "Restless Farewell" is a portrait of the artist in motion at the end of the evening, end of the album, end of the present myth of Bob Dylan and off into the dark towards a new one.

9.

Of the unreleased songs believed to have been recorded at the *Times They Are A-Changin'* sessions, one is interesting for historical reasons: "Paths of Victory," a lesser Dylan effort with a pleasant tune, may be the first recording we have of Dylan accompanying himself on the piano. Three others are memorable Dylan performances: "Seven Curses," "Percy's Song," and "Lay Down Your Weary Tune." The latter two, both recorded in October 1963, are included on the 1985 album *Biograph*.

Dylan's Carnegie Hall concert in October 1963 was recorded by Columbia Records for a possible live album; for a while in 1964 an album called *Bob Dylan in Concert* was actually scheduled for release. It included four performances from the April 1963 Town Hall concert—"John Brown," "Dusty Old Fairgrounds," "Bob Dylan's New Orleans Rag," and "Last Thoughts on Woody Guthrie"—and five from Carnegie: "When the Ship Comes In" (with an interesting rap at the beginning about the Goliaths in today's world that need to be slain), "Who Killed Davey Moore?", "Lay Down Your Weary Tune," "Percy's Song," and "Seven

Curses." So it would have been a live album almost entirely made up of "new" songs; possibly the reason it wasn't released is that by mid-'64 the songs were more like ancient history to Dylan, and he had a knapsack full of newer material he wanted to present to the world. In any case, the five songs that were scheduled for this album are the only recordings currently circulating from the Carnegie concert or from any of Dylan's fall 1963 shows.

"Seven Curses," in the studio and at Carnegie, has a guitar part similar to Dylan's Gaslight tape version of "Barbara Allen," and communicates a side of Dylan that seems to me present but hidden on *The Times They Are A-Changin'*, the side he reveals most strikingly on the fall 1962 Gaslight Tape, his sensitivity to and fascination with music as mystery.

The overall impression the *Times* album gives (and I believe Dylan worked hard to make sure it gave this impression) is of a singer who has something to say in his lyrics—the words, and the stories the words tell, are the thing, and the music is there to provide a setting in which the words can be heard. The Goliath rap and the poems Dylan wrote in this period confirm that he saw himself as a voice speaking out against injustice (it is this context he created around himself, even more than the content of the songs themselves, that made people think of him as a "protest singer"). His love songs also are a man speaking of matters of the heart, while strumming his guitar and occasionally blowing his lonesome harmonica.

But while this is fine as far as it goes, it is actually a limited picture of the artist—Dylan packaged himself on the *Times* album, cleverly and powerfully putting forward a Dylan people could identify with and relate to, bigger than life but with parts cropped because they didn't fit in the frame or allowed for no easy explanations. One friend observed that Dylan suppressed his "inner self" at this time, because he was "into reality" (i.e., had a picture of himself as being concerned with external reality, with the "little people" of the world and their needs).

In fact the music always played a bigger part in Dylan's songs than just accompaniment for words, as enamored as he may sometimes have been with the power of words and with his own wordsmith abilities. In the best of Dylan's performances, from the beginning, we hear him following the music as it expands on, deepens, the story told in the words—his writing follows the music of language (as opposed to the mechanics of content and conscious expression), and his singing and playing follow the music of notes (melodies, rhythms, sounds), openly, unpresumingly, always responsive to and inspired by what the music is saying.

In the extraordinary studio recording of "Seven Curses" we hear a story of betrayal, loss, and wished-for revenge, sung and played in an understated, almost detached manner (you can never point to a moment when there's anger in his voice) which somehow communicates tremendous passion, empathy, rage. Dylan stays cool but the listener wants to scream. The words, the story told, are the necessary jumping-off place for the emotions the performance generates—but the real power of the performance lies in its timing, its vocal textures, its subtly evocative language, and in the mysterious tensions created by the interplay between melody, narrative, and rhythm. Neither Dylan nor the listener needs to understand this process to participate in it. What Dylan does as an artist is explore the elements that present themselves; something inspires him, a tune or a story or both together, and he follows that inspiration with all his heart.

"Percy's Song" makes one think Dylan could have had a career as a courtroom lawyer—in "Hattie Carroll" he convinces us that a man convicted of manslaughter got far too light a sentence; here, in the song that comes right after "Hattie Carroll" on *Biograph*, he makes an equally convincing case that the sentence in this other manslaughter case is far too severe. (Presumably he would have tried to get Medgar Evers's killer off on the grounds that he was "only a pawn.") "Percy's Song" is long—too long, I think, for the simple story it tells; the appeal here is the melody and Dylan's evident affection for this tune and for the repeating lines, "turn, turn, turn again...turn, turn to the rain and the wind." He weaves a spell with these lines, passing along the spell they wove on him—words as well as tune are from a traditional song discovered, as Dylan acknowledged at Carnegie Hall, by Paul Clayton.

In the *Biograph* notes Dylan talks about hearing songs and having them rub off on you, so that elements of them show up in your own songs and performances, and acknowledges that one of Clayton's songs also provided the riff for "Don't Think Twice" (there was actually a legal struggle about that one). A great many Dylan songs, especially in this period, draw their melodies or parts of their melodies and sometimes parts of their lyrics as well from traditional songs. This is called the folk process, and the best creators of folk songs (é.g., Woody Guthrie) are often those who are most at home in this process, consciously and unconsciously absorbing material so they can recreate it and keep it alive. Dylan can be shown to have been less than generous on some occasions when a co-writing credit would have been appropriate and helpful to another living artist; but to find some fault in his actual participation in the process by which musical ideas move from person to person and generation to generation is to misunderstand not only Dylan, not only the folk process, but the nature of music and of the creative process itself. It's something like suggesting that after Dante wrote in Italian the language should have been retired, or used only with his estate's permission.

Dylan not only demonstrates but openly discusses his fascination with music as a mysterious force in "Lay Down Your Weary Tune," a breakthrough piece, one of his most powerful devotional songs (alongside "What Can I Do for You?" and, more ambiguously, "Mr. Tambourine Man") and also one of his earliest abstract, impressionistic writings. He describes the creation of the song in the *Biograph* notes:

> I wrote that on the West Coast, at Joan Baez's house. She had a place outside Big Sur. I had heard a Scottish ballad on an old 78 record that I was trying to really capture the feeling of, that was haunting me. I couldn't get it out of my head. I wanted lyrics that would feel the same way.

We can easily imagine him at Big Sur, exhausted, amazed by the natural wonders around him and at the newly discovered possibility of rest, of freedom from unshoulderable burdens, with this tune going through his head, describing everything he sees, hears and feels in musical imagery: "The crashing waves like cymbals clashed/Against the rocks and sands." The verses are in the first person, all description, no attempt to tell a story (although fragments of story leak through in the images: "The last of leaves fell from the trees/And clung to a new love's breast"). The chorus is in the second person, and this time clearly it is not Dylan talking to someone but Someone addressing Dylan:

> Lay down your weary tune, lay down
> Lay down the song you strum.

And rest yourself 'neath the strength of strings
No voice can hope to hum.

It is as close as we'll ever come to Dylan describing one of his visions, in this case an auditory one—this tune is haunting him, he searches for words to put to it and when they come they come like a message from the universe, the Creator, a release from his weariness, the offer of a stronger shoulder to lean on. And this protective being, this deity, is personified, and in fact experienced, as Music. Later, for a while, Dylan will attach Jesus's name to this mystery he finds in every grain of sand, but here he simply identifies it in the form in which it approached him...and describes himself, in classic devotional form, seeing his beloved everywhere—feeling the breeze and seeing the ocean and perceiving them as Music.

(The animatism—rain crying, wind listening—in this song has some connection with "Percy's Song" ("the cruel rain") and is powerfully echoed in "When the Ship Comes In": fishes laughing, seagulls smiling, rocks proudly standing, sands rolling out a welcome carpet, and, best of all because a fresher image, the sun respecting every face on the deck. These images are effective because they are not contrived; they give us a taste of how, at moments, Dylan actually sees and experiences the world.)

In early November 1963 Dylan played a concert at Jordan Hall in Boston. There's no known recording, but the show has a personal significance for me: it was the first time I saw Dylan perform. I was fifteen. It was great. There were some empty seats near the front and I came down from the balcony and grabbed one. He rambled on about soap commercials before singing "Blowin' in the Wind." He did "Who Killed Davey Moore?", which I loved at the time (first heard it at a Pete Seeger concert), and "Eternal Circle," which bored me. His performance was casual; his presence was captivating. It was exciting to be so close to him. It was apparent even then that he couldn't be compared to other folksingers, other songwriters, other performers. He did everything his own way, for better or worse. And some of his specialness rubbed off on me, just because I was there—proud to be the kind of kid who'd go to see Mississippi John Hurt at the Cafe Yana and Bob Dylan at Jordan Hall.

Dylan was still playing the part of the messenger, the protest singer, the young man with something to say about the world, at this point—indeed, he was at the height of his flirtation with the role—but already his significance to his audience had as much to do with who he was or seemed to be, his presence on stage and in the contemporary scene, as with the actual content of his songs. His stardom may have been launched by the success of "Blowin' in the Wind" but it was sustained and fed by young people's need for someone to identify with, a folk hero. Dylan didn't need to play this part—it fit him naturally, it emanated from him wherever he went, he was living it. He couldn't escape it even when he wanted to.

Sometime in November or December of 1963 Dylan wrote a poem cycle, "11 Outlined Epitaphs," to be included with *The Times They Are A-Changin'* (the poems are printed on the album's back cover and on an insert sheet). He had been doing quite a bit of experimenting with writing outside the song form: in addition to "Last Thoughts on Woody Guthrie," "My Life in a Stolen Moment," and "For Dave Glover" from earlier in the year, we have two pieces he did for *Hootenanny* magazine, his liner notes for Peter, Paul & Mary's *In the Wind* album, his liner notes for *Joan Baez in Concert, Part 2* (included in *Lyrics*), and long prose-poem letters to *Broadside* magazine and to the Emergency Civil Liberties Committee, all written in fall or late summer 1963. The *Hootenanny* pieces are minor; the other pieces are fascinating because they tell us so much about who Dylan was (and, perhaps, still is) and how he saw himself at this time.

The notes to *In the Wind* describe the private origins, in the Gaslight Cafe after hours in '61, of what Peter, Paul & Mary (and Dylan) are now sharing with the world: "It's a feelin that's born an not bought/An it can't be taught—/An by livin with it yuh learn t see and know it in other people/...An once yuh know the feelin it don't change—/It can only grow." Dylan's description of "these times that'll not never come again" is affecting and sincere. It's clear he's talking about his own experience as a performer; in some way he's able to draw on stage from a well of feeling carried with him from those earlier moments of unselfconscious closeness with other musicians.

The notes for the Baez album are not very successful as poetry, but deserve careful reading for what Dylan shares here about his own psychology. He describes how ruthlessly effective he can be at shutting out what he doesn't want to hear: "A fence a deafness with a bullet's speed/Sprang up like a protectin glass/Out-

side the linin a my ears/An I talked loud inside my head." He also
describes the origins of the train imagery that runs through his
work, acknowledges the subtle power of guilt in his life, and hints
at a relationship between his fear and his willfulness, his defiant
independence. The transformation described in the poem, how his
life is changed when he accidentally opens himself to Baez's singing, her truth, is touching but unconvincing. A possible insight into
one of Dylan's writing techniques is offered when he says he mem-
orized some words to write down another day, just before he
passed out from wine and catharsis.

The letter to *Broadside* is wonderfully straightforward and
honest. He talks about how being a star makes him paranoid ("I am
now famous by the rules of the public famiousity/it snuck up on
me/an pulverized me"). He says that nothing upsets him more than
being asked why he does what he does ("it makes me think that I'm
not being heard"—maybe all the people he's singing to are idiots
and philistines like the questioner, maybe all the praise is false and
his worst doubts and fears about the value of his work are true). He
talks about feeling guilty about having money, and the uselessness
of trying to give it away; he talks about feeling guilty about not
loving everybody the way he loves his girlfriend (he feels the pain
and need of other people and doesn't know what to do about it,
and this is heightened by the fact that people seem to think he has
something to give them). He talks about his hassles with his landlord, that he's too lazy to take him to court, how much he loves
listening to Pete Seeger on record singing "Guantanamera," his
enthusiasm for Brecht, and his difficulties with prose: "my novel is
going noplace/absolutely noplace/like it dont even tell a story/it's
about a million scenes long/an takes place on a billion scraps/of
paper...certainly I cant make nothing out of it." He announces,
quite seriously, that he's decided to be a playwright instead. Dylan
often wraps himself in mystery or hides behind hostility, but he can
be astonishingly open and vulnerable in his communications as
well.

November 22, 1963, President Kennedy was shot. Dylan told
Scaduto he'd had to play a concert in upstate New York the following night, and the way his show was structured he had to start with
"The Times They Are A-Changin' " even though it struck him as
terribly inappropriate. (This is the first hint we have of Dylan
"scripting" his concerts, having an idea about what goes first and

which songs to include and doing a roughly similar show at each
stop on a tour. Somewhere along the way, probably on tour with
Baez in August, he'd started thinking like a professional.) "I
couldn't understand why they were clapping, or why I wrote that
song, even. I couldn't understand anything." Both the pace of
Dylan's success and the pace of events in the outer world were
moving faster than Dylan's or anyone's ability to have a concept of
what was going on. There were many times when all he could do
was show up and see what happened.

December 13, 1963, he showed up at the Hotel Americana in
New York to receive the Tom Paine Award from the Emergency
Civil Liberties Committee. The previous year the award had been
given to Bertrand Russell. Dylan was 22; his impression of the
people in the audience was that they were in their 50s and 60s, had
been activists when they were young and now wore minks and
jewels. Dylan felt very out of place, got scared, got drunk, tried to
leave and was brought back, felt obligated to make a speech and
found himself saying things like "I only wish that all you people
who are sitting out here today weren't here and I could see all
kinds of faces with hair on their head" and "The man who shot
President Kennedy, Lee Oswald...I got to admit honestly that I,
too—I saw some of myself in him." People were scandalized, and
the fund-raising event was a failure. Afterwards Dylan wrote a
letter/poem to the Committee attempting to explain what he'd said
and what he'd felt. Once again, it's a unique, valuable, fascinating
document—Dylan explaining (in a poem/ performance) a performance of his that was misunderstood.

"11 Outlined Epitaphs" is related to these other 1963 non-
song writings—Dylan talking directly about his life and feelings, in
rhythmic, sometimes poetic language, with a keen performer's
sense of the beginnings and endings of things—but it is more
ambitious, and more successful. The cycle starts in the early evening and ends just after dawn; Dylan begins talking in a way that
implies that he and his reader are already in communication, and
holds that feeling of intimacy, connectedness, mutual understanding, throughout the set of poems. The opening image is comic, an
angry, punchy, Chaplin-like Dylan, like his early stage persona
doing a parody of his latest stage persona, stumbling about looking
for someone to fight. He delivers a stream-of-consciousness monolog, moving fast but sticking to his topic, which is almost but not

quite within this reader's grasp. The franticness with which the section opens has shifted to serenity by the end, Dylan finding a way to watch the world and the sunset without being noticed: he watches but keeps his eyes closed. Then a piece on his Minnesota childhood, a recurrent theme in his 1963 writings, and his "legacy visions"; as in the first section he "stops a while" at the end, able now to love the place he left because he's willing now "never t expect what it cannot give me."

This is an ambitious work, Dylan seeking to clean up and complete most of the loose ends in his current self-image, to set himself free to move on. The next section acknowledges and buries his past ambition to lead Woody Guthrie's life, marked by a haunting passage to the tune of (music even on the printed page) "The Bells of Rhymney" and by a quatrain at the end that leaps from the page, completing these thoughts and the opening lines of the cycle, and striking a wonderful romantic pose appropriate to the current image of Bob Dylan: "yes it is I/who is pounding at your door/if it is you inside/who hears the noise."

Eight more epitaphs, and riches in each of them. Dylan is remarkable among American artists in how much he has to say (Melville is comparable; Hemingway falls far short). His piece on politics contains a fascinating, heartfelt diatribe against forced education. The brief poem that starts "Al's wife claimed I cant be happy" is high philosophy and another important starting place for anyone interested in Dylan's own experience of his work:

> "I'm happy enough now"
> "why?"
> "cause I'm calmly lookin outside an watchin the nite
>   unwind"
> "what'd yuh mean 'unwind'?"
> "I mean somethin like there's no end t it an it's so big that
>   everytime I see it it's like seein for the first time"
> "...but what about the songs you sing on stage?"
> "they're nothing but the unwindin of my happiness."

Dylan addresses the issue of his borrowing tunes and stories, words and structures from other songs; he talks about the challenge of being an idol; talks about why he won't cooperate with magazine interviewers; soliloquizes on the end of the night from the perspective of the last artist left awake (ending with his famous lines, "for I am runnin in a fair race/with no racetrack but the night/and no competition but the dawn")—his description of Sue sleeping is a precise counterpart of Picasso's famous 1932 painting "The Dream"; and ends by celebrating the gray morning sky and again skating, free-associating, just beyond the reach of the reader's wish to be sure he understands all the connections. He spits a list of artists he admires, from Edith Piaf to Miles Davis to William Blake, ultimately bringing it all in for a neat three-point landing, conjuring movies, music, and religion: "outside, the chimes rung/an they/are still ringin." A tour de force. And, it should be said, not of the sort produced by a show-off, but by a generous, committed spirit. The humor and spontaneity that tend to be lacking in the songs on this third album are very much present in its liner notes. "11 Outlined Epitaphs" can be read as Dylan's effort to preempt the interviewers: he asks himself every worthwhile question he can think of, and answers honestly and probingly. This won't satisfy the press, of course, but it does leave Dylan free to stonewall them in good conscience.

The Times They Are A-Changin' was released in mid-January, 1964. February 1 Dylan recorded six songs for Canadian TV; a videotape survives. February 25 Dylan appeared on the Steve Allen TV show, and sang "The Lonesome Death of Hattie Carroll." In between he and three companions drove across the United States in an odyssey that is unusually well-documented in Shelton and Scaduto's biographies. Dylan and his friends (musician Paul Clayton, journalist Pete Karman, and road manager/bodyguard Victor Maimudes) made their way from New York to concerts in Atlanta, Denver, San Francisco and Los Angeles in a new Ford station wagon well supplied with marijuana, benzedrine pills, typewriter, paper, and wanderlust. Dylan was bored, he and Suze were not getting along, he wanted to see the country and meet some "real people." They visited Carl Sandburg in North Carolina (he was polite but had never heard of Dylan; Dylan was annoyed), striking coal miners in Kentucky, a black college in Mississippi, Mardi Gras in New Orleans. Dylan wrote "Chimes of Freedom" and parts of "Ballad in Plain D" during the trip.

In March, Dylan and Suze Rotolo broke up for the last time. (Scaduto says Dylan tried for almost another year to get Suze to return and marry him.)

In April or May, according to the best guesses of tape collectors, Dylan recorded the last of the Witmark demo tapes: "Mama, You Been On My Mind" (piano version; there's also a demo with guitar, date unknown), "I'll Keep It with Mine," and "Mr. Tambourine Man." "Mama" became a standard duet for Dylan and Baez in joint appearances; "I'll Keep It with Mine" shows up again in a better version as a fifth album outtake; "Mr. Tambourine Man" was included on Dylan's fifth album. This early take of "Tambourine Man" with Dylan accompanying himself on piano is particularly interesting (and moving); melody and lyrics are the same as on the later recording, but just the subtle difference in Dylan's mood, and the effect of the piano on his voice, make this alternate version a treasure in its own right.

In May Dylan went to London for a concert at the Royal Festival Hall. Afterwards he and Victor Maimudes visited Paris and a small town in Greece, where Dylan worked on songs for his next album. Back in New York, June 9, 1964, Dylan went into the recording studio with Tom Wilson, a couple of bottles of wine, and a small crowd of friends, and recorded his entire fourth album, *Another Side of Bob Dylan*, in a single evening.

10.

Nat Hentoff was at the recording session for *Another Side* and described it in a profile of Dylan he wrote for the *New Yorker* magazine. Apparently Dylan was in a good mood, unfazed even when one of his friends' children burst into the studio in the middle of a song. Tom Wilson told Hentoff that the album was being done in such a hurry because the record company needed it for their upcoming sales convention, but in fact Dylan seems comfortable and even enthusiastic with the idea of getting it all down in one night. We have the evidence of the album itself, as well as Hentoff's notes on the sessions, to tell us that Dylan was not at all hesitant to share with his public recordings on which he giggles, starts to sing the wrong verse, strains his voice, and fumbles his guitar chording. He treats the album like a live recording, and an unusually casual one at that, despite the fact that these are new songs that clearly mean a lot to him, and that the content of the songs represents, as the album title suggests, a fairly radical departure from what his audience expects from him. His confidence, in short, is staggering. He

is, this particular evening anyway, an artist who completely trusts
his own process.

Hentoff says Dylan told him at the session, "Those records
I've made, I'll stand behind them, but some of that was jumping
into the scene to be heard and a lot of it was because I didn't see
anybody else doing that kind of thing. Now a lot of people are
doing finger-pointing songs. You know—pointing to all the things
that are wrong. Me, I don't want to write *for* people anymore. You
know—be a spokesman....From now on, I want to write from
inside me, and to do that I'm going to have to get back to writing
like I used to when I was ten—having everything come out naturally. The way I like to write is for it to come out the way I walk or
talk."

Dylan surely didn't talk like "even though a cloud's white
curtain in a far-off corner flared" or "half-wracked prejudice
leaped forth" or even "I don't want to fake you out, take or shake
or forsake you out." And yet the quote captures the essence of his
evolving creative process: these songs, these lines, are from inside
him, as opposed to something written to meet anyone's standards
or satisfy anyone's expectations. And the written songs, when he
performs them, come out exactly as free and honest, naked and
natural, as a person walking across a room or talking to a friend or
a stranger.

The performances are sloppy, and uneven, and it seems reasonable to think the album could have been better if he'd taken
more time with it. Except that that's like saying it'd be easier to fish
if this boat were half-buried in sand in the desert, so it wouldn't roll
around so much.

The truly outstanding performance of the evening, of the
album, is "Chimes of Freedom." Dylan sings it not only as though
this is the only moment there is, there is no second chance, he has
to put everything into this take, but also as though he came back
from France and Greece, agreed to come to the recording session,
agreed to go on with his career and actually make another album,
only for the purpose of getting this song on tape. As though he'd
stayed alive this long only to do this.

Talking about an artist's work chronologically can be deceiv-
ing—it makes us, writer and reader both, tend to treat each individual work as though it is part of a process of development, part
of some heroic saga of personal and artistic growth (or decline). Or

we see it as an episode in the dramatic story of the artist's relationship with his audience. There's truth and much of interest in all this, but it can distract us from the fact that each work, each performance, also exists outside of time, and in fact derives its primary power from its content rather than its context. This is evident when we place 1964's "Chimes of Freedom" alongside the 1962 recording of "A Hard Rain's A-Gonna Fall." Here are two mountains Dylan has climbed, two places he's visited and reported from with searing intensity. The greatness of Dylan's body of work rests on the power of each of his great performances taken separately as much as it does on the awesomeness of his achievement considered as a whole. In fact we cannot actually listen to more than one performance at a time. It is tempting to try to simplify the overwhelming oeuvre of a prodigious artist such as Dylan or Picasso by creating biographical or aesthetic periods in which to group his work, or by setting up standards by which a few works can be singled out as most successful or important. I plead guilty to both approaches, and believe a slightly misleading order may be preferable to none at all, but caution the reader not to take such arbitrary contexts too seriously. In the end, an individual listener has an experience of an individual recording; and greatness in art depends on what occurs in the privacy of that experience.

When *Another Side of Bob Dylan* was released, I didn't like "Chimes of Freedom." I thought it was long and repetitious and that the image of "chimes of freedom flashing" was impossibly awkward and confused—embarrassing, if you will. Having formed that opinion and having expressed it to someone, I held onto it a long time. And probably as a result, I heard the song many scores of times over the years without ever noticing its narrative content: it's a song about feelings evoked while watching a lightning storm. I've spoken to others who also failed to connect with this basic information, even while speculating on the significance of some of the more abstruse imagery in the lyrics.

This is the story Dylan tells: he and someone else (friend or friends) are caught in a thunderstorm in mid-evening and duck into a doorway, where they are transfixed by one lightning flash after another lighting up the night sky. Dylan has a synesthetic vision ("vision" is not quite the right word, since what he experiences is auditory and ultimately emotional, empathetic, not visual) in which the lightning flashes (and the accompanying thunder) are experienced as the tollings of bells (like church bells, wedding bells, with implications of the Liberty Bell perhaps). The lightning bolts become chimes, and sound and sight get all intermixed ("majestic bells of bolts struck shadows in the sounds/Seeming to be the chimes of freedom flashing"). And as the Liberty Bell tolled to proclaim American independence, and church bells in general toll to celebrate a wedding or mourn a death or call to the faithful, Dylan experiences each lightning bolt as tolling (or flashing or striking or cracking or firing) *for* someone, specifically for the underdogs, the needy, the modest, the meek of the earth Christ refers to in the Sermon on the Mount. (I am reminded of Dylan's fall 1963 letter to *Broadside* where he says he's "listenin t Pete sing Guantanamera for the billionth time"—the key line of the song is, "with the poor people of the Earth, I cast my fate.")

What Dylan experiences is a series not of thoughts but of palpable feelings—each illuminating flash is felt as a bell note, vibrating in his heart and evoking one after another of the legions of the forgotten: "flashing for the refugees on the unarmed road of flight...tolling for the luckless, the abandoned and forsaked...tolling for the searching ones, on their speechless, seeking trail/for the lonesome-hearted lovers with too personal a tale/and for each unharmful, gentle soul misplaced inside a jail" (in 1986 he was still dedicating songs to this latter group).

Dylan and friends watch the lightning as the storm rages around them ("the mad mystic hammering of the wild ripping hail"—Dylan often writes of the weather; in this case the hard rain is already falling, but far from the bitter apocalypse of the earlier song, this time it's a Shakespearean tempest in which visions are revealed to those with hearts to see). Eventually the storm begins to break, signaled by the appearance of a white cloud in a corner of the sky and the slow lifting of the mist, and Dylan and his friends are still "starry-eyed and laughing" as they were when the storm caught them, uncertain whether it's been five minutes or five hours ("trapped by no track of hours for they hang'd suspended"—time-lessness is a thread running through many of Dylan's finest songs). In the course of the song, the lightning flashes have been described as "the sky cracked its poems in naked wonder" and "tales" that "the rain unraveled" and "electric light" striking "like arrows." The imagery is fairly direct but it pours over the listener in such a torrent that the mind can't keep up; clearly Dylan would like to "switch" his listeners' senses as his have been, push them over the edge into an unpredictable world of their own visions.

And he is successful. The listener is pulled in by the conviction of the singing, the shivering beauty of Dylan's performance, his brief, penetrating harmonica solos and extraordinarily sensitive guitar accompaniment. The song not only demands attention but speaks directly to the heart before the lyrics have even begun to resolve themselves into any kind of communication. And then fragments of phrases begin to jump out at the listener exactly like lightning-illuminated glimpses of a familiar yet unreal landscape: "fired but for the ones [I always heard "fiery but barbed ones"] condemned to drift or else be kept from drifting" and "starry-eyed and laughing" and "the misdemeanour outlaw chained and cheated by pursuit" (third in a series of remarkable "misses") and ultimately, unforgettably,

> Tolling for the aching whose wounds cannot be nursed
> For the countless confused accused misused strung-out
>   ones and worse
> And for every hung-up person in the whole wide
>   universe...

This may not be great poetry. But it is inimitable songwriting and performing, a rush of wild lyricism, that is both the unmistakable product (and announcement) of Dylan's need to move beyond conscious imagery and specific storytelling and find techniques for getting exponentially more of his inner self out onto vinyl...and a breathtaking tour de force that could only have come from Dylan and would be equally affecting and equally perverse no matter at what moment in his life or career he happened to burst out with it. For me, finding myself hopelessly drawn to and deeply enriched by the song decades after I first heard it and rejected it is a warning and promise of how much else I may have been deaf to, how unlikely it is that I will in a lifetime discover even all the high points of what Dylan's opus has to offer me. A hundred times I probably heard this one, before ever seeing the lightning....

A lot of the songs on *Another Side of Bob Dylan* are sung to women ("All I Really Want to Do," "It Ain't Me Babe") or are about women ("I Don't Believe You," "Ballad in Plain D") or both ("Spanish Harlem Incident," "To Ramona"). Whereas Dylan's earlier love songs have mostly been romantic ones, these new songs express a strong sexuality—clearly the person writing and singing them is sexually active and quite caught up in the push-pull of desire and of sexual union and separation. You can hear in his voice that he's available. You know from the speed with which he enters and leaves the room that he's looking for something.

"Spanish Harlem Incident" is a gorgeous vignette (two minutes and twenty-two seconds, one of Dylan's shortest) of the singer head over heels in lust with a gypsy gal we can imagine he may only have seen walking past him on the street but it doesn't matter, she has him, he's gone. The lyrics are brilliant, a fine example of Dylan's quick artistry, the way he tells us how fiery she seems to him, the way he works in fortune-telling imagery, falling in love in a flash not only with this fox but with the whole idea of gypsies and of himself in love with one. "The night is pitch black, come and make my/Pale face fit into place, oh, please!" may be the most overtly sexual line Dylan has written (or am I reading into it?)—in any case it is phenomenal that he can take "pitch black" and "make my" and get them to rhyme with each other, totally successfully; it's some kind of trick of rhythmic diction, vocal sleight of hand. He also sings "surround me" in such a way that it retroactively rhymes with "I'm nearly drownding" from eight lines earlier. He's inspired. And while his portrait of her and of himself drunk with the thought of her is complete and marvelous in itself, he does manage to push the situation over the edge into universal identification, the Bob Dylan department store of intoxicating insights, when he notes that "I been wond'rin' all about me/Ever since I seen you there" (we expect him to say "about you"—when it's "me" instead we immediately *get it*) and when he ends by pleading, "I got to know babe, will you surround me/So I can know if I am really real." He's real, all right, but he ain't gonna know it until after he's got her and lost her again, or gone home and taken several cold showers.

The sensitive, caring, big-brother shoulder-to-cry-on Dylan who sings "To Ramona" is the same horny street singer, but in a different mood, showing another side, sitting in a bar perhaps, comforting a friend who's up against both circumstances (boyfriend problems?) and her own resultant self-doubts. He acknowledges feelings of desire for her (in order to be up-front, and maybe also to help her feel better about herself), confusing us listeners into thinking this a love song, when in fact it's clearly a song of friendship. The song speaks to anyone who's feeling confused and sad and self-critical, as we all do at times, and this universality and the genuine affection in the performance can make a person feel that Dylan is singing to him or her alone; heard at certain moments Dylan's songs can penetrate a listener's reality and create an I-you relationship of startling, sometimes confusing, intimacy.

Dylan does share himself very intimately in his performances (almost always) and his lyrics (often). This can leave people confused about who they are to him. Stan Lynch, drummer on the Dylan tour in 1986, commented to *Rolling Stone*, "I saw people who were genuinely moved, who felt they had to make some connection with him...They wanted to be near him and tell him they're all right, because they probably feel that Bob was telling them that it was going to be all right when they *weren't* all right, as if Bob *knew* they weren't doing so well at the time. They forget one important thing: Bob doesn't know them; they just know him."

This phenomenon of people acting on their feelings of closeness to Dylan was already part of Dylan's everyday life by 1964, sometimes sweet, often tedious, and sometimes very scary. He no doubt was already thinking of "It Ain't Me Babe" as a song to his audience as well as boy-to-girl when he recorded it; over the years that aspect of it has become more and more important, and he sings it at times like a prayer to the world to leave him alone: "it ain't me you're looking for." But of course he's also out there singing "Ramona, come closer" as well.

Another Side of Bob Dylan is a rich, complex album, and it isn't possible to discuss all its songs or all its aspects here (which is not to say that I think I'm aware of all its aspects; on the contrary, it continues to surprise me, as does all of Dylan's work). One thing I need to say is that there is a feeling of arrival about this album. What has arrived is a sort of mythic being, a projected entity, "Bob Dylan"—the alter-ego Robert Zimmerman began creating six or seven years earlier, to help him express himself, call attention to himself, escape himself, and set his real self free—a stage identity, *nom de plume* and what Rimbaud called "the other." This being is now fully fleshed, holographic (you can look at the image from all sides), unselfconscious (this album contains the last traces—"My Back Pages"—of Dylan trying to get us to see him a certain way; most of the time on this record and the next three he no longer feels the need), and self-standing (the puppet walks by himself; the puppeteer no longer seems to exist).

But there still is another Dylan, and at the risk of confusing you and me both I'll call him the performer, the artist who takes the myth out of his closet and laces it on and becomes as one with it in front of the microphone with his friends in the control room watching and listening and smiling and egging him on (and serving to create a buffer between him and the world, a space to be alone and really get into it). This performer has also been maturing, while his myth has been maturing, and this night in June it's evident that he too has arrived, his piano, guitar, harmonica, and vocal cords are every bit as fluid as his lyrics, his melodies, and his myth, he wears them lightly and seems able to do with them whatever he wants at every moment (this may not be true; but the seeming is what matters).

It is as though Dylan no longer has to prove anything, and this creates a space—first asserted on this album—for him to do whatever he wants, for his creative energies to just run free. In the cover photo he looks exactly like a painter contemplating a completed canvas, brow furrowed, serious about his work, meditative and quietly proud—and where's the child-face of the last three albums? This is the adult Dylan. He's "younger than that now" because he no longer needs to pretend to be old.

All of the (known and suspected) outtakes from the *Another Side* session are songs on which Dylan plays piano. This combined with information in Nat Hentoff's article suggests that these tracks (and "Black Crow Blues," included on the album) may have been "warm-up" songs played by Dylan when he first got to the studio, while the sound crew was still getting ready. If so, it's nice that the tape was running—there's some lovely spontaneous piano playing, including a joyous performance of Dylan's 1962 song "Hero Blues" (lyrically a kind of forerunner to "It Ain't Me Babe"). The blues/boogie piano and piercing harmonica runs on "Hero Blues" are wonderful, and again we hear what a great rock and roll singer Dylan can be, with or without band. (The dating of this outtake is uncertain; it may have been recorded in 1963.)

Another Side again features Dylan poems on its back jacket, under the title "Some other kinds of songs..." (six poems from this sequence that didn't fit on the jacket are included in *Lyrics*). These poems further explore techniques introduced in "11 Outlined

Epitaphs," but for the most part they lack feeling; a poem like "I could make you crawl" touches all the bases—irony, significance, careful clipped language, free tumbling language, the clever return to the opening image via an unexpected route—but it doesn't click for me, it's contrived. Dylan like any artist sometimes falls into self-imitation, tricks for tricks' sake, thinking perhaps the rubes won't know the difference between this and the real thing or temporarily not noticing the difference himself.

But there's a lot that's good in the longest poem, "run go get out of here," from the simple acknowledgment that "i lost my glasses/can't see jericho" (can't march to battle when you're no longer so sure of the enemy) to the description of himself leaving the scene of the would-be bridge jumper because he realizes he really wants to see him jump—honest enough about his own feelings to notice that they're not always trustworthy, and so the only honest thing to do then is walk away from public scenes—to the six lines of pure Dylan that have haunted me for decades, that neatly sum up everything he's saying here and open a dozen new uncharted poems in the reader's mind: "i know no answers an no truth/for absolutely no soul alive/i will listen t no one/who tells me morals/there are no morals/an i dream alot."

In July, Dylan appeared at his second Newport Folk Festival, and reportedly gave an anxious, very stoned, very sloppy performance. Like self-fulfilling prophecy, his fear of rejection by his "old" audience may have made him so nervous that he couldn't give them a fair chance to hear and connect with his new persona. One can also speculate that Dylan was running into a lot of friends and acquaintances giving him advice, wanting him to be this way or that way or just to explain himself, and that the experience of having this place (the folk community) where he'd felt so at home become so uncomfortable for him was extremely painful.

In August of 1964 a photographer named Daniel Kramer got permission to visit Dylan in Woodstock (at his manager's house) for a photo session that turned out to be the first of many over the next twelve months. In 1967 Kramer published a book of his photographs of Dylan; in it he describes their first session: "I found him sitting at a dining booth in the kitchen reading a newspaper. He turned the pages of the newspaper and seemed never to acknowledge my presence. This set the pace. Apparently he was not going to do anything especially for the camera. It was not that he wasn't cooperating. Actually, he was being cooperative in his way—he allowed me to be with him, he allowed me to photograph him and to select my own pictures, as long as they derived from the situation I found him in."

And: "At one point...I suggested we go out to the front porch, where the light was very good. I asked him to sit in a rocking chair, which he did, but after a few moments he stood up, telling me this was not the way he would like to be photographed. I was aware, even on first acquaintance, that Dylan is a restless man. It is difficult to pin him down, difficult for him to remain still."

Reading Kramer's description of working with Dylan, who was friendly, not stubborn, but quite clear about what did and didn't work for him—and looking at the photographs, in the dining booth, in the rocking chair, later playing chess with Victor, climbing a tree, practicing with the bullwhip—I get insight into the mystery of who Dylan is. His sitting and reading the paper, not acknowledging the camera, going on about his business, is itself a performance—he knows the camera is there, perhaps even senses eyes looking at the photograph months or decades later, and he is choosing a way of being with the camera that feels right to him, that allows him to express himself accurately. It is a very conscious way of being: his presence fills the space, he has removed the camera's power to make him something he's not—not by "being natural" but by actually expanding his performance and making the camera and cameraman work under his unspoken direction. He does the same thing with musicians on stage or in the recording studio. He doesn't tell them what to do. Rather he fills the space in such a way that whatever they do is in relation to his aesthetic presence. He not only is true to himself; he creates a zone around himself in which cameras, musicians, microphones, all transmitters, cannot help but be true to him (to what he's feeling in the moment).

On October 31, 1964, Bob Dylan appeared in concert at Philharmonic Hall in New York City. Columbia Records recorded the entire show, and at some later date the tape escaped from their vaults and started circulating among Dylan fans. As a result we have something quite precious: a very good recording (in terms of sound quality) of a complete Dylan concert from his "folk star" (pre-electric) period.

"Don't let that scare you," Dylan says to the audience at one point, possibly in reference to his harmonica playing or to some gesture or grimace he's making; "It's just Halloween... I have my Bob Dylan mask on. I'm mask-erading." (He laughs.) Dylan sounds stoned—it seems likely that he's been smoking marijuana, and he may have swallowed a benny or two (a benzedrine pill; a mild amphetamine) as well. But stoned or not, he proves himself to be an absolute master of the art of performing. When he talks between songs, he's charming and very funny (he has the audience laughing with him constantly). When he sings and plays, his songs come to life as though he were painting them in the air in front of you. He has a power, a presence, that doesn't yield to easy explanations. "To Ramona" and "Hard Rain" and "Hattie Carroll" are performed here in a style very similar to their official studio recordings—neither the arrangements nor the words have been changed significantly—and yet hearing them here is a new and strikingly different experience. The feeling of the songs is different, and in ways that make you love them all the more, like seeing a favorite spot in the woods in a different light, at a different time of day.

Dylan's choice of material ranges back to "Talking John Birch" (now almost three years old) and ahead to three major songs that will be included on his next album: "Mr. Tambourine Man," "It's Alright, Ma," and "Gates of Eden." He starts his performance with "The Times They Are A-Changin'," as he'd been doing for a year and would continue to do until his last unaccompanied concert, May 1965. Over the years, for most of his concert tours, Dylan has tended to work out a basic choice of songs and stay with it, sometimes throwing in surprises or switching back and forth between a couple of songs at a particular spot in the program. There are exceptions, tours or portions of tours when he was completely unpredictable, but the song lists from 1964-65 indicate that even before he had a band to rehearse with he preferred having a familiar structure to work within, a script to fall back on or embellish or play around with. The order in which the songs are done is important to him, perhaps in terms of what the songs communicate but also in terms of his energy, some songs to warm up with or break the ice, probably he finds that it doesn't work (for his voice or his mood) for certain songs to follow certain other songs, whereas other combinations turn out to be particularly satisfying or stimulating, keep the energy going or allow a little comic relief or tickle him in some private way the audience will never be aware of.

At Philharmonic Hall he sings eighteen songs, three of them

with Joan Baez (she also sings one song, "Silver Dagger," solo, accompanied by Dylan on guitar and harmonica). Three songs are from the *Freewheelin'* album, three are from *The Times They Are A-Changin'*, five are from *Another Side*, three will be on *Bringing It All Back Home*, and four are songs he's never recorded or released, some old (so not recording them didn't mean he didn't like them), some new. The sequence is: "Times," "Spanish Harlem Incident," "Talking John Birch," "Ramona," "Who Killed Davey Moore?", "Gates of Eden," "If You Gotta Go, Go Now," "It's Alright, Ma," "I Don't Believe You," "Mr. Tambourine Man," "Hard Rain," "Talking World War III," "Don't Think Twice," "Hattie Carroll," "Mama, You Been on My Mind," "Silver Dagger," "With God on Our Side," "It Ain't Me Babe," and "All I Really Want to Do." Baez joins him on "Mama," "With God," and "It Ain't Me Babe." "All I Really Want to Do" is his encore. (People are calling for songs and someone shouts, "Mary Had a Little Lamb!" The audience laughs. Dylan pauses, then says, "God, did I record *that*?" He starts tuning his guitar. " 'Mary Had a Little Lamb.' Is that a protest song?" The audience laughs again, Dylan sucks on the harmonica a few times and begins singing: "I ain't looking to compete with you...")

Two things are particularly notable about this concert. One is Dylan's rapport with the audience, all his kidding around—he's having a great time, he loves being loved. The other is the sheer beauty of so much of this music.

Of all the aspects of art, beauty is the most important and the most difficult to comment on. The essence of beauty is that it pleases, and pleasure defies both analysis and description. One thing that can be said is that beauty is a thing in motion. As beautiful as the *Freewheelin'* performance of "Don't Think Twice" is, an exact replica of that performance on the Philharmonic stage (if such a thing were even possible) could not have matched the fresh, edgy, unexpected version of the song that emerged from Dylan in the context of the concert and of whatever he was feeling about life and about this song on October 31, 1964, circa 10:00 p.m. This is not a matter of comparison. The point is that a replica would be dead, whereas this performance is utterly alive. It starts from an apparent feeling of belligerence about the "classic" status of the song and uses that feeling as a source of energy with which to explore the incredible plasticity of the song's structure, melody, and lyrics, and of Dylan's performance style—his voice goes right off the edge of melody into screech and instead of backing off he leans into it, makes it work for him, develops it and even echoes it in his harmonica solos. He's out there, creating joyously and extemporaneously at the very moment he's performing, stomping about in unexplored territory, having so much fun and feeling so good about the song's ability to sustain this experiment that he falls in love with it all over again, rediscovers how much it means to him and how well it's able to speak for him.

And then the next song is "The Lonesome Death of Hattie Carroll," and Dylan's mood toward this one is pure affection, he just loves this song, I mean he holds it in his arms and coos at it like a proud papa. He doesn't roughhouse with it like he did with "Don't Think Twice," but he doesn't leave it alone either. When he sings "*Hat*tie *Car*roll was a maid of the kitchen" so much of his personality and of what he's feeling comes through that the effect on the listener is wrenching, there's a sweetness and an intensity here that's overwhelming, that makes you want to cry, not for injustice or murder but, strange as it seems, for the beauty of the world. The performance evokes colors, the colors of human feelings transformed into sound. "The Lonesome Death of Hattie Carroll" was a great song when Dylan recorded it, and now it's another great song, a different great performance.

Dylan wrote a piece that appeared in the program book for the Philharmonic concert, called "Advice for Geraldine on Her Miscellaneous Birthday" (reprinted in *Lyrics*). It's a marvelous prose poem, about the price of being true to yourself in public ("if you go too far out in any direction, they will lose sight of you, they'll feel threatened, thinking that they are not a part of something that they saw go past them"). It has a fine sustained mood, rhythm, and structure, and breathes with the aliveness of being something the poet really wanted and needed to say.

There were other Dylan concerts in the fall of 1964: Boston, New Haven, Philadelphia, Buffalo, Toronto, San Francisco, San Jose, Santa Barbara, and more. A couple of partial audience tapes from the Northern California shows have emerged, and offer more fine performances along the lines of the New York concert. Dylan had them laughing (and cheering) wherever he went. A taste of the backstage meet-the-press-and-all-the-people-with-their-questions, aggressive, rowdy, stoned alcoholic restless boys-driving-around-town-shouting-out-the-windows side of Dylan tours is available on a tape of Bob Blackmar's "interview" with Dylan, road manager Victor Maimudes, and other Dylan pals, which was broadcast on the college radio station in Santa Barbara, December 1964.

The best descriptions of Dylan in concert and Dylan backstage ('64-'65) can be found in the text Daniel Kramer wrote to accompany his book of photographs. He talks about Dylan's "incredible degree of professionalism" at "meeting the challenges [the travel time, the confinement, the boredom, the constantly changing working environment] that are a part of a performer's life." He describes him working on new material in his notebook while traveling, trying out melodies on a backstage piano. He describes the tremendous difference in mood before a concert and after— great calm, clarity, privacy before; restlessness and partying after ("he was seldom able to quit when his work was done"). He talks about Dylan on stage: "He would start strumming his guitar before he reached the mike, as if he couldn't contain himself...as if to say, there's hardly enough time to get it all out. Once I asked him which songs he was going to sing. He said the problem was not which ones to perform but which ones to leave out. He wanted to do them all. He wanted to get it all said."

In January 1965 Dylan went into the studio for two days with Tom Wilson and, for the first time since 1962, some back-up musicians, to record his fifth album, *Bringing It All Back Home*. He had a batch of new songs, and as always a new self-image, a bigger and better (further evolved) Bob Dylan mask to try on. He also had a new friend in his life. Sometime in the last few months Albert Grossman's wife Sally had introduced Dylan to Sara Lowndes, a divorcee with an infant daughter. (Ten years later he described the meeting: "I came in from the wilderness/A creature void of form/'Come in,' she said, 'I'll give you/Shelter from the storm.' ")

11.

Among other things, *Bringing It All Back Home* had a substantial effect on the language of a generation (if we recognize that language is made of phrases as well as words, and that a phrase that is repeated often in conversation and written communication will influence us not only by its content but by its form and style, the way it puts words together; this is so basic to the thought process that a handful of powerful phrases can actually affect the way people think in a particular culture at a particular time). Dylan like Benjamin Franklin can list among his many achievements the authorship of a remarkable number of successful aphorisms. The following widely-quoted lines are all from this album:

> "Don't follow leaders."
> "He who is not busy being born is busy dying."
> "Don't ask me nothin' about nothin'; I just might tell you the truth."
> "I ain't gonna work on Maggie's farm no more."

"I try my best to be just like I am, but everybody wants you to be just like them."

"You don't need a weatherman to know which way the wind blows."

"Even the president of the United States sometimes must have to stand naked."

"Money doesn't talk, it swears."

"Meantime life outside goes on all around you."

"I said, 'You know, they refused Jesus, too.' He said, 'You're not Him.' "

"She's an artist, she don't look back."

And there are many more. And in addition to the lines that have gone into general circulation, there are for most individual listeners to this and other Dylan albums a handful of lines that have taken on deep personal significance, that hang around and run through the mind often quite detached from the song they originated in. The impact of this sort of penetration of individual and collective consciousness by works of art (and, therefore, by the personality or consciousness of the artist) is hard to measure, but we know that it is enormous. Bach and Shakespeare continue to this day to be present in much of the music and literature that is created in the world; their perceptions of reality and the ways they found to express their perceptions still influence human behavior and human self-awareness.

It's only twenty-two years since "Subterranean Homesick Blues" was first released to a shocked world (see, it has electric guitar and a rocking piano and strong backbeat and is therefore "rock and roll." At the time many if not most Bob Dylan fans considered themselves "folk music" listeners and tended to be contemptuous of siblings and acquaintances who were listening to that trashy rock and roll—i.e., the Beatles. The sudden appearance of "Subterranean Homesick Blues," which was a moderately successful pop single, and the other electric tracks on *Bringing It All Back Home*, put a lot of people on the spot—some reacted by calling Dylan a "sellout," not realizing, at least at first, that he was now making the most anti-establishment, revolutionary music of his or anyone's career), but so far it stands up extraordinarily well: after all that's gone down, in music and in the universe, everything about this song (the sound, the lyrics, the vocal performance) is as fresh and exciting today as it was the day it was released. If Dylan like Shakespeare is to be someday remembered for having created combinations of language that "age cannot wither," "Subterranean Homesick Blues" will be a shining example thereof. Just as my classmates and I spent days memorizing "The quality of mercy is not strained," I can easily imagine future schoolchildren bemusedly standing before the class to recite:

> Maggie comes fleet foot
> Face full of black soot
> Talkin' that the heat put
> Plants in the bed but
> Phone's tapped anyway
> Maggie says that many say
> They must bust in early May
> Orders from the D.A.

(Of course some future Kittredge will have footnoted the text to explain the significance of "heat," "plants," "bust," and "D.A." and perhaps to pontificate on the sense of community that prevailed in the mid-1960s among early urban users of illegal psychotropic drugs.)

Some recorded performances ("Ticket to Ride" by the Beatles, "The Last Time" by the Rolling Stones, "Reach Out I'll Be There" by the Four Tops, to name some contemporary examples) achieve a sound that is mysterious in its perfection, something serendipitous that goes far beyond anything the performers and producers could have achieved through mere conscious cleverness. "Subterranean Homesick Blues" has this quality. To be sure, 90% of the power of the recording is in the phenomenal energy and intelligence of Dylan's vocal performance, and it would have been criminal if the musicians present had messed up the take by not being perfectly synched into the spirit of Dylan's singing (not that they had a choice—I contend that at Dylan's moments of greatest power he plays the musicians with his voice; they are helpless but happy instruments). But there's a breathlessness to the performance, the way the bass guitar in particular, and all the instruments as an ensemble, punctuate and mirror his phrasing, that seems magical, just the right mix, just the right fade, just the right echoes in the room, and the result is you can listen to the track over and over and over again and still want to hear it some more (Dylan achieved this again in the seventies with another, very different-sounding, single, "Knockin' on Heaven's Door").

Dylan's book *Lyrics* (and the early edition called *Writings and Drawings*) offers a unique insight into the creation of a Dylan classic by reproducing a manuscript page of "Subterranean Homesick Blues," complete with coffee cup stains. We know from other accounts that Dylan often wrote songs on the typewriter; now we get to see a song unfolding on the typed page, like a blank sheet of paper taking a photographic impression of Dylan's mind.

The first thing that strikes me is that there are no spaces between the lines of type. It's clear from the flow of thought on the page that he's not typing up something he'd already written down in a notebook; this typed page is the start, the first draft. The advantage of double-spacing first draft is that it gives room to make changes and corrections; the advantage of single-spacing is that it's less self-conscious, words may flow faster, like writing a letter to a friend. Someone writing a poem or a song line by line would almost have to double-space. The person who typed this manuscript page was writing verses, not lines (paragraphs, not sentences). This tells a lot about the process that creates all this spontaneous language and imagery, all the internal rhyming and near-rhyming and the extraordinarily imaginative, effective, expressive rhythmic pulse of the writing. It wouldn't happen if the writer wrote a line, fooled with it, made it right, then wrote the next line. The lines, rhymes, rhythms, images chosen are spontaneous, the product of a quick mind grabbing for what comes, what fits. The destination the speaker's rap is rolling towards is the end of the verse/paragraph/overall thought/complete feeling, not the end of the line. No stopping, keep moving. Don't slow down.

"Subterranean Homesick Blues" can be heard as a brilliant early example of rap music. Dylan is a natural rapper—and this song is a clear stylistic extension of his non-song writing style, particularly "Advice to Geraldine" though the technique was already apparent in "Last Thoughts on Woody Guthrie"—but he's far from the first to turn hip talk, black street bop talk, hip bop, into popular song; in fact he's drawing consciously or unconsciously here on Chuck Berry's 1957 rock rap, "Too Much Monkey Business." In the *Biograph* interview Dylan says, "Nothing is new. Everybody just gets their chance—most of it just sounds recycled and shuffled around, watered down. Even rap records, I love that stuff but it's not new, you used to hear this stuff all the time…" The 1965 Dylan no doubt would have considered this 1985 Dylan a hopeless old fart, with all his "nothing is new, music is dead, I've heard it all before" poor-mouthing, but, attitude aside, his musicology is sound.

Dylan's manuscript page begins "man in a coonskin cap in the pigpen wants 11dollars bills an i only got ten". This could be something he thought of while writing another verse and he rolled the paper up to jot it down before he forgot—or it could be that it's the first inspired breath of the song, interesting because this line includes the song's primary rhythmic hook. The next things typed on the page are "i stumble downtown" and "man wants a pay off". He's thinking on paper. Then suddenly the song starts pouring out:

> a voice come sounding like a passenger train
> look out kid, it's something you did
> god knows when but you're doing it again
> better duck down the doorway/ looking for a new friend

This is tremendously exciting. Dylan's process is naked before us now. When the writing really starts coming, it's the chorus that comes, leading him right into an idea for a possible verse (he doesn't skip a space) "here comes maggie/ strutting down the fifth street" which immediately rearranges itself in his brain (he's hitting his stride now) into the magnificent "maggie comes fleetfoot/ face full of black soot…." He types out the whole verse quoted earlier, precisely as he'll later sing it, no strikeovers, Athena bursting full-grown from Zeus's forehead, and proceeds directly into the chorus, dropping the "a voice come sounding" line, demonstrating that he now has the verse and the way it moves into the chorus, structure is achieved and what's left is playing with words, finding what clicks. We're privileged on this page to watch him try a couple of false starts; we see the first verse slowly sort itself out ("Johnny's in the basement" isn't here yet, instead it's "daddy's in the dimestore/ getting 10 cent medicine," and it's the second line, the first being "walking down pavement/ thinking bout the govt" and we can see through the x's—the strikeover—that this started as "walking down mainstreet") while the other two verses jump out breathless and complete like Maggie did, as though as soon as he found "get sick" and "get born" everything else followed naturally, words stumbling against each other in their hurry to hit the page. Yow!

The performance of "Mr. Tambourine Man" included on *Bringing It All Back Home* is on my short list of Dylan's masterpieces. It says something about how our minds work that so many people have speculated on "who" Mr. Tambourine Man is—even though who he is is quite apparent in the song. He's the source of the rhythm the singer hears, no more, no less. The tambourine player, the everpresent percussionist. Dylan lays it out in his album notes: "my songs're written with the kettledrum in mind/a touch of any anxious color. unmentionable. obvious. an people perhaps like a soft brazilian singer." Dylan is not only thinking of a kettledrum, he's hearing one. At his most joyous moments (many of which he shares with us in his songwriting, re-creating and re-experiencing the feeling as he performs), he dances to that rhythm. "Play a song for me." This can be to the muse, but it doesn't have to be; it can be prayer, or any invoking of spirit—the point is it's universal, not limited to those who are consciously creative or consciously spiritual. Not limited even to those who stay up past the end of the night into the uncharted mysteries of not-quite-morning, though that's the song's specific reference point. The song is for anyone who can feel it, and it's about something so simple we can even put a word to it without too much fear of being misunderstood. The word is freedom.

Daniel Kramer, who took some amazing photographs at these sessions, reports that Dylan tried to record "Mr. Tambourine Man," wasn't satisfied and went on to something else (he'd also taken a stab at it during the *Another Side* session the previous June), and then the next day "announced that he didn't want the engineering booth to goof—that these were long numbers and he didn't want to do them more than once," and proceeded to record the final versions of "Mr. Tambourine Man," "It's Alright, Ma," and "Gates of Eden" in a single take, with no playback between songs! No further evidence is needed that Dylan works in the studio like a stage performer, not like a person making a record. It is as though all three songs came out of him in one breath, easily the greatest breath drawn by an American artist since Ginsberg and Kerouac exhaled "Howl" and *On the Road* a decade earlier.

I've been sitting here picking up the needle on my phonograph so I can hear these three songs in their recorded order, letting myself receive them not as three songs but as one performance. I find it difficult to get past awe at what Dylan has accomplished here. I'm equally distracted by a great affection for each song, each line. But "Mr. Tambourine Man," in addition to being about freedom, is about surrender ("I'm ready to go anywhere, I'm ready for to fade..." "Take me disappearing..."), and I can feel myself letting go of my thoughts and going under the dancing spell of the performance as a whole a little more each time it goes by.

Concentrating on the image of Bob Dylan, twenty-three years old, guitar in hand and harmonica around his neck, alone in the studio singing into a microphone, another presence slowly emerges. It's not Bruce Langhorne, who plays the harmonic guitar part on "Mr. Tambourine Man," and it's certainly not Tom Wilson or anyone else in the engineering booth. It's a projected presence, something sensed by Dylan as he sings: his imagined audience. What an enormous respect he has for whoever he believes is out there on the other side of the recording process!

On the Philharmonic Hall tape he sings these songs extremely well; and one can scarcely ask for a stronger rapport between audience and performer than existed at that concert. But there is also a kind of limitation in being so in touch with an actual audience; it limits you to what is, whereas the imagined or projected audience allows you to shoot for what could be. No one had ever spoken or sung to a folk/pop/rock audience before the way Dylan does on side two of *Bringing It All Back Home*—perhaps no one but Dylan had ever even imagined it was possible. And he probably couldn't imagine it most of the time. But when the moment came in the studio where he could actually feel some kind of gut sense of someone out there connecting with and responding to what this music could be, he just went for it and didn't look back, even announced beforehand that something important's going to happen, this is the take, don't miss it. He could *feel* the people listening, and he had to sing it all fast while he still felt that. The other performances of the songs (in concert), excellent in their own right, had all been leading up to this, the step forward, the quantum leap.

We may say that the album contains the "authoritative" versions of these songs, calling attention to the authority with which Dylan sings them here, a truly mysterious clarity and power that is present in each articulated syllable, each guitar strum, each breath.

Listen closely, listen repeatedly, and the mystery increases. Who is he speaking to, and where is he speaking from? Given that his writing could be so powerful and far-seeing and intelligent and inspired in the first place, how does he manage to sing the words and color them with his guitar as though he is fully conscious of the significance and impact of every nuance of every statement, as though he is feeling each word as he sings it even more intensely and personally than he did when he wrote it? And how does he sustain the extraordinary tone of intimacy with the listener that is expressed in very different ways in each of these three songs, never breaking the mood at any point, never confusing his persona in one song with the ones he adopts in the others ("Mr. Tambourine Man," "It's Alright, Ma," and "Gates of Eden," while recognizably products of the same genius, seem to be paintings rendered with three entirely different palettes, each one made up of textures and colors never repeated in the other works), even while singing all three songs consecutively, almost nonstop? And how does he manage to gallop through them so freely, with such spontaneity and style, without ever flubbing a word?

I imagine that if Dylan could reach back to the experience and answer these questions based on what he felt at the time, the answer to all of them would be that he was, at that moment in the Columbia recording studio, a bridge, connecting a felt listener on one side, a presence Dylan is giving to, with another presence on the other side, something with no name except perhaps "truth" or "song" or "Mr. Tambourine Man," from whom Dylan is receiving. A metaphysician might say the performances were being received from Dylan's "higher self." We all have a higher self, according to this description of reality; the artist's achievement lies in being in touch with it and being able to share it. And Dylan's achievement here and at many moments in his career is the generosity, the totality, with which he shares it: not just a taste or a summation but the entire felt experience of being in touch with a deeper, less compromising, more encompassing truth, translated into a medium simple enough to be broadcast over the airwaves and mass-produced for sale in record stores, and subtle enough to retain its essential richness and complexity and mystery, even when played on a cheap phonograph or listened to by an utterly unschooled ear. Great art—I think of Van Gogh's "Sunflowers"—always has an obvious quality, and without sacrificing any depth of complexity is at least theoretically able to offer nourishment to anyone.

The key to "It's Alright, Ma" is again in the album notes: "I am about t sketch You a picture of what goes on around here sometimes...my poems are written in a rhythm of unpoetic distortion/divided by pierced ears. false eyelashes/subtracted by people constantly torturing each other. with a melodic purring line of descriptive hollowness." Just as "Mr. Tambourine Man" is thematically related to Dylan's 10th and 11th "Outlined Epitaphs" from late 1963, "It's Alright, Ma" expands on an issue raised in the 4th "Epitaph" ("Jim Jim/where is our party?"): the possibility that the most important (and least articulated) political issue of our times is that we are all being fed a false picture of reality, and it's coming at us from every direction. Dylan has made an amazing leap here: he has moved from embracing a particular position in identifiable causes through a period of apparent reaction against "politics" (the *Another Side* songs) to becoming perhaps the leading articulator of a whole new kind of politics, the struggle of new and in many cases unformed worldviews against the rigidity of old, entrenched concepts (and the mechanisms that enforce those concepts). This movement was already underway when the album was recorded, but just barely—the Free Speech Movement was taking form at the Berkeley campus of the University of California at roughly the same time that Dylan was writing "It's Alright, Ma." Dylan lashes out at the enemy ("Moloch" in Ginsberg's 1956 poem "Howl") directly in songs like "It's Alright, Ma" and "Maggie's Farm," and indirectly in all his work starting in 1964 and over the next several years, by refusing to be bound by anyone's concepts of what forms songs and music and popular expression should take. He was a leader by example; he inspired his contemporaries to break new ground in everything they did, whether related to art or politics or communications or careers; he was as much or more than any other single person identified with a continuing shift in mass attitudes that characterized the cultural, political, and personal changes of the 1960s in America and Europe and Australia and Japan. To a large extent he backed into this role, as an unplanned side-effect of "sketching You a picture of what goes on around here sometimes"; but he was also fulfilling a promise he'd implied in that 4th "Epitaph," when he asked, "where is the party that sets a respected road for all of those like me who cry 'I am raginly against absolutely everything that wants t force nature t be unnatural (be it human or otherwise) an I am violently for absolutely everything that will fight those forces (be them human or otherwise)'?"

"It's Alright, Ma" achieves its tremendously successful portrait of an alienated individual identifying the characteristics of the world around him and thus declaring his freedom from its "rules," not with words alone but by creating a compelling sound, a driving rhythm and a unique, ominous melodic tone that are essential in causing the listener to feel the words rather than receive them as ideas. Ironically, this song, which Dylan performs unaccompanied on the "folk side" of his half-folk, half-electric fifth album, is more of a rock and roll performance than anything else on the record, and owes its success to basic rock and roll techniques and values: penetrate with the rhythm and the sound, and let them start hearing the words after they're already hooked on the way the song feels. The primary communicative impact is again through the continuing emergence of isolated phrases into the listener's consciousness: "It is not he or she or them or it that you belong to"; "...flesh-colored Christs that glow in the dark/it's easy to see without looking too far/that not much is really sacred." And it's worth noting that while the song is in one sense a catalog of horrors, it is not pessimistic or downbeat (and certainly not lacking in humor); rather it seems to speak of the individual's power to see through all this, endure it, survive it, and ultimately perhaps prevail against it.

The lyrics of "Gates of Eden" go over the edge into the impenetrable a number of times (shadows metal badge?), but the music and overall mood of the song are so moving it doesn't matter; in fact Dylan seems to address this issue directly in the last verse when he says,

> At dawn my lover comes to me
> And tells me of her dreams
> With no attempts to shovel the glimpse
> Into the ditch of what each one means.

We are forewarned, in effect, that it's uncool to analyze or be concerned with "meaning." More helpfully, he suggests that what he's working with here is dream imagery, and the idea that perhaps it takes the unselfconscious perception and communication that

occurs in altered states to cut through the illusion of everyday
reality:

> At times I think there are no words
> But these to tell what's true
> And there are no truths outside the Gates of Eden.

The phrase "Gates of Eden" might be a sort of free-form,
not-to-be-pinned-down combination of Huxley's "doors of perception" with the biblical myth of a perfect state from which we are all
fallen, plus some other things I can't identify. (Am I shoveling
glimpses into ditches yet?) The essence of the song lies in the
feeling of the lyrics rather than their specific content, and in the
mood evoked by the odd droning accompaniment and by the way
Dylan's voice wraps itself around selected words. Somehow he does
in fact create a dream-state that seems keenly relevant to our
emerging common awareness of the way the world really is (and
isn't); and again individual phrases emerge to dazzle the listener:
"the motorcycle black madonna two-wheeled gypsy queen" and
"upon the beach where hound dogs bay at ships with tattooed
sails/heading for the Gates of Eden." The repetition of the title
phrase has a particularly hypnotic effect.

Note, please, the cameo appearances Dylan-the-singer makes
in each of these epic songs: as a clown in "Mr. Tambourine Man":
"And if you hear vague traces of skipping reels of rhyme [those
four words make a perfect description of this particular song]/to
your tambourine in time, it's just a ragged clown behind/I wouldn't
pay it any mind...", as a sort of demagogue in "It's Alright, Ma":
"one who sings with his tongue on fire...cares not to come up any
higher/but rather get you down in the hole that he's in," and as a
minstrel in "Gates of Eden": "I try to harmonize with songs/the
lonesome sparrow sings." Like many of our finest visual artists,
Dylan enjoys including a little caricature of himself, often ironic,
somewhere in each of his energetic portraits of the carnival of life.

"It's All Over Now, Baby Blue" is certainly in my mind part of
the extraordinary four-song symphony that sprawls across side two
of this album, even if it was recorded a few hours earlier or later
than the other tunes. Here is Dylan's singing at its rawest and most
beautiful; it is as though any notion of singing as a technique or a
skill has fallen away and instead we have singing as an open

window through which another person's presence can be felt, a place for direct contact between two human spirits. There is so much life in this vocal performance it's scary. Dylan says "a poem is a naked person"; here he demonstrates that no poem is as naked as the sound of a human voice.

As for who the song is about: I'd say it's clearly about someone in the listener's life, someone you're feeling some sadness toward, resentment toward, affection for, whatever face comes into your consciousness as you're listening this afternoon. Dylan may have been thinking of a particular person as he wrote it, but not necessarily. Sometimes a song starts with a phrase that jumps into the mind, and the tune and the rest of the words just unroll naturally from there; this one is so universal it could easily have finished writing itself before Dylan got around to thinking about who "Baby Blue" was. In hindsight, though, "Baby Blue" seems the first of a series of songs Dylan sings to someone who acts kind of high and mighty and just might be heading for a fall. When you hear the lines, "the vagabond who's rapping at your door/is standing in the clothes that you once wore," don't you get just a hint that the person Dylan is singing to could even be Bob Dylan himself?

Flipping back to side one, "Bob Dylan's 115th Dream" is very clever and very funny. The laughter at the start of the track is like a declaration of independence for recording artists everywhere. "Outlaw Blues" is a good riff; I named my first book after it, I think because the line "I got no reason to be there but I imagine it would be some kind of change" somehow seemed to sum up everything I was feeling about rock music as I was working on the book, circa early 1968. Just about every Dylan line is somebody's favorite sometime; they all get their chance.

"She Belongs to Me" is a fine performance, one of those strange songs that communicates something very different by its sound than by what it says in its lyrics. Going by the sound, this is one of Dylan's more tender love songs. Going by the lyrics, it's about that man-eater from room 103 in his "New Orleans Rag." This has puzzled Dylan fans enough to have prompted dozens of fascinating complicated theories of what the song is really about, and there will be more as the years go by. "Love Minus Zero/No Limit," often mentioned in the same breath as "She Belongs to Me," actually is a sweet song in words as well as tune and sound, and I think it is the only song on the album that might possibly be for Sara. It's often been pointed out that Dylan praises "his love" for what she isn't. It must have been comforting for him, as 1965 came on like thunder, to have someone around him who knew "there's no success like failure, and that failure's no success at all." ("Everybody wants you to be just like them," he sang in his instant classic "Maggie's Farm"; what's also true is they want you to be just like they *would* be if they could only do it as well as they think you can.)

12.

Among Daniel Kramer's photographs of Dylan at the *Bringing It All Back Home* sessions there are many of Dylan laughing or grinning, including one great sequence of Dylan playing piano, singing, and ultimately throwing his head back and his fists in the air, communicating triumph, delight, unrestrained joy. The cause of his happiness is apparent to anyone looking at the pictures or listening to the record: it's the freshness and spontaneity and familiarity (*that's* the sound I've been hearing in my head!) of the music he and his friends are making together. Calling it "rock and roll" is too simple, and, in the end, inaccurate. "She Belongs to Me" and "Maggie's Farm" and "Love Minus Zero" and "Subterranean Homesick Blues" are like incursions into a musical realm that may not even have existed before those sessions in January 1965, a realm that has beckoned to and inspired musicians and every other sort of listener/creator ever since. In 1977 Dylan told Ron Rosenbaum:

> The closest I ever got to the sound I hear in my mind was on
> individual bands in the *Blonde on Blonde* album. It's that thin, that

wild mercury sound. It's metallic and bright gold, with whatever that conjures up....It was in the album before that, too [*Highway 61 Revisited*]. Also in *Bringing It All Back Home*. That's the sound I've always heard.

There are five known outtakes from these sessions. One is "I'll Keep It with Mine," included on *Biograph*. Another is the un-released song: "If You Gotta Go, Go Now," featured in Dylan's concerts from fall 1964 to spring 1965. The others are alternate takes: "She Belongs to Me" and "Love Minus Zero" backed only by Bruce Langhorne's guitar (no bass, drums, or third guitar), and "It's All Over Now, Baby Blue" solo (on the album take Dylan is backed by William Lee on bass).

Listening to these unreleased alternate takes is a reminder that when Dylan is fully involved in the music he's making, every performance of every song is new and different and exciting. The music is so fluid, so expressive of what Dylan is feeling moment to moment, that it would be misleading to suggest that one melodic or rhythmic or lyrical variant is more true to the song's intention than another. That assumes a specific intent that precedes the writing and performing of a song, whereas all the evidence is that Dylan's songs from this period express a constantly shifting intent which is feeling-based and unconscious at least as much as it is deliberate, conscious, premeditated. The achievement of the songwriter, then, is the creation of words, music, and a song structure resilient enough to serve as a vehicle for the performer's everchanging moods and methods. But plasticity alone won't do the job. To be a powerful vehicle for expression of the performer's moment, a song must also have integrity; it must hold together on its own, shaping what the singer feels at the moment of singing as surely as it is being shaped by those feelings. Singer and song shape each other, and the performance that results can then enter a new relationship in which it shapes and is shaped by the feelings of the person listening.

The unreleased solo outtake of "It's All Over Now, Baby Blue" is particularly moving. Paul Cable in his book *Bob Dylan: His Un-released Recordings* says the outtake is "much better tunewise than the released version" and complains that "on the latter the first two lines of each verse are not much more than a one note shout tapering down the scale at the end." I happen to love that "one note shout" very dearly, and could counter that whatever the "wild mercury sound" is, the released version has it and the outtake doesn't. But comparisons, I keep reminding myself, are not the point. Both versions are powerful, and perhaps the most striking thing is that, while unquestionably the same song, the outtake after a few listenings stirs up distinctly different emotions in me than the released version, it has a mood and a character all its own. Dylan's performance of the same song on the Les Crane TV show in February 1965, backed this time by Bruce Langhorne playing contrapuntal electric guitar (similar to his work on "Tambourine Man"), is yet another approach, subtly but significantly different and quite affecting. (Check out the *Biograph* live recording from 1966 for a fourth excellent variant.) "It's All Over Now, Baby Blue" can be sung and performed a thousand ways—can be sung a thousand ways *by the same singer*— without ever losing its power and essential identity. This is a triumph for the songwriter as well as the singer. And for the listener, it is an opportunity to discover the endless possibilities for beauty and truth that can be coaxed from a seemingly limited construction of rhymed couplets and minor chords.

"If You Gotta Go, Go Now" is a lot of fun—Dylan is speaking, with humor and candor, for every young man's frustrated wish to cut through the mixed signals of the mating game. It's a raucous full-band performance. Dylan fans were surprised not to find it on *Biograph*; it will undoubtedly turn up on some future Dylan compilation.

"I'll Keep It with Mine," a heartbreakingly lovely solo performance on piano and harmonica, did turn up on *Biograph*, after sitting in the vault for twenty years. How can Dylan record something so beautiful and then let it remain unreleased? This is a question that gets asked again and again, which is why so many people collect Dylan tapes or buy bootleg (illegal, unauthorized) Dylan albums. Dylan replies, in the *Biograph* notes, that some songs get left off because there isn't room on the album, and "a lot of stuff I've left off my records I just haven't felt has been good enough. Or maybe it didn't sound like a *record* to me. I never even recorded 'I'll Keep It with Mine,' you know [obviously he did record it, but perhaps he means this track was a demo, played on the piano during the album sessions so someone else could record the song, or a warm-up, a performance never intended for possible release]...but if people like it, they like it."

So Dylan in turn might want to ask us, "What's so great about 'I'll Keep It with Mine,' anyway?" And we reply: the singing. The piano playing. The melody. The simple, mysterious lyrics. The strength of feeling expressed. And we are reminded that even the man who creates the songs and gives the performances may not know how precious they are, may not notice when they go over the line that divides the ordinary from the exquisite.

The liner notes for *Bringing It All Back Home* are excellent—rhythmic prose this time instead of poetry. Dylan makes some important statements here, fitted lightly into the flow of his comedic monolog, about his art and his intentions, his sense of himself and his experience of the world. The cover photo is another performance, and the album title still another. He wants to stimulate, provoke. The album title contradicts those who will call his "rock and roll" move a sellout, by announcing that he's returning to his roots. But the cover challenges those who will want to believe that in any case he's the same scruffy Dylan he's always been, by showing him expensively dressed and coiffed, in an expensive living room with an expensive-looking woman. Is this a joke? Yes. But what's it mean? Ahahahaha. It means the joke's on you if you can't take a joke. It means I'm everything you think I am and none of those things. It means I dare you to meet my eyes. Keep 'em guessing.

Maybe it meant, "I'm not a folk star any more." But that wasn't quite true. In March of 1965, when *Bringing It All Back Home* was released, Bob Dylan was on tour with Joan Baez—they had "special guested" each other's concerts since July 1963; now they were doing an actual joint tour, with co-billing. Surprisingly, no tapes have surfaced. There are some incomplete tapes of Dylan solo concerts from April (Santa Monica, California and Sheffield, England) and May (Royal Albert Hall, London)—the performances are good but uninspired. He seems to be doing the same set he did at Philharmonic Hall the previous Halloween (plus "Baby Blue," "She Belongs to Me," and "Love Minus Zero"), but without the intensity and playfulness and enthusiasm for performing that made that concert so wonderful.

By the spring of 1965 Dylan was bored, very bored, with being a "folk" performer, singing and playing guitar and harmonica alone in front of reverent, sold-out crowds. His new album was selling well and he loved the pop/rock version of "Mr. Tambourine Man" that had been released in April by a new group called the Byrds and was on its way to becoming a number one hit in the U.S. He went to England in late April and experienced his first real taste of pop stardom, with the press and the fans reacting to him as if he were America's answer to the Beatles. But somehow he had painted himself into a corner in terms of his concerts—the spontaneity was gone, the audiences and the music were too predictable, it had all become routine. At one point in the documentary film *Don't Look Back* (shot during the British tour), Dylan turns to his friend Bobby Neuwirth just before walking onstage for a concert and says, "I don't feel like singing." Of course, he could have said that before any concert, could have said it and then gone out and given a great performance, but in this case the tapes and the filmed performances suggest that in fact it was true—he didn't feel like singing. He did it, and did it well, because it was expected of him and he was being paid and his pride was on the line and so forth...but the magic was gone.

"After I finished the English tour," Dylan told Jules Siegel in February 1966, "I quit because it was too easy. There was nothing happening for me. Every concert was the same: first half, second half, two encores and run out, then having to take care of myself all night. I didn't understand; I'd get standing ovations and it didn't mean anything. The first time I felt no shame. But then I was just following myself after that. It was down to a pattern."

Some of the footage in *Don't Look Back* of Dylan onstage (most of it very fragmentary) during the English tour is quite powerful—because Dylan is a great performer, and it's moving to watch him sing and play harmonica and stand alone on a stage delivering his great songs accompanied only by acoustic guitar, still in the upward trajectory of his 1960s stardom, just shy of twenty-four years old. But unfortunately these are not great performances that have been captured on film; they are adequate performances by a great artist temporarily sandbagged by his own success.

Don't Look Back (originally released in 1967, now commercially available on videocassette) was shot and edited by D. A. Pennebaker. It's a portrait on film of Dylan and the scene immediately around him during his tour of England, late April to mid-May, 1965. Much of the footage was shot backstage, in hotel rooms, in

Dylan's car going to and from concerts, and on the street. Albert Grossman, Dylan's manager, is very much present in the film, as is Joan Baez, who apparently went along on the tour because she expected to be a guest performer at Dylan's British concerts and because she was in love with him. He shows little or no sign in the film of being in love with her; and he never did invite her on stage at any of these concerts. Indeed it was not until 1975 that Baez and Dylan sang together again. Bobby Neuwirth is also very visible in the film, as is Alan Price, a fine keyboard player who hangs out backstage with Dylan and drinks a lot on camera. The film is flattering to no one, least of all Dylan, who probably spends more time in the movie being obnoxious to interviewers and other easy marks than he does singing. It's painful to watch at times. One would like to think that this mean (and petty) side of Dylan's personality was a temporary aberration caused by fame or drugs or touring, but alas, scores of different Dylan friends and acquaintances, quoted in a wide variety of books and articles, tell similar stories of Dylan "truth attacks"—vitriolic verbal assaults by Dylan on close friends (Phil Ochs, Victor Maimudes), acquaintances, strangers, always in front of an audience of other friends or hangers-on—some occurring as early as 1960 and 1961.

The great value of *Don't Look Back* is that it humanizes Dylan. He becomes a real person to us—not the real person we want him to be or believe him to be, nor the real person the filmmaker wants him to be, but rather the person the filmmaker found as he aimed his camera and, later, examined and edited what he had—and the person we find as we watch the movie that resulted. It isn't necessary to understand this person, or to justify or approve or disapprove of his behavior. What matters is the opportunity to spend time with him that the film offers, this chance to get to know Bob Dylan a little better, to see the real world of the famous musician, inevitably different from whatever fantasy we might have about it. And of course it is still only the external world we're seeing, the public and semi-public scene. Dylan says near the beginning of the movie (at a moment when he's being sincere and cooperative with a reporter), "This is the part where I don't write. You know, anything that happens I'll just remember, you know. When I'm living my own thing, doing what I do, this is never around me. I mean, I accept everything. I accept this."

"Why?" the reporter asks.

"Well, because it's real, 'cause it exists just as much as the buses outside exist. I mean, I can't turn myself off to it because if I try to fight it, you know, I'm just going to end up going insane faster than I eventually will go insane...if I do go insane...when and if the time comes for me to...go...in...sane." He turns it into a joke, a performance piece, but only after he's told the deepest sort of truth about who he is, what he feels, and the way he's choosing to deal with "his success," that is, his reality.

The movie is rich in images of Dylan with guitar in hand, walking through a door to the stage or standing before the audience with his floodlit shadow streaming out behind him—there is something deeply affecting about these images, perhaps because they've been associated with Dylan (and other beloved singers) for so long, perhaps because there is an authentic mystery in the play of light and shadow, sound and silence, that ripples across the space where the performance is happening, something about the image of one person standing at the focus point of a thousand attentions...a thousand attentions in the hall that night, and a million more watching the film over the years, all tunneling down to that one man and the sounds coming from his mouth and his harmonica and his guitar.

The transcendent musical moment in *Don't Look Back*, for me, occurs in Dylan's hotel room when Dylan sings several verses of a Hank Williams song, "Lost Highway." I also love the scene in which he's playing a dressing room piano. In both cases he seems tapped into something bigger than him, the musical force he acknowledges in "Lay Down Your Weary Tune" and sings to in "Mr. Tambourine Man." He's making music because he loves it, not because it's what's expected of him. When he starts to put down his guitar after two verses of "Lost Highway," Bobby Neuwirth won't let him: "No no no! There's another verse." It's an ecstatic moment—you can see it on Neuwirth's face—and he doesn't want it to end prematurely.

The last concert of the English tour was on May 10. On May 12 Dylan and Tom Wilson went into a London recording studio with John Mayall, Eric Clapton, Hughie Flint and John McVie, thinking about possibly recording or starting a new album; apparently nothing much came of it. Sara Lowndes flew in from the States and she and Dylan and the Grossmans went to Portugal for a holiday. Dylan got sick, but managed to fulfill his last U.K.

responsibility by recording two half-hour TV shows for the BBC on June 1; the twelve acoustic performances survive on audio but not videotape. The performances are fairly routine, uninspired, with the exception of "One Too Many Mornings" which is fresh and passionate. Dylan must have really felt a thousand miles behind by this point.

In hindsight, the BBC-TV filming was the last stand of Bob Dylan, folk star. When he arrived back in the States the Byrds' version of "Mr. Tambourine Man" was at the top of the charts. Dylan immediately purged himself of whatever he'd been through in Britain by writing six pages of "vomitific" prose. He was done with his acoustic songwriter identity. He turned the prose into a song, rounded up a new batch of musicians, and on June 15, 1965, went into Columbia Studio A in New York City and recorded "Like a Rolling Stone."

V. Pop Star

June 1965 — July 1966

"It takes a lot of medicine to keep up this pace."
—Bob Dylan, March 1966

13.

"Like a Rolling Stone" is a whole new kind of music. It often happens that an artist's triumphs come as a response to failure and frustration. Exhaustion and dissatisfaction lay the ground for breakthrough. But since real breakthrough requires that one be at the height of one's powers, the feeling of dissatisfaction (in one's work) that precedes it may not be evident to outside observers—indeed, the very enthusiasm of the audience for work that is no longer meaningful to its creator can be the greatest irritant and goad to the working artist.

All of the elements that make up "Like a Rolling Stone" are foreshadowed in the movie *Don't Look Back*. The vengeful anger, and the self-dissatisfaction and hunger for release that fuel it, are most evident in the scenes where Dylan prosecutes his would-be interviewers. We may be seeing the actual moment of inspiration for the song's title and chorus when Neuwirth demands that Dylan sing another verse of Hank Williams's "Lost Highway," the one that starts, "I'm a rolling stone." Dylan sings:

> I'm a rolling stone, I'm alone and lost
> For a life of sin I've paid the cost
> Take my advice, you'll curse the day
> You started going down that lost highway.

Most of all, "Like a Rolling Stone" is previewed when Dylan sits at a backstage piano somewhere in England and improvises energetically—his producer is nearby, listening, but we can see and hear that Dylan is playing only for himself, working out something that's been running through his mind, the sound of his inner music at this time in his life. It's startling how different it is from what he'll be playing onstage. It's like he's having to go out and strum those guitar chords but what he's hearing inside is this rich, stately, almost classical music, not a folk or rock and roll rhythm but something else, a celebration of the hidden relationships between the notes of the piano, tied together as they are by the magic of chords and the mysterious, complex power of music in motion.

And in the ascending chords Dylan plays at the very beginning of his backstage piano solo we can hear the basic musical pattern—which Dylan has identified as being from Richie Valens's "La Bamba," but to my ear that's only one of a broad variety of influences—that will form the basis of the chorus melody and the repeated harmonic figure in "Like a Rolling Stone." The filmmaker has caught the miracle of creation here, a great work emerging from its creator's subconscious and starting to take form in the material world. Gooseflesh.

Something happened in the brief moment between the end of the U.K. tour (the last concert was May 10, but his last performance was the BBC taping, June 1) and the writing and recording of "Like a Rolling Stone" (we know he wrote it "after England," maybe during a three-day visit to Woodstock with Sara as he recalls in the *Biograph* notes; the recording session took place June 15). Dylan told the same story to at least four different interviewers in late 1965 and early 1966:

> I wrote that after I'd quit. I'd literally quit singing and playing and I found myself writing this song, this story, this long piece of vomit, about twenty pages long, and out of it I took "Like a Rolling Stone." I'd never written anything like that before and it

suddenly came to me that was what I should do. (to Martin Bronstein, February 1966)

Everything is changed now from before. Last spring, I guess I was going to quit singing. I was very drained. I was playing a lot of songs I didn't want to play. I was singing words I didn't really want to sing. But "Like a Rolling Stone" changed it all. It was something that I myself could dig. It's very tiring having other people tell you how much they dig you if you yourself don't dig you. (to Nat Hentoff, fall 1965)

I used to know what I wanted to say before I used to write the song. But now I just write a song like I *know* that it's just going to be all right and I don't really know exactly what it's all about, but I do know the layers of what it's all about. Rolling Stone's the best song I wrote....I wrote Rolling Stone after England. I boiled it down, but it's all there. I had to quit after England. I had to stop and I knew I had to sing it with a band. I always sing when I write, even prose, and I heard it like that. (quoted by Ralph Gleason, December 1965)

He told Jules Siegel the same thing. He quit after England. He quit. What a mystery! How can a man quit, and then write the most important song of his career, and then go into the studio and record it, all in the course of two weeks? The cynic would say, "he must have quit for about five minutes," not realizing that quitting in the sense Dylan means it is not something you do over a period of time. It happens in an instant—and if it's the real thing, it's complete and permanent. You never go back. The literal-minded might think, he means he quit being a solo acoustic performer, he decided to start playing with a band. But that also misses the point. What happened was something much bigger: Dylan quit singing and playing, gave up his career, gave up his work, let it all go. He didn't change what he was doing; he stopped doing it. Forever. He'd come to the end of the road.

The evidence that this is true, paradoxically, can be found in the burst of activity that immediately followed. Something happened that Dylan himself has described as a breakthrough—suddenly he was writing and (at the June 15 session) performing in a completely new way. Whatever had been holding him back was gone and he was bounding forward with giant leaps. Like Christ after going to the desert, he'd passed a turning point—a more significant one, I think, than the motorcycle accident fourteen months later, even though the latter event is much more visible and dramatic in Dylan's personal history. To say that this turning point had something to do with a shift from folk music to rock and roll music is an irritating (or amusing) trivialization, focusing in, as the popular media tend to do, on the form of the artist's work and downplaying the tremendous ongoing spiritual and creative growth that gives the work its character, its energy, its life.

The mechanics of what happened can only be intuited. We see in *Don't Look Back* that Dylan was tired and often reacted with a defensiveness characteristic of a person who feels stuck or trapped. We know that he was quite sick in late May, and this may have been an impetus for change or the expression of an internal change already starting to occur. We know Sara joined him in Europe around that time, and was with him when he went back to New York and Woodstock, and I find it easy to imagine that we are now at the moment in Dylan's life that is later recounted in "Shelter from the Storm":

> I was burned out from exhaustion, buried in the hail,
> Poisoned in the bushes and blown out on the trail
> Hunted like a crocodile, ravaged in the corn...

> Not a word was spoke between us, there was little risk
>   involved
> Everything up to that point had been left unresolved...

> Suddenly I turned around and she was standing there...

Comments in the various interviews already mentioned suggest that Dylan came back to New York, decided in his heart that he was done with singing and playing and being "Bob Dylan," considered that perhaps what was up for him was pursuing his prose-writing ambitions and typed out a cathartic manuscript (he uses the word "vomit" to describe it in half a dozen different interviews and attributes various lengths to it, finally telling Shelton "it seemed like twenty pages, but it was really six"), and then unexpectedly the manuscript started to sing to him, started to become a song even though he'd never intended that, a whole new kind of song:

It wasn't called anything, just a rhythm thing on paper all about my steady hatred directed at some point that was honest. In the end it wasn't hatred, it was telling someone something they didn't know, telling them they were lucky. Revenge, that's a better word.

I had never thought of it as a song, until one day I was at the piano, and on the paper it was singing, "How does it feel?" in a slow motion pace, in the utmost of slow motion following something.

It was like swimming in lava. In your eyesight, you see your victim swimming in lava. Hanging by their arms from a birch tree....Seeing someone in the pain they were bound to meet up with.

I wrote it. I didn't fail. It was straight. (to Jules Siegel, February 1966)

Not much is known about the progression of Dylan's relationship with the woman who became his wife and the mother of his children, but on the evidence of what Dylan himself says in his songs and the few biographical details that are known, I believe that late May and early June 1965 was the watershed period for them, the moment when they shifted from friends ("little risk involved") to soulmates. And in some mysterious way, "Like a Rolling Stone" expresses and celebrates both new relationships: the one with Sara, and the one with himself, his art, his music.

Serendipity is "an apparent aptitude for making fortunate discoveries accidentally" (according to Webster's College Dictionary). Dylan in his recording sessions elevates this aptitude to a high art, seemingly going to great lengths to insure that there's no way for the musicians or producers to fall back on normal ways of doing things—it's going to be the unexpected, the spontaneous, the fortunate accident, or nothing. This comes across often as willful perversity, but combined with the power of Dylan's personality, his ability to create musical excitement, and his casual confidence in the ability of the musicians, whoever they are, to keep up with and contribute to the program, it seems to work, some of the time, and when it does it works phenomenally well. The "Like a Rolling Stone" session, like the *Bringing It All Back Home* sessions five months earlier, is an example of reckless reliance on serendipity producing results that make every musician involved seem like a certifiable genius.

Young white Chicago blues guitar whiz Michael Bloomfield made much of his reputation at this session. He'd never played at a professional recording session before; Dylan had met him years earlier, heard about what a hot guitar player he'd become, and invited him down.

But the real amateur (there were experienced professionals there too—Paul Griffin on piano and Bobby Gregg on drums, both of whom had played on *Bringing It All Back Home*, and Harvey Brooks on bass), and one of Dylan's more extraordinary fortunate accidents, was Al Kooper. Kooper hadn't even been hired for the session—producer Tom Wilson knew him slightly and had invited him to come and watch. Kooper tells the story in his book *Backstage Passes*: he came to the session with fantasies of joining in on guitar, dropped that idea as soon as he heard Bloomfield, and then had his ambitions rekindled when "it was decided that the organ part would be better suited to piano...In a flash I was on Tom Wilson telling him I had a great part for the song." Wilson pointed out that Kooper couldn't play the organ, but Kooper slipped in anyway when Wilson wasn't looking, and desperately invented something to play.

> If the other guy hadn't left the damn thing turned on, my career as an organ player would have ended right there. The best I could manage was to...feel my way through the changes like a little kid fumbling in the dark for a light switch. After six minutes they'd gotten the first complete take of the day down, and all adjourned to the booth to hear it played back. Thirty seconds into the second verse, Dylan motions towards Tom Wilson. "Turn the organ up," he orders.
>
> "Hey, man," Tom says, "that cat's not an organ player."
>
> But Dylan isn't buying it. "Hey, now don't tell me who's an organ player and who's not. Just turn the organ up."...At the conclusion of the playback, the entire booth applauded the soon-to-be-a-classic "Like a Rolling Stone," and Dylan acknowledged the tribute by turning his back and wandering into the studio for a go at another tune.

What is it, finally, that makes this song a classic? This is a tough question; if I have to answer, I'll say it's the vocal performance and everything that surrounds it: the overall sound, the lyrics (especially the irresistible chorus), and the musical structure of the song,

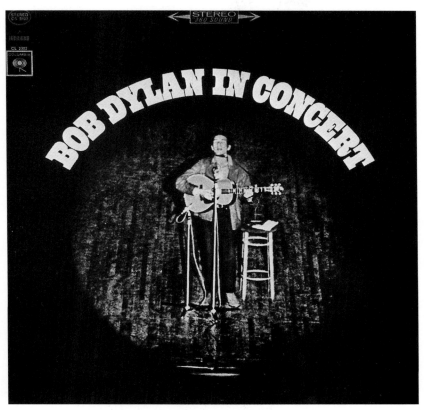

Jacket for live album, prepared but never released, 1964.
(Photo from 1962 or 1963).

Recording session for the first album, November 1961.

Probably 1961.

Bringing It All Back Home session, January 1965.

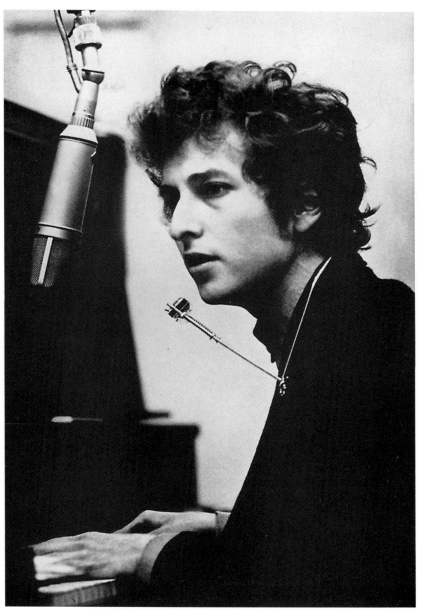

Bringing It All Back Home session, January 1965.

England, May 1965 (from *Don't Look Back*).

Self Portrait, probably spring 1969.

1966.

Concert for Bangladesh, August 1971.

Dylan as Alias, in *Pat Garrett & Billy the Kid*, 1973.

Pat Garrett & Billy the Kid, 1973.

Pat Garrett & Billy the Kid, 1973.

the way it builds and builds and builds on itself, releasing with "How does it feel?" and then building some more, finally reaching apotheosis with that piercing, hugely satisfying harmonica solo at the end. But the vocal performance is the center of it all. The lyrics, verse and chorus both, derive most of their power from Dylan's *diction* as he sings them. Drums, organ, piano, guitar, bass, all these great-sounding performances that work so well together, all exist and take on significance (separately and as a whole) only in relation to the sound of Dylan's voice. What animates the song is the absolute conviction with which the singer says what he has to say.

What does he say? Well, he says how it feels. Most of all, at every moment, he says "I am."

"Once upon a time..." The song needs no interpretation, since it speaks so directly to every person who hears it, but also for that reason it lends itself wonderfully to interpretation, and the best such piece I've read appeared in the Spring 1986 issue of *The Telegraph* (a magazine for Dylan fans), credited to "Hugh Dunnet" and titled "Weary Hugh Tonight." Hugh recounts an insight or a vision that came to him while falling asleep, the thrust of which is that Dylan is singing not to a woman at all but to and about himself, his various selves, expressing contempt for the hollow person he'd become and also celebrating his own rebirth ("his birth cry is the primal demon voice that whoops out the surging refrains of this song...each is a searing, vituperative taunt, designed to needle to the bone. But the tone of the words (as sung) and music is unmistakably joyous, celebratory. [This Dylan] is exultant, jubilant, free, on his own, ecstatic that he is as he once was, a complete unknown—unknown because unknowable"). Hugh identifies the other characters in the song—the mystery tramp, the diplomat, Napoleon in rags—as also being Dylan, so that the song chronicles his ongoing relationship with his other or former or inner selves...the explanation is more confusing than the song itself, but I like it, it has the ring of truth.

Meanwhile Dylan moved on to the next thing. He tried three or four more songs the following day, June 16; took six weeks off; came back to the studio at the end of July; and by early August had completed a new album called *Highway 61 Revisited*.

14.

"Like a Rolling Stone" was released as a single on July 20, 1965, in two versions, one full-length (six minutes) and one cut in half to facilitate radio airplay. It was an immediate hit, peaking at #2 on the U.S. charts at the end of August. The success of this record, coming on top of the Byrds' "Mr. Tambourine Man" and a flock of hit records that were either Dylan songs ("It Ain't Me Babe" by the Turtles, "All I Really Want to Do" by Cher) or sounded like Dylan in some way ("Eve of Destruction" by Barry McGuire), established Dylan as a pop star of the first order, right up there with the Beatles and the Rolling Stones. It was a dream come true for the boy who'd once wanted to join Little Richard, who almost went on the road with Bobby Vee. Dylan had triumphed in his chosen field, and he'd done it completely on his own terms.

"You'll find out when you reach the top, you're on the bottom," he later wrote. Dylan had been famous, had been the center of attention, for a long time. But now the ante was being upped again. He'd become a pop star as well as a folk star (though the latter crown would soon be stripped from him, since the folk world doesn't recognize dual citizenship), and was, even more than the Beatles, a public symbol of the vast cultural, political, generational changes taking place in the United States and Europe. He was perceived as, and in many ways functioned as, a leader. He was twenty-four years old. The pressure was enormous.

On July 25, 1965, Dylan made his first public appearance with a band. It was the Sunday night concert at his old stomping grounds, the Newport Folk Festival. Michael Bloomfield was at Newport with the Paul Butterfield Blues Band, a young ensemble (part white, part black) who were playing kick-ass Chicago blues and bringing it to a whole new audience. (They played three nights at Club 47 in Cambridge that month and I was there for every minute of it; it was like I'd died and gone to heaven.) So Dylan recruited Bloomfield and Jerome Arnold and Sam Lay (lead guitar, bass, drums) from the Butterfield Band, plus Al Kooper and Barry Goldberg (organ, piano), to accompany him on his first electric appearance. They practiced well into the night on Saturday, and Sunday night they went on the Newport stage and roared through "Maggie's Farm," "Like a Rolling Stone," and "It Takes a Lot to Laugh." They left the stage, and Dylan was asked to go back on and do some solo numbers; he agreed, and sang "It's All Over Now, Baby Blue" and "Mr. Tambourine Man." The whole set has been preserved on audiotape, and partial videos of "Maggie's Farm" and "Tambourine Man" can be seen in the documentary film *Festival*.

The fame of this performance (Shelton compares it, not inappropriately, to the tumultuous premiere of Stravinsky's "The Rite of Spring") rests on the fact that the audience booed. I'm not sure they booed all that much (only applause can be heard on the tape), and one theory has it that the real problem was the sound mix (the audience couldn't hear Dylan's voice). But it doesn't matter. Myths have a life of their own, and in the long run they are a truer reflection of human history than facts tend to be. As soon as the idea of Dylan being booed by his folk audience for "going electric" got out, it caught the imagination on the one hand of historians and journalists (who thrive on conflict) and on the other hand of that portion of Dylan's audience who felt threatened by his continuing growth, many of whom sincerely believed that "rock and roll" commercialism equalled sellout to the Establishment. They came to Dylan's next concert, Forest Hills, August 28, and loudly booed the electric part of the show, and the boos and criticism continued, slowly diminishing in the U.S. but reviving with a vengeance when Dylan toured in England in the spring of 1966. For Dylan it was a blessing in disguise—he was rattled at Newport, but by Forest Hills he'd achieved a genuine appreciation for the booing, presumably because it gave the shows an edge, made them more real, gave him a sense of standing tall for something he believed in, a political figure again instead of a safe, cuddly, Bob Dylan protest doll.

At Newport, on "Maggie's Farm," Dylan sings well (his first electric live performance, opening song of his new career) but is upstaged by Mike Bloomfield's brilliant and aggressive lead guitar. The song definitely rocks. "Like a Rolling Stone" 's live debut is ragged but effective; a rich ensemble sound is achieved, with Kooper's organ playing the most striking element. "Phantom Engineer" (the original name for "It Takes a Lot to Laugh") is another hot track; Kooper and Bloomfield square off as equals this time, and do some outrageous jamming. For the kids who were ready for it these songs were great blues-based rock and roll with the added dimension of Dylan's lyrics and powerful vocal presence; for the uninitiated, it was not just electric instruments on a "folk" stage but probably the loudest, most piercing, most cacophonous noise they ever endured in the name of entertainment.

I don't think Dylan was deliberately being confrontational (for once). He was just following his muse, his ear, moving out of a format that no longer worked for him and into a world rich with new possibilities. He probably thought his audience, the Newport audience (synonymous in his mind since the 1963 triumph), would follow along enthusiastically (he may even have pictured them asking, "What took you so long?"). "I ain't gonna work on Maggie's farm no more" is always a declaration of independence, but there's no hostility in Dylan's singing here—the words don't seem to be aimed at anyone present. Nor does he sing "It's All Over Now, Baby Blue" as a sad goodbye or angry kiss-off. Stimulated by the electric set, he puts his heart into the acoustic numbers as well. "Baby Blue" is lovely; "Tambourine Man" is pretty but a little pat, rescued by an inspired harmonica finale.

As usual, whatever it meant to the crowd and to the media, the performance meant something else to the performer. Judging from what he did next, I'd say Dylan *loved* working with a band, and that rather than choosing to play with less assertive musicians (the evidence is he would have taken Bloomfield on the road with him if he'd been available) he resolved instead to grow as a performer, to make his voice, his stage presence, big enough to incorporate into itself whatever wild music his accompanists could come up with. He found another incredible guitar player, Robbie Robertson, and a band that could kick ass equal to anyone around in 1965-66 (or before or since), but very seldom if ever did he get upstaged by his accompanists again.

Four days after Newport, Dylan got his revenge on the "folk crowd" who rejected him (and who had been attacking him, baiting him, condescending to him since the release of *Another Side of Bob Dylan* twelve months earlier), by recording "Positively Fourth Street" as his single to follow "Like a Rolling Stone." The song functions as a kind of universal put-down, "the perfect squelch," but it also speaks quite specifically to Dylan's critics in the folk community (Dylan lived on West 4th Street in Greenwich Village in his folk days), particularly Irwin Silber, editor of *Sing Out!*, who wrote a piece in the November 1964 issue of *Sing Out!* called "An Open Letter to Bob Dylan": "Dear Bob...I'm writing this letter now because some of what has happened is troubling me. And not me alone. Many other good friends of yours as well..." And so forth. Dylan over the years has had to put up with an endless succession of public admonitions from "friends" and strangers telling him what he should be doing; this song serves as his permanent, all-purpose reply (especially for those who think "Maggie's Farm" and "It Ain't Me Babe" aren't addressed to them). On the videotape of the December 1965 press conference, someone tells Dylan he's hard on people in a lot of his songs—"Rolling Stone," "Fourth Street"—and asks, "Are you hard on them because you want to torment them, or because you want to change their lives and make them know themselves?" Dylan screws up his face into a very serious and rather demonic grin and says, "I want to *needle* them."

"Positively Fourth Street" is Dylan having fun with the airwaves, using them to send his own "open letter," breaking all the rules of top 40 radio. "Like a Rolling Stone" was an unheard-of length for a single, six minutes, and he followed it with a top ten hit that has no chorus (no recognizable repeating phrase) and the title of which is never mentioned in the song. How can radio listeners be expected to remember or request such a record? But they did.

Dylan also has fun here with his own reputation for rich, complex, poetic lyrics: "Positively Fourth Street" is written in relentlessly plain language. Far from seeing pop music or rock and roll as a commercial interest to sell his soul to, Dylan saw it (correctly; 1965 was a very unusual time for pop music) as a huge new playground to create and communicate and be perverse in.

In addition to "Positively Fourth Street," the July 29 recording session (same musicians as "Like a Rolling Stone," but a new producer, Bob Johnston) provided two tracks for *Highway 61 Revisited*: "Tombstone Blues" and "It Takes a Lot to Laugh, It Takes a Train to Cry." It was a great day in the studio. If on June 15 Dylan invented a new kind of music, on July 29 he consolidated his gains.

A sound was emerging. Bruce Springsteen: "The main thing I dug about [Dylan's 1965-66 albums] was the *sound*...Before you listened to anything of what was happening in the song, you heard the chorus and you heard the sound of the band, he had just an incredible sound, and that's what got me." Dylan, in his 1978 *Playboy* interview with Ron Rosenbaum (where he spoke of the "thin, wild mercury sound" on his 1965-66 albums), offered some insight into the relationship between the sound of his music and its content:

> Dylan: Music filters out to me in the crack of dawn.
> RR: The "jingle-jangle morning"?
> D: Right.
> RR: After being up all night?
> D: Sometimes. You get a little spacy when you've been up all night, so you don't really have the power to form it.
> But that's the sound I'm trying to get across. I'm not just up there re-creating old blues tunes or trying to invent some surrealistic rhapsody.
> RR: It's the sound that you want.
> D: Yeah, it's the sound and the words. Words don't interfere with it. They—they—punctuate it. You know, they give it purpose. [Pause] And all the ideas for my songs, all the influences, all come out of that.

The creative artist is an explorer who penetrates an unknown realm, and brings back more than what he knew he was looking for. For a painter, this realm is visual; it is explored as brush touches canvas, leaving behind color and line, and as shapes and impressions and feelings, expected and unexpected, emerge from those lines and colors. For Dylan, a musician-writer-performer, the realm is aural, explored with voice, guitar, piano, typewriter—a realm of sound with words in it. This is where he works; this is where he makes his discoveries. It isn't two separate realms, one of words and their meanings, the other of musical sounds and relationships. It is a single place where a single thing happens.

The thing that happens in "Tombstone Blues" (and "Desolation Row" and "Just Like Tom Thumb's Blues") is evocation of a scene, a place. A feeling. I was going to include "Ballad of a Thin Man" on this list, but there what's evoked is a *situation*. The difference is "Ballad of a Thin Man" focuses on a single protagonist, the "you" who is addressed throughout the song. There's lots of scene in the song, plenty of freaky atmosphere, but the situation dominates. In "Tombstone Blues" there is no consistent protagonist or situation, so scene is what comes over. "Desolation Row" also focuses on scene, but in a more purposeful way: the images build up powerfully, propelled by the vocal and instrumental performances. The song makes a statement: this scene is important, it needs to be paid attention to, there *is* a reality in this life which may not be cheerful but which, once discovered, shows everything else to be a pose. "Desolation Row" is an anthem; it proclaims and forever defines a certain place, certain state of being. "Tombstone Blues" is more of a stoned lark: look how weird it is around here sometimes. "Just Like Tom Thumb's Blues" combines scene and situation: both are tremendously evocative, neither resolves itself into a single clear picture of what the song's "about." (It doesn't want to be clear; it is an absolutely gorgeous evocation of muddied consciousness.) Notice how "Tom Thumb" has three verses that are basically second person ("you"), two that are first person (including the last verse, which therefore gives the autobiographical side of things a special punch), and one that is entirely third person, similar to most of "Desolation Row." Lots of neat confusion as to who's singing, who's being sung to, and who's being sung about. "It Takes a Lot to Laugh," on the other hand, is all first person, totally a mood piece, with great visuals ("leanin' on the window sill," "sun...going down over the sea," "windows are filled with frost"), the content of which is entirely emotional, so that the conjured images become vessels into which melody and voice are poured to overflowing, song leaking into and out of all the cracks in the listener's heart.

Allen Ginsberg, who knew Dylan in 1965, was asked in a 1985 interview, "Dylan didn't like to be pinpointed on specific things, did he? Like who was Mr. Jones, or where was Desolation Row?" Ginsberg replied, "I don't think there was a pinpoint. His interest was in improvised verses which he would sometimes blurt out into a microphone without knowing what the next word was going to be....Sometimes he would listen to what he had said and write it down and straighten it out a little. [It] didn't necessarily mean something in the sense that he set out to mean something, but it would mean something in terms of indicating the cast or direction of his mind or mood, or specific references or thought-forms that were passing through his mind at that time...it was a composite of what was going on in his mind."

The Vietnam War was one of the things going through Dylan's mind when he wrote/sang "Tombstone Blues" ("...fattens the slaves/then sends them out to the jungle"), but one would be hard put to claim the song is *about* the war. The influence of Depression-era songs like "Wandering" ("Daddy is an engineer/ Brother drives a hack/Sister takes in washing/And the baby balls the jack") can also be spotted, but shall we then say it's a song about the "new Depression"? Fiddle-faddle. Judges 15-16 (the biblical chapters that tell of Samson and the Philistines) are referred to three more-or-less separate times, but can we infer any special intention from this? Not necessarily. Maybe free-associating from the word "Philistines" (easy to think of that word when thinking of Lyndon Johnson, in those days) led automatically to the little scene between Galileo and Delilah which in turn led to describing "Brother Bill" 's masochistic longings for martyrdom in terms of casting him as Samson in the DeMille spectacular (Dylan maybe saw the movie once, remembered Galileo as a name from school long ago, no more reason needed than that, but what magic how it all seems to fit!).

Same verse starts with the phrase, "the geometry of innocent flesh on the bone." Isn't it exquisite? Whatever does it mean? Well, actually, we know. It's about teenage desire. But how does it convey that? That's the mystery. I mean, the math book, Delilah's contradictory reaction (she feels worthless, she laughs in his face), the word "innocent"—this could never have turned out so well if it had been thought out beforehand. (On the other hand I never have much liked the verse about "the sun's not yellow, it's chicken.")

Another word for what Dylan evokes in these songs by word and sound is "landscape." He became the poet laureate of the 1960s because his music so powerfully captured the subjective landscape of the times, what people felt and saw in the world around them. "Felt" is the key here, because "the times" are not an objective phenomenon. They take on certain defined characteristics in hindsight, but it's always a mistake to think that any one set of images or feelings was actually much or most of what was going on. If anything, Dylan's willingness and ability to include so many different aspects of his and our experience into his art (which meant he was also inevitably exploring the *resonances* between, say, horniness, rebelliousness, curiosity, exhaustion, junkyards, and taking risks), is what gave his work such an aura of timeliness (and timelessness). It never bogged down (not for long) in any one movement. It (Dylan's art) mirrored the felt consciousness of the times precisely through this quality of being and staying in motion. He really never talks about anyone's experience but his own (what artist does?), but that's enough. Like the Beatles, Dylan was a leader to his public, and to other musicians, but the source of his leadership was his willingness to follow. Something was happening and he didn't know what it was, but he sure loved following it to see what would happen next.

"It Takes a Lot to Laugh" is a good example of how Dylan's songs shift and transform from performance to performance. There is an outtake of this song, maybe from the same session, maybe from the June 16 session six weeks earlier, that has a completely different sound and energy from the album track. This outtake differs from but is closely related to the Newport version of the song (performed July 25). Both have a more raucous, uptempo, noisy shuffling musical feel, similar to "From a Buick 6" on the album; it is almost as if "Phantom Engineer" (as the song was called) split into two parts, one aspect of it becoming "It Takes a Lot to Laugh" and the other "From a Buick 6." Four lines of lyrics changed between the earlier performances and the album version: the "wintertime is coming" section was originally

> Well, I just been to the baggage car
> Where the engineer's been tossed

I stamped out forty compasses
Sure don't know what they cost.

    This is jive free association, of the sort that shows up in "Buick 6" ("I need a steam shovel, mama, to keep away the dead"—totally off the wall, but admittedly a powerful image), and from a language point of view doesn't fit the later performance, but then I'm saying that without being able to hear how Dylan would have sung these lyrics in the mood and context of the later performance. Again I say, the words only really take on meaning when we hear them sung (and when he hears himself singing them). "I can't help it/If your train gets lost" are the last lines of the earlier version, and so we can see the engineer tossed in the baggage car as an (interesting, awkward) representation of someone whose has given up, thrown away, control of herself, her vehicle—Dylan responds by stamping out compasses for her, tools for finding direction, while protesting that he doesn't want to be her boss. With the coming of the later version, this becomes a sort of underpainting, perhaps revealing some of the process that led to the more mysterious and also more beautiful, more communicative, juxtapositions of the "finished" work. "Windows filled with frost"—very pretty to look at, but you can't see through them. "Don't say I didn't warn you..."

    Each performance of the song is different; each is worth hearing, experiencing—each is a work of art in its own right. And this calls attention to the fact that the album, any album, is constructed of performances, not of songs. Each performance has its own tone—a tone of voice, audible in Dylan's vocal attack, in the flow of the lyrics, in the sound the band achieves. In the liner notes to *Highway 61 Revisited* Dylan says "the songs on this specific record are not so much songs but rather exercises in tonal breath control." That's a sort of joke, but the sort that's funny because it's actually true. Band and Dylan (Dylan writer, Dylan singer, Dylan bandleader) join together into a single animal, and this animal demonstrates nine completely different ways of breathing on the nine tracks of the album, conjuring a different picture and expressing a different mood attitude scene situation tone in each set of breaths. Same words and music at a different moment (even a second take five minutes after the first) may be breathed differently, resulting in a different song. When you're as free and honest as Dylan is in these sessions, it's hard to breathe the same way twice. All you can do is let the new feelings come through.

The first irresistible attraction of "Ballad of a Thin Man" is the bluesy piano-and-organ riff that starts the song. It sets a tone that is tremendously compelling. Dylan is playing the piano on this track—rhythm piano, playing the repeating figure, the chords, just as he almost always plays rhythm guitar rather than lead (when he wants to make a melodic comment instrumentally, he uses his harmonica). In the first verse you can hear him laugh as he sings "You try so hard"—the same kind of laugh we often hear from him when he's forgotten or mixed up the words to a song. In this case, I think he laughs because he fumbled in his piano-playing. What is remarkable is that, the way Dylan performs and records (and sings), there is room for the laugh in the song—in the sense that he doesn't stop and start over again, or decide not to use this take on a record, as most other recording artists (or their producers) would do, and also in the sense that his aesthetic sense allows the laugh to be there, makes it part of the performance. Listen carefully to this little bit of expressed amusement and you'll notice that it's in his breath as he's singing.

An extraordinary quality of Dylan's singing is how much emotion, how much of what he's feeling at the moment he's performing, comes through in his breath (and, if there's a distinction, in his attack on particular words, his diction; I think the attack can be heard in consonants and the breath in vowels and the spaces between words). There are at least two aspects to this: his ability to communicate this way, to be so present in his singing, and his willingness to let it happen. Many performers are disciplinarians; they decide (when they write a song or when they arrange it or find the way of performing it that seems right to them) how a song should go, and then see their performing self (voice, breath, fingers) as an instrument that is required to execute the arrangement, the planned performance, correctly. Dylan, on the other hand, trusts the accidents and impulses of his "performing self" more than he trusts his preconceived ideas. The result is a tremendous space for expression.

Indeed, I believe his method of performing has to do with a need for expression, in the sense of letting something out ("I might go insane if it couldn't be sprung"—a response to an inner pressure), so that the laugh is there on "You try so hard" because what was happening as he played the piano prompted a laugh in Dylan's consciousness and *he had to let it out*, his state of mind when performing doesn't allow him to consciously hold back or keep in some of what he's feeling, he's structurally required to express, exhale, everything. This is a clue to how he succeeds in giving so much.

I don't mean to suggest that the emotions and communicativeness of the performance come through largely unconsciously or by accident. There's some of that, but most of Dylan's expressiveness is a function of projection and interaction. "Projection" means the song's situation is real to him as he sings it—not that he's mad at his girlfriend every time he sings "Like a Rolling Stone" but that he projects himself into the skin of himself or someone who's angry at this woman (or at someone). When he sings "Ballad of a Thin Man" he can see that thin man in front of him, he taunts him to his face (and empathizes too, just a little), he sees the events take place and sings to him as they're happening, narrative soundtrack to the victim's movie. He projects himself into that conversation with Mr. Jones, and if he happens to be pissed off at a newspaper reviewer that night (as he was when I saw him in Austin in 1986), well, that just adds to the intensity, puts more spin on the ball. But he's quite capable of projecting himself passionately into any of the situations in his songs without being specifically aware of those emotions in himself before he starts singing. He pulls them up from a reservoir that is always there in him (and, fortunately, in the listener as well). Of course, certain songs come alive more on certain nights, because they touch some part of the self (in the singer, or in the listener) that has already been recently sensitized. In any case, note that projection allows for deliberate spontaneity—you get into the song, into the situation, the feeling, the story, and go from there (singing the words and playing the chords that are already written—although Dylan does vary them often enough—but singing them in a unique manner that expresses this moment).

Interaction is there in Dylan's songs as a part of projection, since there's always a you or a them or a me that he's singing to or about. He feels that person and interacts with them as he sings. But interaction is also there with the audience and, more importantly in Dylan's case, with the other musicians. Listen to the organ part in "Ballad of a Thin Man," the way it comments on and responds to the singing. Imagine how that in turn affects, impacts on, stimulates the singer.

This is direct interaction; equally important is the constant awareness that the other instruments and musicians are there—when Dylan laughs his little laugh, he is *acknowledging* to the other musicians something he's just done that affects their joint performance, he is apologizing, making a joke of it, and saying, "on with the show." He's being in communication. This becomes clear when one watches him on stage, in person or through a video camera. His sense of the other musicians—which comes both through hearing them and through feeling them, knowing they're there and working with him in this single task of saying the one thing that's being said—affects his performance, he interacts with everything they do, every moment. He respects them, he loves them, he gets frustrated with them, he teases and needles them, and it all becomes part of his expressiveness. It's clear that he plays with a band not just because he loves the sound but because the music is so much more alive for him when there are other musicians to interact with. In a certain sense it is as if he is making all the music, all the sound, that you hear on the recording of "Ballad of a Thin Man"—he is the bandleader, and he needs all these parts of himself, needs to be a drum, a bass, an organ, an occasional lead guitar, to get across what he's feeling. The message is definitely in the words and sound together; Dylan's vocal performance is at the center of it all, and it is shaped, moment to moment, by the presence of all the sounds and personalities and energies it's interacting with in this common effort.

Highway 61 Revisited is the product of a series of recording sessions in which Dylan is performing at his peak, pure creativeness, sheer intensity, inspired by and pulling forth equivalent performances from the musicians around him. Whichever way he turns, something new and remarkable happens. "Queen Jane Approximately" is an underrated song, modest in what it tries to do lyrically and musically, brilliant in what it achieves. Its modesty is beguiling: every verse is an ABAB quatrain (with the last line repeated as chorus), beginning with the word "when" and ending with "...come see me, Queen Jane." So every B rhyme is "ain"; the A rhymes are all double syllables and every one delightful: "invitations/creations," "lent you/resent you," "commissioned/repetition," "plastic/drastic," and "cheek to/speak to." These charming pairings inspire affection for Dylan in his listeners; they also celebrate the English language, and indeed Bob Dylan may someday be remem-

bered with James Joyce (and who else? Yeats? Faulkner?) as one of
the great celebrants and promoters of the English language in the
twentieth century.

The musical achievement of "Queen Jane Approximately" is
harder for me to point to—it has to do with the deceptive simplicity
of its sound. The melody is sweet and appealing, with an insistent
build-up and release of rhythmic tension underlying it that is
striking, surprising, full of vengeance, violence, suppressed power.
Dylan's sound on *Highway 61 Revisited* and *Blonde on Blonde* is
primarily keyboard-based, percussive; it is amazing how many
different ways he uses keyboards and drums in the different songs,
and yet there is a strong common thread here as well, something
about the tonal relationship between Dylan's voice and the percussive instruments, and Dylan's need and willingness to explore that
relationship, energetically and unselfconsciously, encouraging the
musicians to recreate, any way they can, the accompaniment he
hears in his mind.

"Highway 61 Revisited"—another new sound, incredibly free
and exciting, ironic and playful, capped by Dylan blowing into a
toy police siren. Rhyme scheme: AAAA BBB, with the B rhyme
always "un." The words "Highway 61" at the end of the verse tie
everything together, same function as the words "Desolation Row"
and "tombstone blues" and "Mister Jones" and "Queen Jane" and
"rolling stone"—Dylan at this time liked to build his songs around
two-word choruses or punchlines.

"Just Like Tom Thumb's Blues," on the other hand, gets by
without punchline, without a chorus, with nothing but six unforgettable AAAA rhymes, sweetened and deepened and foreshort-
ened and prolonged by a handful of chords and Dylan's tricks of
vocal emphasis. Keyboards and drums and vocal tensions and
textures to die for.

And finally I can say about "Desolation Row" only that I am in
awe of it. Consider one tiny question: in the third verse ("The
moon is almost hidden/The stars are beginning to hide/The fortune-telling lady/Has even taken all her things inside..."), what
time is it? Dawn? Dusk? Midnight? End of the cycle? Just before the
big show? The verse as heard, as experienced, is nothing more or
less than an announcement of the time, and hearing it one *knows*,
senses, to the bone, the moment that is being referred to; yet you
cannot put it in words or numbers without discovering, on second

thought or closer reflection, that you're contradicting yourself. But it's not contradictory when we hear him singing it—it's real, it's specific, something very particular is evoked. What? No words for it. Only: that time Dylan speaks of in "Desolation Row" when he says, "The moon is almost hidden..."

15.

The last session for *Highway 61 Revisited* took place August 4, 1965 ("Tom Thumb's Blues" and "Desolation Row"). The album was officially released August 30, 1965, two days after Dylan's first full concert since England, at the Forest Hills Tennis Stadium in Queens, New York City.

The only known tape of the Forest Hills show is of very poor sound quality (one of the exciting aspects of tape collecting, however, is that at any time a good quality recording of this concert could turn up, to enrich our lives and upset the authority of histories such as this one). What is worth noting is the structure of the performance: two sets, the first consisting of seven songs performed by Dylan alone, with acoustic guitar and harmonica, and then, after an intermission, a second set of eight songs performed by Dylan with his first-ever concert band: Dylan on (electric) rhythm guitar, Al Kooper on organ, Harvey Brooks on bass, Robbie Robertson on lead guitar, and Levon Helm on drums. All the instruments were electrically amplified except the drums, so this was the "electric" set and as such was booed by many in the audience.

The solo set was primarily songs from *Bringing It All Back Home* (released only five months earlier, but already ancient history), plus "Ramona" and, boldly, "Desolation Row." The electric set included two from *Another Side*, one from *Back Home*, and five from the new album: "Tombstone Blues," "I Don't Believe You," "From a Buick 6," "Just Like Tom Thumb's Blues," "Maggie's Farm," "It Ain't Me Babe," "Ballad of a Thin Man," and "Like a Rolling Stone." It could be argued that Dylan has been playing variations on this same set at his live shows ever since.

Clinton Heylin's book *Stolen Moments* lists 33 more Dylan concerts in the last four months of 1965, all over the U.S. plus a few in Canada. None of these performances, as far as I know, has been preserved on tape. After the second concert, at Hollywood Bowl in Los Angeles September 3, Kooper and Brooks left the band and were replaced by Richard Manuel (piano), Garth Hudson (organ), and Rick Danko (bass). Dylan was now being backed by the full contingent of the Hawks, five guys who'd started playing together in 1960 as a back-up band for Ronnie Hawkins and more recently had been working on their own with drummer Levon Helm doing the vocals. Somewhere out on the 1965 Dylan trail Helm got tired of the new situation and left; he was replaced on drums by Bobby Gregg, or at times Sandy Konikoff, and later Mickey Jones. Every show by Dylan and the band for the rest of 1965 and on into May of 1966 featured the same structure, a solo acoustic set by Dylan followed by an electric set by Dylan and the band.

Since 1963 at the latest, Dylan had been working on and off on a book, first conceived of as a novel and later as a string of Dylan prose-poems. Sometime in late 1963 or early 1964 Dylan signed a contract for this book-in-progress with Macmillan, a New York publisher (the working titles were *Side One* or *Off the Record*, although in January 1965 a tiny fragment of Dylan-prose appeared in *Sing Out* with the note "condensed from *Walk Down Crooked Highway*").

In the fall of 1965 Dylan started speaking of his book in interviews as though he'd completed it—by this time it had acquired its final title, *Tarantula*—and we know that by March of 1966 the book had been set in type and Dylan was carrying the galley proofs with him on his concert tour, trying to correct them, trying to decide if the book should really be published. Ultimately he decided it shouldn't be (as he explained in interviews in 1968 and 1969—"it just wasn't a book, it was just a nuisance"). However, copies of the galleys circulated among Dylan fans, and eventually pirated editions of the book appeared, apparently prompting Dylan to change his mind and allow Macmillan to publish *Tarantula* as he'd submitted it in 1965, which they did in May 1971.

Various bits of evidence suggest that the book *Tarantula* as published was completed by Dylan in August or September 1965. It is a remarkably unrewarding manuscript. It is very unlikely that a reader unaware of Dylan's other works would find anything of merit or interest here. There are occasional clever lines and paragraphs; but even these are quickly rendered unappealing by the phony ironic context that seems to entrap every sentence. The games with language are not liberating or stimulating but transparent and banal; the rhythms of the writing are fun for a sentence or two at a time but quickly become stodgy, stagnant, sleep-inducing. What is fascinating is that in this same period Dylan was using not-unrelated techniques to produce masterpieces like "Desolation Row" and "Gates of Eden."

The failure of *Tarantula* is not mysterious: Dylan was trying to be something that he was not. He wasn't a book-writer. But he did have a strong desire to write a book, a novel; and, perhaps because of frustration in his early efforts in this direction, by the time of *Tarantula*-as-we-know-it Dylan's writing displays contempt for the form he's working in, for book-writing, as if to say, "This is a totally bullshit form, and I'm going to prove it by exploding it, revolutionizing it, taking it beyond all its limits." This is not the spirit in which he writes his songs, records his albums, performs his performances. There he is a true revolutionary, coming from inside, exploding and expanding forms that he feels at home in, that he respects and loves.

Tarantula is show-off stuff, and it is very interesting to discover that Dylan, for all his genius with language, is not impressive when he's just showing off. What makes the difference in his work, what in fact liberates his genius, is his sincerity. This is what burns in "Gates of Eden" and "Desolation Row" and all his major work, what illumines even his minor work: he cares about what he's saying, and the way he's saying it. He has no need to aspire to the forms he works in, because they come naturally to him: he inhabits them.

By way of example, the *Highway 61 Revisited* liner notes employ the same techniques as *Tarantula* for three-quarters of their length, but they succeed where *Tarantula* fails because they have a context, one that is meaningful to Dylan at the time— notes to go on a record jacket. One important result is they're limited in length, but that's not all: Dylan's jive talk is fun and appropriate as something to appear on the back of this consumer object, and Dylan's sense of purpose here causes him to go further, to open with a truly evocative bit of language ("On the slow train time does not interfere") and ultimately to say something to the reader/listener that acknowledges the relationship between artist and audience ("the songs on this specific record..."). Notice the elegant return of the slow train, notice the power, in the last section, of the repetition of "you" and "right" and "eye," the uncanny perfection of the structure of Dylan's language in this section, and how exciting it is for the reader to be trusted to understand and feel what Dylan is saying in his soliloquy that starts "I cannot say the word eye anymore." A connection is made. This is real, this is deep, this is heartfelt. So all the nonsense about the Cream Judge becomes not contemptuous or aloof but playful, friendly—*Tarantula* never offers this kind of release anywhere in its 149 pages. It's cold, where the liner notes are hot.

And this is important, because it demonstrates that it isn't just the difference between Dylan on the page and Dylan singing. Even on the page Dylan's power comes through—when he respects the person he's communicating with and the form he's working in. This happens most easily and most often for him in song, in musical performance; but it is how he feels toward the form, not the form itself, that is the critical factor.

1965: Dylan speeding along, Dylan taking a lot of speed. Dylan living and creating on the edge, Dylan getting more and more edgy. No fixed address. Three weeks in Los Angeles and Toronto after the Hollywood Bowl, then some shows in Texas with the new band, then Carnegie Hall October 1. Newark the next day. Atlanta, Worcester, Providence, Burlington, Detroit, Boston, Hartford; and some recording sessions in October, too. Working on the next album already. Interviews at every stop along the road. November: Minneapolis, Buffalo, Cleveland, Toronto, Columbus, Syracuse, Chicago, DC, more recording, and, between shows, on an off-day between Syracuse and the midwest gigs, a biographical note: Bob Dylan and Sara Lowndes wed in New York State, November 22, 1965.

Everything about this period is confused, a blur, so it's no surprise that there's confusion about the dating of the miscellaneous studio recordings that survive, the ones that didn't get onto *Highway 61 Revisited* or *Blonde on Blonde*. June 16, 1965, Tom Wilson's last session as Dylan's producer, is the likely source of "Jet Pilot" (a song fragment included on *Biograph*, where it is misdated), and of "Sitting on a Barbed-Wire Fence," an uptempo blues shuffle with spontaneous nonsense lyrics that at one point break into teasing misogyny a la "You're No Good": "This woman I've got, she's killing me alive/She's making me into an old man and, man, I'm not even 25."

June 16 is also usually credited with the early versions of "Can You Please Crawl Out Your Window?"; a later version, released as a single, was recorded the night of October 20, 1965, with the Hawks. Other recordings thought to be with the Hawks (and dated by various guessers as October 20, November 30, or late January) are the two versions of "I Wanna Be Your Lover" (one is on *Biograph*), an instrumental track called "Number One," a false start called "Medicine Sunday," "She's Your Lover Now" (band version), and the two early recordings of "Visions of Johanna" (then called "Freeze Out").

These are the only outtakes that have emerged from the 1965-66 period of Dylan recording with the Hawks. Dylan has said that in fall/winter 1965-66 (before the Nashville sessions) he spent endless hours in the studio trying to record his next album, and came up dry—in one interview he specifically blames the band. We might surmise that the problem with the Hawks, if there was one, was not their musicianship but their familiarity; for the most part, Dylan has done his best studio work when he's been with musicians he didn't know very well. An exception to this rule is Robbie Robertson, Dylan's closest comrade during this period and the only member of the Hawks who played on some of the Nashville sessions for *Blonde on Blonde*.

"Can You Please Crawl Out Your Window?" loses much of its magic in the digital remastering that was done for *Biograph* (many other performances gained in the process, I hasten to add). It's one of those songs whose power depends on the perfection of the sound, in this case the joyful shattering shrillness of Dylan's voice when it's tuned just right to the cowbell accompaniment, something that only happens on the mono mix (as heard on the original single and certain bootleg albums). I love the friendly lustfulness of the chorus—the song was probably written in early June, and I like to think of the first verse as a self-caricature of Dylan the vomit-artist writing "Rolling Stone" ("preoccupied with his vengeance"), while the playful child side of Dylan coaxes Sara to sneak away from that obsessive nitwit and come romp with me for a while.

It's possible that the band version of "She's Your Lover Now" precedes the Dylan-alone-with-piano version that has been reliably dated as being from mid-January, but it seems so unlikely (because the piano takes are usually made as demos, to introduce a new song to the other musicians) that I'm going to consider both versions as dating from January 1966, and will discuss them when we get there.

That leaves the two early alternate takes of "Visions of Johanna," neither of which can pass unmentioned in a survey of Dylan's major recorded performances. In jazz it is common to see alternate takes released from a recording session, particularly after the passage of time (for example, the compact disc of John Coltrane's *Giant Steps* includes alternate takes of almost every track on the album). This is accepted practice because jazz is implicitly understood to be an art form the units of which are improvised (i.e., at least partially spontaneous) performances. In rock music, however, musicians are working in a historical context in which finished music is created by striving to arrive at the best (most attractive, most commercial) possible representation of the song in question. Studio recording is seldom done in one take, and so there often are no "alternate takes," because each take is a building block that is either added to at the next stage of the process, or else put aside, incomplete. But even when true alternates do exist (for example, the marvelous 1963 recordings of the Beatles performing live on the BBC), artists and record companies have been slow to make this material available to the public. The Beatles are admired as composers, constructors of perfect pop objects, and there is conscious or unconscious concern that making available a variety of alternate, unpolished, spontaneous performances would dilute rather than add to their oeuvre.

One of my purposes in writing this book is to help legitimize a conceptual view of rock and roll implicit in the activities and enthusiasms of collectors of performance tapes and studio outtakes (whether the collectors in question focus on Dylan or the Beatles or the Grateful Dead or R.E.M. or Jimi Hendrix or any of the hundreds of other artists whose performances are varied enough and exciting enough to be collectible): the view that each performance by an artist is potentially of interest, that our attention need not be limited to the sum of the artist's output as measured in songs or record albums.

To demonstrate this in terms of Dylan's oeuvre, I can think of no better place to start (the goal being to open the minds and ears of the unconverted) than with a mini-album of two 12-inch 45s, each side containing a different performance of "Visions of Johanna": the fast take of "Freeze Out" from the early session, the slower take that may or may not date from the same evening, the "official" album version of "Visions of Johanna" from *Blonde on Blonde*, and the live recording from May 1966, London, that is included on *Biograph*. To sweeten the deal, the "official" version should be the now-rare original mono mix.

I can imagine a loyal *Blonde on Blonde* fan being shocked, at first, by the aggressiveness of the uptempo ("rock and roll") "Freeze Out," or being left cold, also at first, by the oddly different arrangement and unfamiliar diction of the slower (well, it's not really slower; quieter, maybe) unreleased take. But I can't imagine anyone listening to either of these takes a few times in succession without becoming totally captivated by the power, beauty, uniqueness and communicativeness of this particular performance. If you love Dylan saying "Ain't it just like the night?" on *Blonde on Blonde*, wait till you hear him say "*Jewels* and binoculars" on the rock version, wait till you fall into the hypnotic "Sad-Eyed-Lady"-like rhythmic wash of the other early version and start noticing his weird delivery of phrases like "up on trial" and "taken my place." You'll be hooked. You'll want more.

While I'm dreaming up odd marketing moves for the corporate owners of Dylan properties, how about *What Do You Want Me to Say?* (Bob Dylan press conference 1965) as a feature release in repertory movie houses around the world (followed, of course, with a commercial videotape once it has achieved sufficient publicity and product recognition). This one-hour press conference, held and filmed in the KQED-TV studios in San Francisco on December 3, 1965, hosted and produced by critic Ralph Gleason and featuring an intriguing mix of amateur and professional newspeople plus special guest questioners like Allen Ginsberg and Bill Graham, is quite simply one of the most affecting Bob Dylan performances currently circulating on videotape.

This is the Dylan usually encountered only in song: quick, smart, vulnerable, honest, a deadly wit, charming to be with, no stranger to the weaknesses and suffering of the flesh, mysterious combination of tongue-tied and articulate, hip bodhisattva with an angel's face and a demonic grin, privy to the secrets of the universe and of the listener's heart. His delicious putdowns are more than balanced by his sincere efforts to give honest answers to the impossible riddles posed to him. And not only does the film bring you closer to the heart of who Dylan was in 1965 than *Don't Look Back* or any biography that's been written, it also succeeds as a subtle, remarkable portrait of the times—we can almost see consciousness shifting and re-forming before our eyes.

Like liner notes, press interviews are a secondary, functional form that comes with the territory of being a musician, a pop star; during his most prodigious years Dylan was able to recreate these inherited forms and make them his own, turn them into opportunities for art. Not without effort—Dylan's success (on his own terms) at this press conference is clearly a product of lessons learned the hard way, from repeated muggings by the press, experienced whether he was being friendly and cooperative or acerbic and aloof. It's also clear that he gives such an outstanding performance—just his little smiles and grimaces and the way he leans on his fist are worth the price of admission—partly just 'cause he's in a real good mood this day. (No doubt the friends in the gallery and his sense of a hip, San Francisco audience out on the other side of the TV camera, digging the nuances, contributed to his good mood. He also looks a little stoned.)

Every exchange is a new performance—often it's the wit, the imaginativeness, the zen clarity or deliberate opacity that delights, but other times it's just the surprising, totally real way he rises to an aggressor's challenge, or, equally unexpectedly, turns the other cheek. Sarcasm and irony are not overused. Most of the time he's really trying to answer the question. When the camera pans Ralph Gleason the viewer can see the man is totally lovestruck—and the viewer can empathize. Dylan has seldom been more lovable. This may be something like having a good quality film of one of Dylan's early comedy/folksong appearances in a Village coffeehouse. He wouldn't be half so charming if it weren't so damned apparent that all this is happening outside his control: "I really ain't no comedian..."

Even if the transcript of this press conference published by *Rolling Stone* were accurate and complete, which it isn't, it couldn't begin to communicate the magic of watching and hearing Dylan's performance on tape. But there are other published interviews from this period that function as first-rate performances when read on the page. Two of the best were actually ghosted by Dylan (that is, they are not transcripts, but seriocomic essays, literary works, written by Dylan in the interview format with which he was so familiar).

One is "Positively Tie Dream," a short, hilarious piece published in *Cavalier* magazine in February 1966 (credited as an interview with Maura Davis) but reportedly conducted/concocted in spring of 1965. The other is the *Playboy* interview with Nat Hentoff (published March 1966), originally a serious interview conducted in fall 1965 (parts of which are circulating on audiotape) but then extensively rewritten by Dylan with Hentoff's help after the *Playboy* editors tried to put words in Dylan's mouth. The section that starts, "What made you decide to go the rock 'n' roll route?" is particularly famous, and rightly so ("Carelessness. I lost my one true love. I started drinking. The first thing I know I'm in a card game..."). This Dylan comedy routine says everything that needs to be said about the public's illusion that personal history is public property and the key to all mysteries. It casts a new light on the tall tales he told interviewers when he first arrived in New York, and foreshadows, in form and language, his 1974 dissertation on a related theme, "Tangled Up in Blue."

Dylan returned to New York in late December, after a series of concerts (and press conferences) in California, and stayed there (commuting between Woodstock and New York City, presumably) until the touring started again in early February. On January 25, he recorded "One of Us Must Know (Sooner or Later)," which was released as a single a few weeks later and is the only track on *Blonde on Blonde* not recorded in February and March in Nashville. In a radio appearance on WBAI in New York later the same evening,

Dylan mentions that he's just recorded his new single, which is better than the last two and comparable to "Like a Rolling Stone." When I met him in Philadelphia a month later he was still very enthusiastic about "One of Us Must Know," but Top 40 radio didn't agree. "Like a Rolling Stone" had gotten to #2, "Positively 4th Street" to #7 (peaking in late October), and "Can You Please Crawl Out Your Window?" to #58 (on the *Billboard* magazine list), but "One of Us Must Know" didn't even make the top 100. Was Dylan disappointed? Relieved? Confused? Indifferent? Probably all four.

On the radio show, Dylan mentions that he and the musicians had been in the studio for three days and nothing came of it except this one song. The musicians were the Hawks—their one appearance on *Blonde on Blonde*, although only Robbie gets mentioned in the album credits. It seems likely that the solo version of "She's Your Lover Now" (and probably the band version as well) was recorded at these sessions.

"She's Your Lover Now" is the song that started me searching for bootleg albums of unreleased Dylan material. The impetus was Dylan's release in 1973 of his collection of lyrics called *Writings and Drawings*, which included quite a few songs not available on any Dylan album. I discovered "She's Your Lover Now" and soon got in the habit of reading it aloud to friends—I could hear Dylan's voice, his inflections, as I read the lyrics, even though I'd never heard him sing the song. So then when I got a catalog of "rare records" one of which included a Dylan recording of "She's Your Lover Now," I couldn't resist ordering it, and a new world opened up to me.

The band version of "She's Your Lover Now" is rough-edged—although this, like the early versions of "Visions of Johanna," is delightful, one can understand Dylan searching for something more—something more that turned out to be the truly magical, light-handed, complex and refreshing sound he achieves on *Blonde on Blonde*, a new and deeper journeying into the heart of musical mystery, in no sense *Highway 61 Revisited* revisited. The band version of "She's Your Lover Now" is also incomplete—Dylan makes a mistake in the lyrics in the fourth verse, gets confused, and stops singing. (The line goes: "Now your eyes cry wolf, while your mouth cries, 'I'm not scared of animals like you'"; Dylan sings, "Now your mouth cries wolf, while...what?") The words to the song in *Writings and Drawings/Lyrics* are clearly transcribed from this tape, and so they lack the fourth verse.

Then, in the summer of 1980, a revelation for Dylan collectors: an acetate (recording studio pressing) turned up entitled "Just a Little Glass of Water No. 89210" (the last part is CBS recording studio code, the first part presumably Dylan whimsy), which turned out to be a full-length "She's Your Lover Now" sung by Dylan alone at the piano. It's a great song in any case, and this solo performance is absolutely stunning—the power of Dylan's voice and the genius of his expressive gift can be heard at their most naked, terrifying, oceanic, threatening at every moment to burst the thin skin of decorum that keeps human beings from overwhelming and obliterating each other with the force of their emotions or the sheer bitter strength of their personalities. "Oh, how the pawnbroker roared," he sings, after gargling in tongues for a moment to tune his voice and spirit to the piano, "And it was so good for the landlord/To see me so crazy, *wasn't it?*/They both were so glad/To see me destroy everything I had/ Pain sure brings out the best in people DOESN'T IT??"

The song is a vivid portrait of one of the more difficult moments in any person's life: just after the abrupt end of a sexually and emotionally intense relationship, when one sees (in the imagination or in fact) the other person with their new lover. In the first eleven lines of each verse, the singer addresses his ex-lover, alternately angry, scornful, pleading, sad; then, abruptly, in the twelfth line, he turns and addresses her new boyfriend, mocking him hilariously, playing bitter oneupsmanship and never letting this straight man, this prop, get a word in edgewise. This takes up the last seven lines of each verse. The rhyme structure is worth noting: AAB CCB DEFEE / GG HH IJI (the last rhyme, last line, is always "She's your lover now" or "You're her lover now"). The third E line, which is always long (spitting out a string of words) serves as a climax to the first section; the simpler rhyme structure of the second section is appropriate to the change in mood from earnest, elegant intensity to fierce but playful sarcasm. Two kinds of hatred: one full of love and the frustrations of love, the other full of indifference or maybe the frustrated desire for indifference (What can she possibly see in you? Why do I have to admit that you exist?).

I have no idea what biographical event could have inspired

this song—this is a guy who just got married in November, whose
first child is about to be born, maybe he's harkening back to an
earlier incident or—who knows? But it's interesting that this third
man theme (putting down the nonentity who's with the girl on
whom the singer's attention is focused) shows up very clearly in
other songs from this (*Blonde on Blonde*) period: "Visions of Johanna" 's "little boy lost," "I Want You" 's "dancing child with his
Chinese suit." Who is this guy? Who is this girl? Only Dylan knows,
if he can even remember. What seems likely is that the subject is not
so much a particular heartbreak as a recurring situation, experienced or imagined or a little of both, that characterizes the power
and confusion of sexual connection, the mysteries and frustrations
and rewards of the sexual encounter (always tied up in the problem or fear of being misunderstood). Isn't this what "One of Us
Must Know" is about? ("Sooner or later one of us must know/That
I really did try to get close to you.") What about "Fourth Time
Around"? And, in different ways, "Absolutely Sweet Marie," "Leopard-Skin Pill-Box Hat," the Ruthie section of "Memphis Blues
Again," "Most Likely You Go Your Way," "Temporary Like Achil-
les," and "Just Like a Woman." The whole album is about sexuality
and its power, or, if you will, the war between men and women.
This isn't the only thing the songs and the album are about, but it
seems to be there, in the music as well as the lyrics, in song after
song after song. Maybe it's a raucous farewell to bachelorhood. In
any event, it's a memorable, amazingly successful work of art—and
a bookend to the great album that came out of the other end of the
marriage, *Blood on the Tracks*.

If I had to choose a single performance to stand as evidence of
Dylan's greatness as an artist, one momentary breath of song to
define his essence and defend his stature, "She's Your Lover Now"
(solo at piano) would be the one. It isn't on my "masterpiece" list
because it lacks (in this form) the universal accessibility of "Mr.
Tambourine Man" or "Like a Rolling Stone"; it is, however, the
equal of those performances in power, beauty (strange beauty,
awful beauty, not a beauty every listener is ready to hear yet), and
expressive accomplishment, and, in its very rawness, it has a trans-
parency, a translucency, that cuts through the mystery of Dylan's
special talent and illuminates the real nature of his artistry.

Dylan is a passionate vocalizer of felt truth, tongue connected
directly to heart, mind following not leading. The rhythm and the

performance structure come first, and the language fills in the spaces. Those who perceive specific symbolic references in Dylan's songs (*this* stands for *that*) are almost always barking up the wrong tree—they assume that discovered meaning must necessarily have been encoded by conscious intellect. Dylan's technique skips steps—his "symbolic" language is intuitive, not rational, felt not preconceived. His songs entertain our intellects but their source is visceral—mind follows feeling. Feeling is first for the listener, too, but Dylan's cleverness with words is so striking we may not always notice that his songs make us feel first, and our thinking about them comes later.

In "She's Your Lover Now" Dylan is not "trying to" say something, as the interpreters of songs would have us believe; rather, he *is* saying something, and he allows us to listen in—to share the experience, by identifying with the speaker or with one of the people being addressed or as an uninvolved observer or all of the above. The song's greatest impact, of course, comes through the listener's identification (self-recognition) with the speaker. When this occurs (the listener can't will it to happen), we go beyond appreciation of the speaker's cleverness (his performance, in the sense of a person performing before a mirror, telling off all the people who've caused him pain, coming up with the perfect squelch) or discomfort with his cruelty, and enter into a far more affecting realm.

"I've already assumed," he sings in the second verse "That we're in the felony room/But I ain't the judge, you don't have to be nice to me." *Feeling* these words, as we do when we hear them, we may go beyond his arch, smug manner and find ourselves feeling (remembering from our own experience) the pain underneath, when someone you love, someone you were as one with, who a moment ago was an intimate and could only speak to you from her heart, now tries to humor you, to be "nice," treating you like an interrogator in court or some beggar on the street she doesn't want to aggravate but dearly hopes will go away quietly. "Will you please tell that/To your friend with the cowboy hat/He keeps on saying everything twice to me." We feel his combined anguish and fury at having to talk to her with this other guy (who's also trying to be "nice," presumably because he's uncomfortable, but is experienced by the singer as a condescending son-of-a-bitch) present; Dylan wants to scream but he's holding back his anger because part of him desperately wants to be perceived sympathetically by the woman—he's also holding back his desire to beg for reconciliation. This can be felt quite strongly in the next lines: "You know I was straight with you/You know I never tried to change you in any way/You know if you didn't want to be with me/That you didn't have to stay." Beneath the self-justification, the desperation is unmistakable. (A sweetness, his genuine love for her, also comes through as we hear these words sung.) Then the incredible eleventh line: "Now you stand here saying you forgive me—what do you expect me to say?" The full intensity of the trap he's in is evident now: his pride (I've done nothing wrong) in direct conflict with his desire to have her back (don't "forgive" me—love me!), both feelings (pride, desire) unendurably strong and neither with the least hope of getting satisfaction from her even if the other feeling could get out of the way. But meanwhile here he is with her and him, and there's this conversation to carry on, but no way he can even begin to explain himself or apologize or say what he feels or speak to her heart in the context she's set up by the way she's speaking to him.

He turns on the boyfriend: "And you, you just sit around and ask for ashtrays, can't you reach?" (At last someone that he can vent at least a little of his feelings to; it's safe, because he doesn't care about this person—except that of course he can't control himself and his angry feelings towards her pour out as he's speaking to him.) "I see you kiss her on the cheek every time she gives a speech./With her postcards of the pyramid/And her snapshots of Billy the Kid/They're all so nice but why must everybody bow?" (This is not symbolism, by the way, but surrealism—spontaneous, humorous, absurd, and very effective as characterization. She's into the mystical, she romanticizes outlaws, she loves show and tell and likes to be—and probably deserves to be, which is why he still wants her, and why he's angry—the center of attention.) "Explain it to her" (is it just the tone of voice that makes this such a vicious putdown?) "—You're her lover now."

The beauty lies in the vulnerability, the naked sharing of feelings of conflict and pain. The singer's anger and cleverness are a transparent foil for helpless anguish, of a sort that the listener too has experienced and has despaired of finding words for. Dylan's genius is he finds chords, finds voice, and the words follow, tumble out and allow us to share his experience and, more importantly, to share our experience with him. This happens without any thinking about it. It happens at the moment that we hear and are moved by his voice, music, language—a moment in which we embrace what we hear and make it uniquely our own.

This solo piano performance of "She's Your Lover Now" would still be remarkably compelling if the words were in some unknown foreign tongue, and all of our understanding had to come through the piano and the *sound* of the words, the sound of Dylan's voice. In fact my discussion of the lyrics of the second verse barely scratches the surface of what the *performance* of the verse communicates. Dylan uses English like a billiards player, putting a new spin on every word—every sound from his mouth has a life of its own, and is capable of conjuring up worlds of meaning, nuance, complexity.

Listening to Dylan play piano and sing on this track it's possible to hear the song as he hears it in his mind, played by a full electric band—not specific details of which instruments play what and when, I don't think he hears it that way, but rather a complete *sound*, orchestra playing in his head, the whole feeling of it is present and audible in this performance, along with the sense that this performance isn't complete in itself, it's a sketch for this other thing in which much of what is conveyed here by Dylan alone would be communicated instead by a group of musicians playing with and around Dylan's voice. So this vocal contains things that wouldn't be in the "finished" vocal—much of the process of refinement and completion involves removing things from a creative work rather than adding to it, like an artist erasing parts of his pencil sketch as he fills in colors and textures.

And in this particular case we have more by having the sketch than we might have if we had a finished recording—we have a scream from the heart of the artist, so ferocious and so personal it's easy to imagine him not wanting to share it with his audience. "My voice is really warm," he sings in the last verse, "It's just that it ain't got any form/It's like a dead man's last *pistol shot, baby!*" Dylan is holding nothing back here. And the question could be asked, What is his purpose in writing and singing such a song?

My answer is to go back once again to "Restless Farewell": "Oh every thought that's strung a knot in my mind/I might go insane if it couldn't be sprung." What drives him is the need to release something, let it out, relieve the pressure. Interpretation assumes message—that the artist's primary purpose is to communicate with his audience. Not necessarily so. This idea that art is communication may be a function of the audience's vanity, the interpreter's self-importance. The artist is more interested in *expression*—finding words, music, rhythm, sound, not to communicate something but just to let it out, externalize it, because it won't let him rest until it has been so expressed.

He does this for himself, not for us. But because he's a performer, he does need our participation, in the form of our attention. When he dives off the high platform, he doesn't want us to receive him at the bottom like a pail of water—what he wants is for us to notice every elegant little movement as he leaps, admire his composure as he falls, and be thrilled by the perfection of his splash.

The performing artist isn't interested in whether we understand what he's saying. He wants us to listen to the way he says it. What we feel while we're listening is what we get.

16.

Breakthrough. On January 25, 1966, when he recorded "One of Us Must Know," Dylan found the key to yet another previously unexplored musical realm. This was the first performance recorded for *Blonde on Blonde*; it came after months of false starts and frustration in the studio. But after this performance—the realization of a certain sound and feeling that Dylan had been pursuing, on paper and in the studio both—the rest of the album flowed easily, evidently pouring out of Dylan and the musicians with him at the next recording sessions, February 14-17 and March 8-9 in Nashville, Tennessee.

Creative work of any kind involves arriving at an externalized expression of a felt presence. Thus the power and usefulness (to the artist) of the sound of the words while writing, and the sound of the music as a whole while performing—these are qualities by which one can intuitively measure one's success at making external what is felt and sensed inside. Never mind what it says or whether it's played right, does it *sound* like what I feel? If the answer is no, back to the drawing board; if yes, then the truth is there and

185

presumably will be felt by the imagined audience, no need to think about the names of these particular truths or to identify consciously the paths by which they'll arrive. When it's right, there's a resonance; the artist hears it, and is satisfied.

Blonde on Blonde is all resonance. The songs and their stories and evocative lines and seductive melodies inhabit a realm of sound unique to this album, different from anything created before or since by Dylan or anyone else. Dylan called it "that thin, that wild mercury sound—metallic and bright gold, with whatever that conjures up." It is characterized by the bright, bouncing notes from the electric organ in "I Want You" and "Memphis Blues Again," the lonesome harmonica that opens "Visions of Johanna" and "Just Like a Woman," the expansive organ chords in "Sad Eyed Lady of the Lowlands" and "One of Us Must Know," the brassiness of "Rainy Day Women" and "Most Likely You Go Your Way," and perhaps most of all the omnipresent metronomic drumming by Ken Buttrey, mixed so that it strikes right down the middle of every song, organizing and flavoring every musical moment. Try to imagine *Blonde on Blonde* without that drum sound—it can't be done.

And here in this warm, intimate, relentlessly playful house of music, Dylan has gathered us to share his tales of love and lust, a latter-day Canterbury, a little entertainment for all us road-weary humans, sung with a conviction that suggests that this is the ultimate subject matter for the ambitious artist, when you strip away everything transient this is what is at the center of our lives and experience. According to Dylan. Or, according to the Dylan who made this album.

"One of Us Must Know" is a joyous song about guilt, joyous not in its lyrics but in the sound of the music and the singing, joyous because like a blues song releasing feelings of bitterness and loss, "One of Us Must Know" expresses and releases the singer's guilt (and so, through the power of identification and empathy, the listener's), building through each verse into a triumphant chorus combining apology, putdown, plea for forgiveness and reaffirmation of higher purpose. "I couldn't see," says Dylan again and again, as if to acknowledge (and, at the same time, try to excuse) how blind he's been. (Remember, this is a near-sighted guy who won't wear his glasses.) "You said you knew" is another recurring phrase; the guilt he feels is so strong he seems compelled both to explain himself and to try to share the responsibility. The lyrics hold back just enough information about the actual situation to give the song a lasting sense of mystery, always on the edge of making sense and coming together into a specific story but never quite doing so. I'd say sex was definitely involved (presuming it was a woman scorned who tried to "claw out" his eyes, and that they had to be lovers for her to have felt so scorned), and Dylan admits that he treated the person bad, whatever it was he did (he also manages to add insult to injury in the interesting first verse; sure has a way with apologies, doesn't he?).

In any case, the memorable chorus with its reverberating implications is applicable to almost any situation involving two people and an ongoing misunderstanding; in particular, a situation in which the emotions of the speaker (resentment, righteousness, remorse) are still trying to sort themselves out. It's a great song; and it couldn't begin to say so much or be of such lasting value without the tour-de-force performance by Garth Hudson on organ, and the fabulous way all the elements of the song's sound come together, floating, hesitating, surging, overflowing—in particular Dylan's passionately expressive singing, which I can only describe by pointing. See him push himself into every word—the extended "so" and gentle "bad" stand out in the first line, but there's lots of personality in the way he sings the first "I" and in the pause after "mean" as well. This vocal in its own way would be almost as overwhelming and difficult to withstand as the solo "She's Your Lover Now" vocal were it not for the comforting ticking of the drum, always there to hold onto in the middle of things like the metal pole in a subway car. A great song, great performance—and not very much like anything Dylan had done before. Reason enough for him to get excited and decide to let the rest of the album (double album, in fact) flow out of him and into permanent public grooves after all.

"I've always been drawn to a certain kind of woman," Dylan said in a 1985 interview with Scott Cohen. "It's the voice more than anything else. I listen to the voice first. It's that sound I heard when I was growing up. It was calling out to me...There's something in that voice, that whenever I hear it, I drop everything, whatever it is." He makes reference to the Staples Singers, the Crystals, and Clydie King, but he could just as well be describing someone's response to the voice on *Blonde on Blonde*, especially in "Sad Eyed Lady of the Lowlands," "Visions of Johanna," "Just Like a

Woman," and "Memphis Blues Again." "Nobody had ever talked to us like that before," I wrote in 1969 in an essay about a variety of subjects, and went on to quote the part of "Just Like a Woman" where Dylan sings "It was raining from the first/And I was dying there of thirst/So I came in here..." "It isn't often that people, strangers or friends," I wrote, "reach in to where we really feel stuff and speak gently and openly—so many who think they penetrate merely hit and run." I realize now I was talking about not only the content and quality of his language but the sound of his voice. Dylan himself might be horrified, then or now, to realize how much he really did try to get close to us—and how well he succeeded.

"Sad Eyed Lady of the Lowlands" has an almost unearthly beauty. It is unusual among Dylan songs in that it is the melody rather than the lyrics that first strikes the listener. A love song, it also has a spiritual quality that links it with songs like "Mr. Tambourine Man" and 1981's "Every Grain of Sand." Although the song is heart-stoppingly sensual, it noticeably dodges the sexual, except insofar as the singer is jealously aware of the (potential?) attentions of others ("who among them really wants just to kiss you?"). Instead, the singer seems to have fallen in love with grace itself, like the medieval "juggler of God" whose purpose in life is to please Our Lady (the Virgin Mary or her present-day manifestation). Interestingly, while what comes through in the song is *his* feelings for *her*, the actual words of the song are as much about "them" as "you," and never speak directly of "us." It doesn't matter. The words are fascinating, but they pale in significance (most important is that they sound right, they have the rhythm, the rhyme, the elusiveness and vague evocativeness, the flow) beside the motion of the vocal performance and the stately, immensely fulfilling music that moves with it. This indeed is the music of marriage, that which endures, inhalation and exhalation, self-contained and self-renewing, soothing, stimulating—when I hear this performance I see rolling hills of white sand, a great expanse of quiet and calm, unhurried but always in motion, changing, growing, alive.

Okay. I was driving into town today and I turned on the radio and found myself right in the middle of "Just Like a Woman." Sounded good, especially the drums-and-keyboard ending which, inexplicably, unconscionably, is missing from the *Blonde on Blonde* compact disc (the song fades early, as does "Sad Eyed Lady"—a travesty. On the other hand, you haven't lived till you hear Dylan's

"Sad Eyed Lady" vocal on compact disc, so whatcha gonna do?).*
It was followed immediately by two other glorious works of music,
"Bye Bye Love" by the Everly Brothers and "Johnny B. Goode" by
Chuck Berry, and I found myself considering the artistic context in
which Dylan's performances exist.

A song like "Bye Bye Love" needs no interpretation. In fact, it
absolutely disallows interpretation. To suggest that there is some
meaning other than the obvious in "There goes my baby/With
someone new" is to be laughed at before you finish your sentence;
the same is true if one purports to find this hidden meaning in the
manner of singing or the song's overall sound rather than in its
lyrics. The song says what it seems to say. And yet every moment of
the performed song is rich in nuance, full of subtle and exquisite
expressed awareness, expressed in the vocals, in the harmony
between the voices, in the precision of the rhythm, in the kineticism
of the guitar playing and the way the guitar works with the voices
and the way the words build on themselves: "I'm through with
romance/I'm through with love/I'm through with counting/The
stars above/And here's the reason/That I'm so *free* [climax of the
verse]/My loving baby/Is through with me [perfect anticlimax, de-
nouement]." If this isn't art we need a new word. The greatness of
this record (this recorded performance) is immediately recognizable to anyone who hears it, in the sense that it connects, it provokes a profound visceral response. We feel it. Analyzing it (as I did
clumsily just now) won't add to it or take away from it—at best it
will let us peer a little deeper into the mystery of what it is that we
feel, and how the mechanisms work that exist under the surface of
the relationship between a work of art and its listeners.

"Johnny B. Goode" again allows no confusion as to what it's
about. What is mysterious in a work like this is its energy, its
perennial freshness, its power. Its personality—unmistakably a
manifestation of the personality of its creator. This one is closer to
Dylan in being primarily the work of a single artist; there's a band,
but that's Berry singing, Berry playing the guitar, Berry inventing
words, rhythm, tune. "Bye Bye Love" on the other hand involves
two singers, two other people writing the song, a very savvy (and
very intuitive) producer, all of whom work together like they were
born for this moment. But never mind. The point is, here is an

*The problem reportedly has been corrected on later pressings.

object called "Johnny B. Goode," and an object called "Bye Bye Love," and listening to them or contemplating them we understand instantly that it is within the set of objects that contains these performances that the object called "Just Like a Woman" belongs.

To name this set is to invite confusion. Instead we need to understand that the creative force within us aspires to fill a hole in space the way a song on the radio fills two and half minutes and the listener's emotional and spiritual and physical and intellectual consciousness. To see someone else fill a space successfully in some fashion is to imagine that perhaps we can do so too; the artist reaches out and maybe even succeeds, though never in quite the same way as the models, the examples that helped inspire him. He finds his own way.

The issue of interpretation comes up because Dylan's songs, especially from certain periods, invite interpretation, and even achieve some of their effect by the way they tease the listener to grab for the brass ring of meaning that seems so nearly within reach. This is a playground, then, that the listener is invited into; the danger comes in mistaking the arrived-at "explanation" for the experience itself. When this happens, the power of the experience is lost, is replaced by an outline, a symbol. It almost doesn't matter whether it's the "right" symbol or not, because no symbol, no explanation, can be or replace a song or a painting. The song or painting only exists in the context of the dynamic relationship between it and its current audience. It has those qualities that give it substance only when it is being seen, heard, felt.

If we remember this, then we can play at interpretation without losing our senses, our sensual, personal relationship (or potential relationship) with each performance.

Alan Rinzler says in his book *Bob Dylan, The Illustrated Record* that "Just Like a Woman" is "a devastating character assassination...[it] may be the most sardonic, nastiest of all Dylan's putdowns of former lovers." This is fascinating to me, because it is so different from my experience of the song. Robert Shelton in *No Direction Home* discusses "Just Like a Woman" by quoting one writer who says "There's no more complete catalogue of sexist slurs" than this song, and another who says it's a poem about "the failure of human relationships because of illusion created by social myth." Well there's no end to the nonsense written about Dylan, of course, not that the last quote is nonsense necessarily, it's just strangely unconnected to the song I know, as if the writer only knew the song through rumors (or lyric sheets) and had never experienced it directly. So I find myself taking up the sword of interpretation as a defense (and because it's fun), convinced as I am that there's a simpler, more common-sense hearing of the song that is a hell of a lot closer to what most of us feel when we hear it.

First of all, the song (the performance of the song included on *Blonde on Blonde*) is affectionate. This is evident in the opening harmonica notes, and the vocal that follows is affectionate in tone from beginning to end; there's never a moment in the song, despite the little digs and the confessions of pain, when you can't hear the love in his voice (or in his harmonica-playing, which returns at the end for a full, wordless verse that has the effect of emphasizing what is unambiguously communicated in the performance and the sound of the song, and smoothing over any confusion aroused by the playful needling in the lyrics).

If one can't hear the affection in the performance (and I guess Rinzler can't), then there's nothing more to be said. Certainly there's no argument that could be constructed to prove that it's there, any more than one could construct an argument to prove that "There goes my baby/With someone new" in "Bye Bye Love" is about a guy losing his girlfriend. It's immediate; you hear it or you don't. If you do hear it, then there is a further question: what is meant by "she breaks just like a little girl"? More specifically, what is meant by the "but" that connects the first three lines of the chorus (take/fake, make love, ache just like a woman) with the last line? It's the "but" that creates all the mystery, and much of the richness, of this last line—on an obvious level, the "but" separates the perceived characteristics of a woman from behavior more commonly associated with a child, but it does something else too, it sets up a wonderful teasing tension in the realm of approval/disapproval or implied success/implied failure, with no final resolution. There's no question that one of the themes or issues of the song is the power the woman has over the singer ("I was hungry and it was your world" is not, I think, social—it's sexual), and that the release in the last line of the chorus, the release implied by the "but," has to do with a sort of revenge, a loss of power by her or a gaining of power by him—but an ambiguous one. For one thing, he is not free of her effect on him now, nor does he want to be. And let me just say this: that the truth of a situation may be its very ambiguity, in which case clarity would be the booby prize. Dylan expresses the reality of human relationships by not reducing them to blacks and whites. He leaves us instead with the loving, aching, angry, forgiving tension that moves us so deeply because we know it from our own experience. This is the real thing. "I can't stay in here." The pain is excruciating. Not being able to have as much of her as he wants, he has to withdraw from the situation, but he doesn't want to. Maybe the problem is that she defends herself from his pushing by breaking like a little girl, and he can't find a way to get through to the child-woman she really is. Maybe he can't resolve his own confusion about his feelings towards perceived woman, perceived girl—which does he want? Or maybe she just doesn't want him as a lover, and this is his way of romanticizing his embarrassment, his frustration, his loss. Whatever it is, it's open-ended—and ultimately as simple and directly moving and awesome in its singularity, its perfection, as those performances by Chuck Berry and the Everly Brothers. An object, a work of music, now released to the world and so the property of the people who hear it, however they hear it, forever.

At one point Dylan was going to call the *Blonde on Blonde* album *I Want You*, which is interesting in that he eventually did release an album called *Desire*. I don't know what significance, if any, the title *Blonde on Blonde* has. The best I can do is to recall that he was impressed, years earlier, by a theater piece called "Brecht on Brecht." Possibly he got the idea, one stoned evening, of calling this record *Dylan on Dylan*, immediately rejected that and proclaimed it *Blonde on Blonde* instead.

The first song on the album, "Rainy Day Women #12 & 35," was one of the last recorded (March 9). It was released as a single in April and was an instant success, Dylan's only novelty hit (radio terminology for wacky records that make it big, like "Witch Doctor" and "Surfing Bird")—it got to #2 in the U.S. in May 1966, equal to "Like a Rolling Stone" nine months earlier. The memorable joke in the chorus is about marijuana (although it could just as easily be about alcohol), but the song as a whole is about persecution, specifically criticism, and the message in the chorus is a straightforward one: it happens to everybody, so don't feel bad (and, implicitly, don't be such a victim about it).

The combination drunk party/revival meeting sound of the song is wonderful, a product of the unique musical chemistry

Dylan and the Nashville studio musicians (under the leadership of Charlie McCoy and producer Bob Johnston, with help from Kooper and Robertson) achieved during these freewheeling sessions. This is not country music. This is not Dylan music as defined by any earlier Dylan album. It's only rock and roll in the broadest, most all-encompassing sense (one of rock and roll's virtues is that it is or can be the most open-ended of musical forms, able to make room for almost anything as long as it's a hybrid or a mongrel). Mostly what we have here, on this track and throughout the album—no two tracks alike—is a sound, a set of sounds, created on the spot, shaped by the moment just as Dylan's songwriting method is reshaped at each separate moment in his career. He doesn't do the same thing twice because, really, he wouldn't know how to—words, sound, music, verse structure, all of it is created in response to and in collaboration with the external and internal forces operating on him and around him at the time when the work is being done.

So we get track two, "Pledging My Time," an improvised blues with a great groove that sounds similar to but at the same time quite different from any other small combo blues performance I've ever heard. The harmonica sets the tone. In fact, a Dylan harmonica riff at the beginning of the song sets the tone for eleven of the fourteen songs on this album—a fascinating clue to Dylan's creative process, musically. What does the harmonica do? I suggest that it pulls together all the different elements of the sound and the song, thereby leaving them room to remain separate, to work side by side and in and out of each other without ever losing their individuality or their commonality. How does it do this? I have no idea. But I can hear it. In no sense is Dylan's harmonica-playing on these tracks embellishment. It is a primary element of the performance, a powerful extension of his singing voice across octaves and into musical cracks and corners essential to his form of self-expression. If there were no such thing as a harmonica, it would have been necessary for Bob Dylan to invent it—and, in a real sense, with a nod to precursors like Sonny Terry and Sonny Boy Williamson II, he did.

In 1982 readers of *The Telegraph* voted "Visions of Johanna" their "favourite Dylan song" by a wide margin ("Like a Rolling Stone" and "It's Alright, Ma" tied for second). Why? There is a depth in this song, an intimate bond created between the singer and the listener, that defies analysis or explanation. The subject is simple: sitting in a room, probably a loft in New York on a rainy night, thinking about someone who isn't there. The music is not complicated: four chords. The rhyme scheme is straightforward through four verses—AAA BBBB CC—with a dramatic crescendo in the last verse, AAA BBBBBBB CC (all those Bs give the last pair of Cs a special resonance, you betcha). The arrangement is exquisite, admittedly—it's amazing how he uses enough instruments for a full rock band (bass drums organ guitars harmonica) and puts the rhythm section in the foreground of the mix, yet still achieves the feeling of a solo acoustic performance with added instrumental coloring (as in the album versions of "Mr. Tambourine Man" and "Desolation Row"). The language of the song is as beguiling as the instrumental and vocal performances: typically the listener is overcome by the mood of the recording, and the actual lyrics drift in and out of awareness, but whichever phrases do jump out are always remarkably intimate, moving, precise even when one can't say just what Dylan is talking about, still he's caught the feeling of it, the listener knows that here at least is one other person in the world who knows exactly what it feels like to be where I am right now.

One aspect of Dylan's performing technique that is particularly noticeable here is his ability to fit as few or as many syllables as he wants into a line (or a different number every time he sings it), and still have it work out right in terms of melody, meter, and rhythm. It's quite a trick. As I've mentioned before, this elasticity in his songwriting lays the groundwork for great freedom and inventiveness in his performing: he sings it however he feels it, and the music and the meter spread and contract to meet his needs.

"I Want You" and "Stuck Inside of Mobile with the Memphis Blues Again" are two more indispensable Dylan performances. They go together nicely, and in fact one of the minor triumphs of this album is the programming, the order of the songs and the way they work together as album sides on the original two-record album. It's not just a collection of fourteen songs, but a kind of symphony in four parts. Particularly successful is the third side, five songs that are not among the album's standouts individually but that flow together into a dense, enticing tapestry of sound and story, with unforgettable horn riffs and immortal snatches of lyrics ("to live outside the law you must be honest") jumping out at you from the general fray.

"Leopard-Skin Pill-Box Hat" on side two makes a nice, brash, somewhat ugly (sarcastic, rude, to my mind the only really mean-spirited song on the album) transition between the bright, extroverted beauty of "I Want You"/"Memphis Blues Again" and the warm, enveloping beauty of "Just Like a Woman." Something that shouldn't be overlooked here is the humor in so many of Dylan's songs—"Leopard-Skin Pill-Box Hat" is a misogynous belly laugh (moderated slightly when one realizes that jealous pique is the underlying emotion here), but the subtle wordplay and comic vocal inflections of "I Want You" and the pointed absurdities in the "Memphis Blues Again" vignettes are more typical examples of Dylan humor. "Now people just get uglier/And I have no sense of time," is a hilarious line (well, the best humor often has a dark edge to it), especially thanks to Dylan's delivery, his extraordinary sense of timing. Listen to him howl "Oh" at the beginning of the chorus ("Oh, Mama, can this really be the end")—it's so wonderful, so funny painful poignant and real, one could hear it a thousand times. *Blonde on Blonde* is the sort of record that has to be replaced every few years; people play it till they wear it flat.

"Here I sit so patiently/Waiting to find out what price/You have to pay to get out of/Going through all these things twice." Dylan's wish was about to be granted, in fact. But not quite yet. First it was time to go out on tour again.

17.

Once more unto the breach, dear friends. Dylan and his band began their 1966 tour on February 5, in White Plains, New York (some say February 4, in Louisville). The first half of the show, Dylan accompanying himself on acoustic guitar, featured the same seven songs he'd been playing since August, except that "Freeze Out" (soon to become "Visions of Johanna") had replaced "Gates of Eden." Dylan added two other new songs to his acoustic set, in both cases right after recording the songs in Nashville: "Fourth Time Around" (replacing "Ramona") and "Just Like a Woman" (replacing "Love Minus Zero"). So the solo set became: "She Belongs to Me," "Fourth Time Around," "Visions of Johanna," "It's All Over Now, Baby Blue," "Desolation Row," "Just Like a Woman," and "Mr. Tambourine Man." Dylan apparently sang these same songs in the same order every night throughout the spring of 1966, as he travelled from Missouri to Hawaii, from Australia to Ireland.

The electric set was also almost unvarying, as far as we know. From early 1966 on it went like this: "Tell Me, Momma" (a great rock and roll song, never recorded for an album), "I Don't Believe

You" (from *Another Side*; new arrangement), "Baby, Let Me Follow You Down" (from the first album; new arrangement), "Just Like Tom Thumb's Blues," "Leopard-Skin Pill-Box Hat" (again, added to the show right after it was recorded), "One Too Many Mornings" (from *Times They Are A-Changin'*; new arrangement), "Ballad of a Thin Man," and "Like a Rolling Stone." On a few occasions he also performed "Positively Fourth Street."

I attended two of the 1966 concerts, February 24 and 25 in Philadelphia. I remember enjoying them; and I remember that the vocals were hard to hear during the electric set, which apparently was a problem at most of the 1965-66 shows. I can't claim to remember much else about the performances. It was a long time ago; in addition I was (pleasantly) distracted by the fact that I had just spent several hours on the afternoon of the 24th "interviewing" Dylan (chatting with him) in his hotel room, and was attending the shows as his backstage guest. I was a college freshman, and had sent copies of the first two issues of my mimeographed rock and roll magazine to the theater hoping to get free tickets (asking for an interview was an afterthought). The theater had passed them on to Dylan; he was struck by them, and invited me, via his road manager, to come in and meet him.

He was open, friendly, kind—quite different from the Dylan many other journalists reported meeting during those years. I suppose my youth was a factor, and the fact that I wasn't trying to get something from him; indeed, I wasn't really a journalist, or was choosing not to be one for the afternoon. Instead of an "interview" I got a sense, which I won't try to put into words, of who he was and how he saw himself, during the hours we spent together. More than anything else I came away with the impression that he was a real person and could be related to as such.

He became less mysterious to me, and more human. At one point he indicated a line in an article I'd written about Paul Simon where I praised Simon for avoiding the "Dylanesque crime" of songs that go on interminably. He raised his eyebrows, and I squirmed—it was essentially a silent communication, he was not attacking me but, in a cautious way, letting me know the comment hurt. By not defending myself I acknowledged my careless arrogance, and in effect apologized. I think I learned at that moment to be conscious of, responsible for, what I write and the opinions I express, because what I say might sometimes make a difference to, be felt by, a real person on the other end.

That afternoon with Dylan gave strong support to my tendency to relate to works of art as things produced not by distant masters but by real people, similar to me, who have feelings and are searching for ways to express them accurately, honestly, straightforwardly. From this point of view, art is something experienced directly, by whoever appreciates it, always accessible to common sense interpretation.

The few audience tapes of the winter 1966 tour (three that I know of) are of minor interest because of poor sound quality, although the best of the three (supposedly from Pittsburgh, February 6, 1966) is noteworthy for containing the only known recording of Dylan and the Hawks performing "Positively Fourth Street" live. But the performances on this tape, though solid, seem unremarkable; and I find myself wondering, if and when more recordings of the North American 1966 concerts turn up, will we hear anything comparable to the incandescent music created by Dylan and the Hawks and Dylan alone in Australia and Europe? Or was it a matter of the music getting better later in the tour, because they'd found a groove, or because they'd left North America, or most likely because things had finally gotten *totally* weird and "out there," over the edge, senses stripped, amazing weariness escaping on the run for one last spectacular (six week) burst of semiconscious genius?

In February Dylan played a week of concerts, spent four days recording *Blonde on Blonde*, then played another week of concerts. The pace continued in March—a couple of concerts, then a couple of days in the studio to finish the album, then immediately on to St. Louis, Nebraska, Denver, Seattle, Vancouver (where he was visited by his wife).

Dylan and the Hawks flew from concert to concert in a small private plane; Robert Shelton's book contains a fascinating document of this time in Dylan's life, a chapter-long account of an interview (mostly monolog) with Dylan, taped aboard the plane, in the middle of the night, flying between Lincoln, Nebraska and Denver, Colorado. The other musicians were sleeping. Dylan was clearly wired on amphetamine (he talks to Shelton about "medicine"; six weeks later he told an interviewer in Stockholm "I've been up all night...I've taken some pills"). He had the galley proofs for *Tarantula* on his lap, along with a stack of poetry given him by a fan at the airport. He tells Shelton, "A concert tour like this has almost killed me...It's been like this since October...It really drove me out of my mind." And, "Playing on the stage is a kick for me now. It wasn't before, because I knew what I was doing then was just too empty..." The words tumble out of him, electric avantgarde world-famous songwriter/pop star Bob Dylan caught in midflight. Read it out loud to get the full flavor.

On April 13 Dylan played his first concert in Australia. In the next six weeks he would play twenty-three more concerts, in Australia, Scandinavia, Ireland, France, and Great Britain. A handful of essential Dylan recordings document this tour, most of them incomplete soundboard tapes (recorded from the PA system rather than by a tape recorder in the audience): Melbourne April 19-20 (nine songs), Dublin May 5 (six songs), Belfast May 6 (one song), Liverpool May 14 (one song), Manchester May 17 (thirteen songs), London May 26 (six songs), and London May 27 (seven songs). These recordings, particularly the electric set from Manchester (which was widely circulated as a bootleg album with the inaccurate title *Live At Royal Albert Hall*), are the most famous and probably the best-loved of all of Dylan's live performances.

All of these recordings are exceptional and deserve careful scrutiny. For the purposes of this text, I'm going to focus on the acoustic set from the last concert of the tour, London (Royal Albert Hall) May 27, and the electric set from Manchester May 17, with some mention of other standout performances, particularly the three that are currently available to record-buyers via *Biograph*.

Cameron Crowe in the *Biograph* notes speaks of the "otherworldy" quality of the live "Visions of Johanna" (from May 26), and it's true, the acoustic performances from this tour sound like Dylan is singing straight from dreamtime; there is a texture of intimacy and "other"-ness here that is so rich the listener is transported by it the moment each song begins. "She Belongs to Me" from May 27 is absolutely extraordinary, not for any particulars one can point to that set it apart from the album version—there's more harmonica here, and it's marvelously expressive, but every syllable of the vocal and every strum of the guitar are also expressive, as on the lp version only more so. What comes through is the musician's confidence in his music, a feeling of clarity and certainty that is overwhelming. The song as sung is a gentle, very personal but strictly non-negotiable invitation to the listener to yield tc the power of the music's presence, and a self-fulfilling promise of the treasures obtainable thereby. I get chills every time I hear it.

"Fourth Time Around," Dylan's second song of the evening, is the only May 27 performance I'm not insanely enthusiastic about, probably because I'm so attached to his May 5 "Fourth Time Around" from Dublin. That performance, when I started listening to it a few years ago, transformed the song from a collection of vaguely interesting lines to a vivid movie playing before my eyes. And still every time I hear it (Dublin version) I can smell the booze and the recently-completed lovemaking, hear the voices of mutual attraction souring into distrust and righteousness, and see the bizarre, compelling landscape of the casual encounter with its hallways and scattered clothes and deadly earnest issues of weakness and need just under its good-times surface. The London performance has that otherworldly feeling and some great moments of vocal inflection (Dylan tended to sing this new-to-the-audience song like an experiment in arTICuLAtion), but to my taste he gets hypnotized by the rhythmic guitar figure and sings the words more as sounds (quite an interesting approach in its own right) than story. In Dublin it's the story, not the words, he wants to get across, and he succeeds fabulously. The rhythmic waltz-figure that dominates the song is not obtrusively in the foreground or background but right in the center of the performance, where it should be.

"Visions of Johanna" (third song of the acoustic set) is a superb vehicle for Dylan's voice. The narrative is ambiguous yet full of delightful specifics; the song provides the singer with an intricate structure to rest on and, at the same time, tremendous freedom. May 26 and 27 Dylan sings the same words, same arrangement, but achieves two strikingly different performances, each unforgettable. It's all a matter of emphasis, and I don't just mean which syllable or even which word gets emphasized, but which of the thousand strands of imagery and emotion that weave together to form the song get highlighted or shaded or turned a little this way or that. Any given word or phrase can take on a whole new life each time through.

Obviously the singer doesn't think, "What do I want the song to say this time?" He opens his mouth and sings, puts his hands on his guitar and plays, and something flows out from him. His attention is not on directing the flow but on avoiding or removing anything—thoughts, doubts, self-consciousness—that could get in the way. He listens, feels, responds, and shares, all in one action. He is a vehicle for revealed truth.

What is revealed is how it feels to stand here at this moment. This is not trivial. In a real sense it is all that any of us can say to each other, ever. Nor is there a limit to how much or how deeply we can feel. The limits lie in our willingness to feel, and our willingness and ability to share and express.

A great performer, at the moment of performance, is characterized by how present he or she is, and how abundantly this presence is communicated. We as audience have a sense of having our own limits expanded; great performances increase our willingness and therefore our ability to receive.

The *Biograph* performance of "Visions of Johanna" could hardly be improved on. (Listen to how much his voice puts into the phrases "trying to be so quiet" and "our best to deny it" and "a handful of rain" and voice and guitar together on "from the opposite loft"; you could listen to these lines a hundred times and keep discovering new wonders, before ever going on to the other 9/10ths of the song.) But I would be reluctant to leave for a desert island without the May 27 performance, with its thick textures of sweet mournfulness, its moments of startlingly penetrating intensity (I want to say, life-affirming desperation). It is stately, seductive, gorgeous. Dylan sings as if he somehow knew, felt in his bones, that after singing the song almost every night for six months, he was now saying goodbye to it—that he would not perform it again in public for more than seven years.

Dylan had turned twenty-five three days earlier. His seventh album, *Blonde on Blonde*, had just been released (mid-May), and the unlikely single from that album, "Rainy Day Women #12 & 35," was already at the top of the American charts, reaffirming Dylan's status as pop star as well as supreme cult figure of the emerging youth movement in America and Europe, a movement that somehow pulled together civil rights and anti-war and anti-establishment politics, adolescent alienation, psychedelic drugs, and rock and roll music into a palpable force. Something was happening, and no one really knew what it was, but even the most dimwitted journalist could tell that Bob Dylan as much as anyone was at the center of the storm.

Dylan, meanwhile, was on an adventure of his own. He was using a lot of drugs, particularly when he was touring (and he'd been touring almost constantly since August). He ate little and slept seldom, standard operating procedure for an amphetamine user— and certainly the amphetamines (i.e., methedrine, dexedrine, benzedrine..."speed") were Dylan's drug of choice, along with marijuana and hashish. What else went around is anyone's guess— presumably some LSD, probably barbiturates or other "downers" to help induce sleep, possibly DMT (a short-term psychedelic, highly disorienting), vitamin injections (a "respectable" form of speed), maybe the occasional taste of opium, cocaine, or heroin. But surely speed and grass were primary. (Alcohol was a favorite drug of Dylan's at least since college days, and continues to be today; but I don't know if it was of much interest to him in 1965-1966.)

What Dylan did with the drugs is what anyone does: he controlled subjective reality. He filled up the spaces on the road. He also used them, specifically amphetamine, to maintain an extraordinary level of creative productivity. (In 1969 he was asked, "Did taking drugs influence the songs?" "No," he said, "not the writing of them, but it did keep me up there to pump 'em out.")

"Rainy Day Women," Dylan's hit single (which he was not performing on tour), was a great prank at the time, with its singalong chorus of "everybody must get stoned." At the May 27 concert Dylan mentions to the audience that this is his last concert in England (a comment widely misquoted, as though he'd vowed not to come back) and takes the opportunity to complain that this song (he's about to play "Visions of Johanna") is probably a typical example of what "your English music newspapers would call a 'drug song.' I don't write drug songs, I never have...It's just vulgar to think so." He's no doubt objecting to simplistic interpretations of songs like "Mr. Tambourine Man" and "Just Like Tom Thumb's Blues," rather than defending the playful "Rainy Day Women." Ironically, he's almost certainly very stoned as he says this. While tuning up for another song, he mutters to someone in the audience, "Don't do that—that's terrible," and giggles. In photos from the time, he inevitably looks exhausted.

And yet, for this moment in his life, and speaking strictly in terms of his art, his performing (which was his great passion in these months, more than at any time since college days), it worked—he managed more often than not to take the right combination of poisons or anyway to work with and transcend the poisons in his system (or play them off against the music biz/media/popularity poisons all around him) to perform from the heart, with great confidence, with genius, with a fascinating mixture of control and abandon, and, on these acoustic performances, with tremendous vulnerability, taking unbelievable risks and succeeding beyond all possible expectations.

He knew full well he was burning the candle at both ends, that it couldn't go on like this, that he was hurting himself. But he also loved the results he was getting, what he was achieving creatively, whether anyone else knew it or cared. He knew he was playing exceptional music—especially in the electric sets, they were what he cared about most, but on the evidence of these recordings the passionate artistry the electric performances inspired in him carried over to his solo work as well. No one could ask or expect an artist to recreate the chaos and pain that inspired great works from him at some earlier time in his career. But neither can one honestly regret those times or wish that they'd happened differently.

"It's All Over Now, Baby Blue" on *Biograph* is from the Manchester concert, May 17, 1966; it is quite similar to the May 27 performance—the same wonderful tricks of the tongue at the ends of words, same (or very similar) heart-stopping melodic twist on the word "home," similar awesome harmonica solos. This is a song with an emotional message so simple and powerful it seems to fit almost any occasion. Dylan plays the guitar as a rhythmic drone, giving birth to, commenting on, and finally reabsorbing each line of the lyrics. The harmonica sings high, lonely, glorious release.

The last three songs of the May 27 acoustic set at Royal Albert Hall are good enough to stand next to the best work of any twentieth century artist (performer, painter, poet, mathematician...). One of the controversies that has swirled around Dylan is whether or not he is a great, or even good, singer. The answer depends, of course, on what one thinks great singing consists of. Dylan is an artist who breaks new ground, over and over in his career—like Picasso, this is sometimes a function of his inventiveness, sometimes of his primitivism, and always of his integrity—and certainly as a singer he is like Kafka in the Borges essay, creating his own predecessors by embodying a set of values not new but having no existence as a set until Kafka or Dylan came along. So of course it is his fate always to be found wanting when judged by critical standards that predate the breakthroughs he himself has helped bring about or bring into focus. Even so, I find it difficult to imagine anyone listening to Dylan's May 27 performances of "Desolation Row," "Just Like a Woman," and "Mr. Tambourine Man" without immediately surrendering all preconceptions and acknowledging that this is remarkable art, an exaltation of the human spirit. If these performances are not the work of a great singer, how shall we account for them?

"Desolation Row" is perhaps the most ambitious and most successful popular work of its era—not that it's so ambitious to write a long poem, but writing it as a song to be performed is something else...writing it to be performed and then performing it yourself, with complete confidence, as though every single breath of it matters, and also as though this thought need not be troubling, because when one is sharing truth there is no wrong way to breathe. Dylan attempts this and succeeds, and never more so than on this concert hall stage in London, blowing the whole subjective subterranean flavor of midtwentieth century reality, what it feels like to be here, out through his voice and guitar and language as though he were a saxophone player blowing his finest solo, putting everything into it and wailing all the feelings of all the voiceless people, now and forever captured at this moment, blowing it out through the roofs of the apartment buildings and past the men on the docks already arriving to load the boats, blowing it out through the little speakers of the college kids' phonographs, through the jukeboxes, through the radio stations, through Europe and Japan and Australia and Canada and Brazil, and gutsy enough to not just take the silence and express it as sound but to actually express it in *words*, without slowing down mind you, blowing it through the most omnipresent and slippery and dangerous of powers (words!) without looking back or wavering except the way truth itself wavers as it blows out into the sunlight, past the edge of the curve, out into the interplanetary spaces, cool and confident, putting it forward and letting it ride and giving it everything and letting it down easy and walking away when it's over, ready to sing the next song.

And the next song, next performance, is every bit as moving, but in a totally other way, because here he shifts from singing about a street to almost the only other thing there is, singing about a person. Five seconds of harmonica after the strummed intro and just before his voice begins, and already you're ready to cry. And then the impossible beauty of his voice, never more chilling or naked or transcendent than on this particular take of "Just Like a Woman." Great singing? Years later Dylan wrote, in a song about a love affair, "I still can't remember all the best things she said." Having this performance on tape is like not only remembering but being able to play back her voice in your mind whenever you dare to.

And finally a song about a songmaker, song of songs, acknowledgement of the music's source, a benediction (as "She Belongs to Me" was invocation), "Mr. Tambourine Man." When the words begin and the audience recognizes the song and bursts into loud applause, I imagine I can hear Dylan consciously not pausing, not allowing himself to notice, because to do so would be to feel resentment at their enthusiasm (which he knows will turn to catcalls and hostility when he comes back for the electric set), and feeling even a tiny resentment or reluctance now would cut him off from this extraordinary flow of music that's happening. So he sings on, ignoring the audience, or rather singing his song straight to the "higher self" of each person there, that part that is able and willing to be open to every note, to hear it for the first time, just as though we really were outside of time and space for this moment.

Because that's what it is that's so magical about Dylan's performance of these seven songs, this is what his drugs (at who knows what price) have temporarily bought him: an unimaginable freedom from self-consciousness, a total willingness to share in his performance everything he's feeling and everything each song means to him, to give it all away without any conditions to anyone who happens to be listening. For the listener, the result is that we can hear him enter and inhabit and depart from every syllable in every song. We see what he sees and hear what he hears and smell what he smells. We share each certainty and each doubt, even when there's three of one and four of another in a single moment. What characterizes Dylan's solo singing at this concert (and on this tour) is a supernatural generosity. Another word for it is clarity, or translucency.

The last minute of "Mr. Tambourine Man" is missing from the circulating tape of this concert—the last line of the chorus and the harmonica solo that presumably follows—and it's appropriate somehow, a reminder that there are limits to our power to teleport

ourselves to 1966, and of what a miracle it is that these performances survive at all. The harmonica solo before the last verse is
magnificent, a spontaneous poem, wordless update, Dylan dancing
before us with love and energy and humor, writing in the air in
shorthand everything he forgot to tell us earlier. And, listening, we
cannot fail to understand.

So imagine, if you will, a short intermission while we switch
reels, and now you're in Manchester (Free Trades Hall) May 17,
but for all intents and purposes it's the same concert (and indeed
some argue that the last two songs of the Manchester tape are
actually from one of the London shows). Dylan walks back onstage
wearing an electric guitar, with five other men he doesn't introduce: Garth Hudson playing Hammond organ, Richard Manuel
on electric piano, Rick Danko playing electric bass, Mickey Jones
on drums, and Robbie Robertson on lead guitar. There's a few
moments of (electric) guitar strumming and then on a drumbeat
cue this big noise kicks in and then Dylan starts singing over the
din, and the angel who shared his soul with you only minutes
earlier person to person so intimate and clear you could hear a pin
drop is now muttering sardonically and screaming crazily, and the
only words you can make out are, "But I know—that you know—
that I know—that you show—something—is tearing—up your
mind—Tell me momma—Tell me momma—Tell me momma, what
is it? What's wrong with you—*this time*?"

In 1958, at the Hibbing High School Talent Festival, Bob
Zimmerman took his band up on stage and proceeded to make the
loudest music he could possibly make; the boos and hostility he
provoked either didn't matter to him or else spurred him on to
play with even more power and fire. His electric sets during the
1966 world tour were a further exploration of the same musical
and theatrical impulses, just as much an expression of Dylan's
essential nature as writing and singing "Hard Rain" and "Mr.
Tambourine Man" and "Desolation Row." "If I didn't write this
stuff, I'd go nuts," he told a reporter in 1963; "I've got all these
thoughts inside me and I've gotta say 'em." To understand Dylan's
music, one need only remember that he doesn't necessarily experience thoughts as words or ideas. He experiences them as sounds.
And so the extraordinary music he made with the Hawks (soon to
be known as the Band) in the spring of 1966 was for him a saying

of sounds—sounds that already existed inside him. He had found a way to let them out.

In a 1968 interview, Dylan told John Cohen, "I was trying to make the two things [folk music and rock and roll] go together when I was on those concerts. I played the first half acoustically, second half with a band, somehow thinking that it was going to be two kinds of music." This is an intriguing statement which unfortunately was not followed up on; did it turn out to be two kinds of music, in his view, or didn't it? At Manchester he repeats a song introduction he'd been using, I believe, ever since starting his acoustic/electric tour: "This is called 'I Don't Believe You.' It used to be like that, and now it goes like this." This comes just before the second electric song, his first opportunity to speak to the audience, and it could be considered conciliatory, an attempt to share his artistic process. The audience responds, some of them, at the beginning of the next song—they drown out Dylan's harmonica introduction to "Baby, Let Me Follow You Down" by clapping their hands slowly in unison, a consciously disruptive action, presumably a protest against his rock and roll presentation. Dylan stops for a moment, then starts again decisively, drowning out the protesters.

From here on in the concert is framed by this confrontation between Dylan and the disaffected members of the audience, and the drama that results unquestionably has contributed to the fame and popularity of this recording (which has been called the greatest or one of the greatest live rock and roll recordings ever by quite a few different commentators). Dylan's response is brilliant and energetic throughout the performances and in two extraordinary spontaneous bits of between-song repartee. He defeats the slow-handclappers by mumbling not-quite audible nonsense words in unmistakable story diction; the audience eventually hushes itself out of curiosity, and as they do, he delivers the punch line, "—if you only just wouldn't clap so hard!" The audience as a whole (presumably the protesters are a minority, albeit a loud and powerful one) laughs and applauds, and Dylan and the Hawks rip into "One Too Many Mornings." The other now-historic episode comes before the last song—there is a very audible shout of "Judas!" (which many in the crowd applaud—almost as though they were at a boxing match, screaming for each good punch regardless of who throws it), followed by several other (indecipherable) shouts from the audience. Dylan replies, loudly and with great dignity, "I don't believe you" (stretching out the third word), strums his guitar, the first chord of the next song is heard and Dylan says, louder and with perfect timing, "You're a *liar!*" The song that follows is "Like a Rolling Stone."

This exquisite dramatic moment and the whole context of the battle to sing one's song in the face of skepticism, hostility, and outright opposition, obviously gives this concert that extra something that makes it memorable, that indeed opens us to the musical part of the recording, makes us want to love it and appreciate it and gets us to listen sympathetically a few times until exposure to the music teaches us its form and its language and allows us to hear it and experience it as the awesome work of performed art that it is. But I am at pains to point out that the dramatic context is what makes the performance noticeable and accessible; it is not what makes it great.

Indeed, the fame of this performance, and the legend that surrounds Dylan's early live shows with the Band (a legend largely based on this recording, since very little else of their performances together has ever circulated), has had the inevitable detrimental effect over the years, as fans (summer soldiers) and critics dismiss Dylan's live performances after giving them scant attention (specifically not opening themselves to learn the form and language of what the artist is doing), saying (as critics and fans always do in response to any great artist who goes on creating) that he isn't living up to his past achievements: "Why doesn't he play like he did in 1966?"

In considering Dylan as an artist rather than as a hero or a symbol (or a subject for a biography), we must go beyond the circumstances of this concert (i.e., some members of the audience were angry and confused because they thought their icon of independence was selling out to the pop music establishment), and look instead at what Dylan was attempting and what he achieved.

He says he was attempting to make two things go together. A simplistic view would be that he was giving his fans what they wanted in the first half of the concert, and then coming back with the challenging "new Dylan" in the second half. There is some superficial truth in this, but one has only to look at the song selection (no "Blowin' in the Wind," indeed nothing from his first four albums, three songs out of seven new to the audience) and listen to the performances themselves to realize that he was in no way playing it safe or being cynical in his acoustic set. On the contrary, he sings and plays his heart out, and chooses an extremely demanding (for performer and audience) set of songs. The entire acoustic set is "new Dylan," Dylan passionately involved in creating something that is meaningful and fresh for him.

The electric set is the same man, with the same creative and musical vision, working in a different context, a different musical format. The biggest difference is that he's not making music by himself, this half. The obvious difference is that he's playing electric guitar and working with a rock and roll band, but that's simply an expression of what he wants to hear when he's making music with other musicians. He wants a rich, loud, rhythmic sound. The musical difference that is most important, I think, is the presence of the drummer. In the first half, the words of the song are at the center of the performance, and Dylan's voice unites the words with the music, while Dylan's guitar and harmonica playing shape and frame the song that's been given life by the voice and identity by the words. The guitar conveys rhythm, and carries it, but the essential rhythms of the song are in the words, in the flow of language, and the guitar provides accents and counterpoints.

In the second half there are two centers to the performance instead of one, and they are Dylan's voice and the drums. It is as though he is facing the drums and singing to them (musically if not literally) and everything else is built around this interaction. Words are secondary—they are material for Dylan's voice to work with, like the skins on the drums for the drummer. Instead of the voice, the bass (and sometimes the piano) works to unite the center of the performance with the rest of what's happening. And there's a lot happening. Whereas in the acoustic performances there's one thing happening, and it is added to, colored, embellished, and enriched, in the group performance there are all sorts of things happening (wonderful lead guitar bits and organ fills and melodies and lyrics and vocal emphases and pounding rhythms and harmonies and cacophonies) and the overriding goal of the six performers is to bring it together, to be constantly aware of and in service to the creation of this single thing that can only be called a sound. You start making the sound when you start performing the song and you don't stop till the song is over. And at the center of that sound is the voice (not words but voice) and the beat.

So Dylan, using as a model the Newport performance where

he played electric and then came back with his folk guitar, but reversing the order, created a concert structure in which these two very different approaches to music could be experienced side by side, to express the fact that they do exist side by side for him, this is a wholeness, not an either/or. It was his way of telling the truth about music, about his experience of music. It wasn't just the electric half but the concert as a whole that was outrageously radical.

And it is the energy of this radical experiment, and of its increasing success (it really came together in Australia and Europe) that Dylan is expressing in his extraordinary performance in Manchester, much more than any anger provoked by the carryings-on of the audience. Many have spoken of the pain conveyed in his singing at this show. It's there, to be sure, but even more present is what D. A. Pennebaker, who filmed these shows, reports he was most struck by: Dylan's unbounded joy. "It was the first time I had ever seen him really happy in the middle of music," says Pennebaker. "He was jumping around like a cricket in the middle of the thing. And the music was incredible. The sound of that band was the best sound I ever heard."

Dylan can be seen jumping around making music with the Hawks in the fragmentary footage of the European concerts included in the experimental film *Eat the Document* which Dylan, Howard Alk, and Robbie Robertson put together in 1967 from footage shot by Alk and Pennebaker in 1966. There are no complete songs, unfortunately, just glimpses—one great minute of "Baby Let Me Follow You Down," two minutes of "One Too Many Mornings," three minutes of "I Don't Believe You" (great shots of Dylan's hands moving wildly as he plays the harmonica, charged with nervous, creative energy). Bits of most of the other electric set songs are included, and a nice two and a half minutes of "Mr. Tambourine Man" focusing on a wonderful harmonica solo. Other performances visible through the keyhole of *Eat the Document* are Dylan dueting backstage with a wasted Johnny Cash on "I Still Miss Someone," and three hotel room performances, Dylan playing guitar and singing (words not always audible, but his voice is beautiful) while Robbie accompanies him, also on acoustic guitar. Dylan sings three songs that he apparently is working on, tiny clues to what he might have written and performed next if history had been different (they sound almost like traditional folk songs, but of

course we don't know what Dylan's other songs at that time might
have sounded like when he was first fooling around with them)—at
a guess, the titles are "On a Rainy Afternoon," "What Kind of
Friend Is This?," and "I Can't Leave Her Behind" ("where she
leads me I do not know," sung in this lovely high vulnerable voice).
Somewhere there is more footage, on stage and off, stored away,
that could possibly emerge someday. The time machine has not yet
made its last trip.

On the *Biograph* lp (but not the compact disc), "I Don't Believe
You" live from Belfast, May 6, 1966, segues directly into the May
26, 1966 "Visions of Johanna." They flow together very nicely, and
in the context of the album as a whole (a cross-section of twenty
years of Dylan's work) I doubt most listeners would even consciously notice that the first song is performed with a rock band
and the second is solo acoustic. They have similar energy—both
strongly rhythmic, strongly melodic—and are sung by the same
voice. And of course they sound different, with their very different
instrumentation, but in this context that doesn't seem like a bigger
difference than the differences in subject matter or any of the other
distinctions that separate one song from another. But when the
transition was new, electric Dylan versus folk Dylan (like Christian
Dylan versus "pre-Christian" Dylan) seemed a distinction worth
dying for (at least the death of renouncing the relationship with the
singer, the loved one). This in itself is a testimony to the power of
the performer's art. If he touches the core of us, over and over, as
he sings facing south, we may find ourselves ready to go to war
(either in the name of who he's become, or in the name of who he
used to be) when he turns and starts singing facing east.

The first live Dylan recording ever released to the public, and
the only one until 1970 (nine years into his career), was "Just Like
Tom Thumb's Blues," recorded at Liverpool, May 14, 1966. This
was included as the flip side of the 45 of "I Want You," released in
June 1966 (no longer available, alas, unless you can find the 1978
Japanese Dylan album called *Masterpieces*). It is magnificent, quite
comparable to the best moments of the Manchester set. The rhythmic core of the performance is as solid as anything that can be
experienced in this material world, Dylan's vocal is as alive and
penetrating as the voice of God in a nightmare, and the band's
playing—particularly the organ and lead guitar—has the bright
intensity and richness of an acid trip with stage sets designed by

Jackson Pollock and Vincent Van Gogh. This one definitely added a notch to Dylan's mystique when we punched it up on the jukebox in Harvard Square in the summer of 1966. What does it mean, that somewhere someone is making music like this?

Dylan on this world tour had the rare ability, a lot of the time, to be totally in the moment when he was on stage, not consciously aware but simply tuned to everything that was going on. His "You're a liar!" in Manchester is a function of this—another very different but equally wonderful exchange with the audience has recently surfaced on a tape of three songs from the electric set in Melbourne, April 19 or 20, 1966. Dylan delivers an unusual, wry but revealing, introduction to "Tom Thumb," worth quoting in its entirety:

> This is about a painter down in Mexico City who travels from North Mexico up to Del Rio, Texas, all the time; his name is Tom Thumb, and, uh, right now he's about 125 years old but he's still going. And uh, everybody likes him a lot down there, he's got lots of friends, and uh, this is when he was going through his blue period, painting, and uh, he's made countless amount of paintings, you couldn't think of them all. This is his blue period painting, I just dedicate this song to him, it's called "Just Like Tom Thumb's *Blues*."

The moment he says the song's title a young woman in the audience lets out a ferociously loud, out-of-control squeal of excitement that goes on for several long moments (and provokes laughter and applause from the crowd), the sort of thing you'd hear constantly that year at a Beatles concert but very seldom for Dylan. When she finally finishes, Dylan, with his flawless timing, in a hesitant, friendly voice, asks, "You know Tom Thumb?" And they start the song.

It is this responsiveness, this ability to be there with whatever's happening (a spiritual rather than intellectual quality), that makes possible the incredible collaboration between him and the other musicians. I've said before that it is as if Dylan plays the musicians he works with, so that every note you hear from the band is an expression of what he's feeling. Another, perhaps more accurate way to say this is that he has a gift of receptivity that allows him to open himself to the feelings of the group as a whole, so that this collective feeling comes through in his voice as well as in all the music as they perform together on stage. Paradoxically, when he is gentle and vulnerable playing his complex songs alone on acoustic guitar in the first half of the show he is in a sense in a fully masculine, yang role, consciously controlling everything that happens, his voice, his timing, his harmonica, his guitar; and when he is fiery and aggressive singing rock and roll in the middle of the band in the electric half he is in an essentially feminine, receptive role, constantly responding, flowing with, adjusting to what all the other musicians and the music as a whole are doing, holding everything together with his willingness to accept it and work with it as it is. This was (and still is, most of the time) his formula for ensemble performing, on stage and in the studio—don't plan it, don't control it, do it and make room for the unexpected, respond to it and create with it as it's happening. Robbie Robertson recalled, in a 1975 conversation with Larry Sloman, "We were playing so out of this world, we didn't even know what the fuck we were doing, because he didn't want to learn any of the songs. It was just play them."

An applicable phrase here is "to live outside the law you must be honest." If you're going to make music without a predetermined plan or arrangement, your only hope is to be completely true to yourself and completely open to what's happening at every moment of every performance.

But just imagine someone living this and acting it out in his art to the extreme degree that Dylan did in both sets of his 1966 concerts, giving everything he has over and over and coming back a few minutes later, and then a day later, and doing it again, and again. The concerts were incandescent because the singer was living for art, was literally burning himself out, not to please the audience and certainly not out of obligation but for the sheer joy of doing it, travelling with intrepid companions out into unknown aesthetic realms, shining lights into unexplored darkness.

I haven't said much about the individual performances that make up the Manchester electric set because there's so much here and it requires the creation of a new language to be able to talk about it and anyway you already know—"everything I'm saying, you can say it just as good" (Dylan sings this at Manchester with a weariness that has an extraordinary core of resilient strength, surrounded by guitar notes and drum beats and organ riffs that are truly eloquent, full of very specific color and breathtaking beauty). The songs flow together into one song, moving from the explicitly sexual ("Tell Me Momma," "I Don't Believe You," "Baby Let Me Follow You Down") to a more complex, less identifiable, more emotional landscape ("One Too Many Mornings," "Ballad of a Thin Man," "Like a Rolling Stone"). The version of "Ballad of a Thin Man" is arguably the most powerful I've ever heard. The band (that includes the vocalist) found the groove, I mean really found it, this performance is an ocean wide and a hundred light-years long (and ends right on schedule, the infinite in a nutshell).

And "Like a Rolling Stone," impossibly, is the equal of the original recording, totally new and just as intense. This performance has been called apocalyptic, which I think means announcing and even glorying in the destruction of the world as we know it. Is this something that can be repeated every night? Another definition is, "depicting symbolically the ultimate destruction of evil and triumph of good." Whew. What's that drummer's name, again? Mickey Jones. I think maybe he's the difference between the shows on the world tour and the concerts that came earlier...

Anyway, May 27, Royal Albert Hall, it all came to an end, and the details of the next few months are vague. Presumably everyone went home, and Dylan got to play with his infant son for a while, and was reminded by his manager that he had to complete or approve *Tarantula* for publication by Macmillan, had to come up with the one-hour TV special that ABC-TV had already paid for (that was the impetus behind the filming in Europe), and had to get ready for the next 64 concert dates that had been set up in the U.S. for midsummer and into the fall.

That particular fall never came. Instead, on July 29, 1966, Bob Dylan pop star was thrown from his motorcycle while riding around near his house in Woodstock, New York. Ever the artist, he recognized in this an opportunity to bring an end to the world as he had known it up to that moment, and he didn't hesitate.

VI. Husband

August 1966 — December 1973

"That was a brush, I survived that, but what I survived after that was even harder to survive than the motorcycle crash. That was just a physical crash, but sometimes there are things in life that you cannot see, that are harder to survive than something which you can pin down."
—Bob Dylan, 1978

18.

In two and a half years, January 1964 to May 1966, Bob Dylan released five extraordinary albums, each more intense, more complex, more revolutionary than the one before. He performed to live audiences throughout these years; the occasional months off were more than balanced by the fullness of his schedule when he was out on tour—often three or four concerts a week. He gave interviews and press conferences endlessly. He wrote, and when he wasn't on the radio singing his own songs, someone else was singing them, and there seemed to be new ones all the time. Dylan's audience, and their expectations of him, and indeed his expectations of himself, just got bigger and bigger.

And then suddenly...silence.

A year passed, after the motorcycle accident, before Dylan gave any sort of interview to anyone, before his fans had their first direct confirmation that he was still alive and able to communicate. A year and a half passed before he released a new album. It was also a year and a half before he next performed in public: three songs at Carnegie Hall in January 1968. In the seven and a half years between May 1966 and January 1974, Dylan performed only one full concert (an hour-long show in August 1969). He ended his 1966 tour having just turned 25, and started his next tour at the age of 32.

The first year of silence was the most dramatic, because it followed such a period of fecundity and came at a time of great public interest in Dylan—and because no one except those closest to Dylan knew how badly he was hurt.

In fact, his actual injuries had been minor. He suffered a cracked vertebra in his neck, was dazed, went to the hospital, had to wear a brace for a while. The story that he had been almost killed and completely incapacitated by the accident was put out by his manager as justification for delaying the promised book and television movie, and for cancelling the 64 concert commitments (the first two were at the Yale Bowl and at Shea Stadium in New York, both huge venues, suggesting Dylan had arrived at or was being pushed into a level of pop stardom comparable only to the Beatles). For his part, of course, Dylan used the accident as an excuse and an opportunity to tell his manager no—no, he wasn't going back out on the road for a while, no he wasn't going to say when he would turn in the book, complete the TV film, make his next album.

But the accident was certainly more than an excuse. It was a turning point. Dylan told Shelton he'd been awake for three days before he fell off his bike; this suggests his amphetamine lifestyle had continued unchanged after he got home from the tour. In the months after his injury, we know, the changes were radical: Dylan gave up the star game, gave up being in the public eye (escaped, withdrew)—and also gave up smoking cigarettes, and, it seems reasonable to assume, taking drugs and chasing women. One of his favorite new pastimes, after the crash, was reading the Bible—he mentioned this to friends and, later, spoke of it in interviews. He became a family man. The accident was a moment of awakening, an opportunity for a life-changing, probably life-saving, reassessment, leading to a dramatic shift in personal values. Some would say he was blessed with an opportunity to "hit bottom," and then begin a period of recovery. Dylan in 1978 described the experience as "the Great Spirit telling me you need a rest."

But Dylan didn't give up music, or alcohol, at least not for long. The trail of Dylan performances picks up in approximately

June 1967 with the relaxed, boozy, homemade recordings of Dylan and the Band known as the Basement Tapes.

Prior to this, Dylan and Howard Alk had assembled and edited the first half hour of a TV movie based on the footage shot in Europe in May of 1966. They bogged down—Dylan evidently had very little energy for creative work at this time, roughly fall 1966—and Robbie Robertson was invited up to Woodstock to complete the job. He did, along the lines of what Alk and Dylan had begun; the film was submitted to ABC, and was rejected. It was highly experimental. Alk and Dylan had broken down the footage that interested them into small segments, numbered categories (i.e., a pile of "train" clips, a pile of clips of fans expressing their opinions, etc.), and they then tried to establish a musical rhythm, orchestrating these little segments of film as if each number represented a note, or a chord. "I'm a mathematical singer," Dylan once said, and he intended to be the same kind of filmmaker.

Eat the Document, as the name implies, was also consciously edited with the intention of frustrating the desire of the public, of the television network that had commissioned the film, and indeed of the cameraman (D. A. Pennebaker, who'd filmed and directed *Don't Look Back* during Dylan's U.K. tour the previous year) to capture and document Dylan and his performances and what was going on around him. Dylan, to his credit (and much as I would like to have a filmed document of the 1966 tour), refused to be pinned down and mounted like a butterfly. He wanted a film that would be as satisfying to create, and as radical, as his music; something rhythmic and melodic and visual, a pulse, an alternate and somehow truer way of seeing/experiencing reality. This was ambitious. And yet *Eat the Document* is surprisingly successful for a first effort. It takes on added significance in that it was definitely an early, very rough draft of Dylan's masterful 1977 film, *Renaldo & Clara*.

Robbie Robertson spent time at Woodstock editing *Eat the Document*, and liked the place, and as a result he and the rest of the Hawks (hereafter I'll call them the Band, although that name didn't really come along till 1968), except for Levon, got a house on a hilltop in West Saugerties, not far from Dylan's home in Woodstock. The legendary Basement Tapes were recorded (some of them, maybe most of them) in the basement of the Band's house, on fairly crude equipment operated by Garth Hudson. Dylan apparently would come over in the afternoon—every afternoon, week after week—and he and the Band would sit around making music together, and when the spirit moved them they'd record some of what they were doing.

A number of Dylan compositions recorded in this fashion were circulated by his American and British music publishers as demos, in acetate or tape form, to other artists who might be interested in recording the material. (Indeed Dylan has said he recorded the songs because he was being "pushed" to "come up with some songs.") The result was as intended: some songs did get recorded, some even became hits (notably "The Mighty Quinn," or "Quinn the Eskimo," recorded by Manfred Mann). A secondary result was that musicians and others who heard the songs liked them so much (and were so excited to have new Dylan material after the drought of the last fifteen months or so) that they played the tape to and made copies for friends, and so these Dylan/Band performances started circulating samizdat fashion, hand to hand. In 1967-68, simply having heard this tape conferred status on a person.

In 1969 the first bootleg record (as they came to be known) appeared, a double-album of unreleased Dylan material with a white cover, manufactured and distributed by fly-by-night black market entrepreneurs. It acquired the nickname "Great White Wonder," and sold a lot of copies. Seven of the Basement Tapes songs were included on this album, and as more Dylan bootlegs appeared albums specializing in Basement Tapes material became common. Finally in 1975 Dylan and the Band and Columbia Records put out a double album of this material (16 songs by Dylan with the Band, eight more performed by the Band alone) as an official release. It sold very well, surprising Dylan, who said, "I thought everybody had a copy already."

In all, there are 22 Basement Tapes songs (that we know of so far) written and performed by Dylan between June and October of 1967, plus a few alternate takes, plus approximately twenty more performances from the same period that have recently started circulating, most of them old songs—country or folk or pop—sung by Dylan but not written by him. Members of the Band play with Dylan on all of these recordings—Garth Hudson's distinctive, wildly original organ playing is usually central to the sound, a very special sound, quite different from anything else Dylan ever did, including *John Wesley Harding* (which was recorded in October and November of the same year).

The sound of the Basement Tapes songs is the sound of the unconscious (musical, verbal) mind brought forward into the world of conscious, touchable reality in a very calm, aware, marvelously unselfconscious fashion, with more than a touch of the collective unconscious—the group mind—thrown in to sweeten the sauce. Say what? I said, the sound of the Basement Tapes is the sound of deep inside dancing openly around the living room with simple outside, while everyone involved including the TV audience stamps their feet and cheers them on and becomes part of the show.

There was a crash of some kind for Dylan in the summer of 1966, and it wasn't only a fall from a motorcycle, nor just an escape from touring and other excessive commitments; it wasn't even limited to the traumatic and courageous decision to go through detoxification. Dylan arrived in New York in 1961 burning with ambition, and his ambition in all its forms served as the continuing source and goad for his many extraordinary accomplishments over the next five years. When he "quit" at the end of May 1965, I believe he had gone as far as he imagined he could go, creatively and professionally—the feeling of doing what he was doing told him that he'd reached an intolerable plateau, and so regardless of the fact that there was more money to be made, more worlds to conquer in a linear sense, he had to quit (and maybe try his hand at something different, i.e. not music, not performing), or else be trapped in meaningless motions, empty efforts, a lifeless life. And he had the courage to let go of it all; this willingness and ability to be true to himself (even when no one around him agrees or understands) is the consistent hallmark of Dylan's life and art.

But the unexpected happened. In letting go of all that baggage, indeed in the very process of exorcising it, "vomiting" it out in a typed catharsis, a space was created in Dylan for an even grander form of his ambition to assert itself, the long-repressed desire to speak through the airwaves in the tongues of rock and roll, not a style of music but something experiential, felt and intuited and desired since childhood, playing with a band, creating and projecting (on stage too; especially on stage) a sound, a very personal sound—this desire had its secular side, to conquer that territory, to join not only Little Richard but Elvis, but even more it had a spiritual and artistic side (as did the earlier form of Dylan's ambition, the one that resulted in songs and performances like "Blowin' in the Wind" and "A Hard Rain's A-Gonna Fall" and "Mr. Tambourine Man," and in his becoming a bigger star as folksinger and songwriter than anyone else would have imagined possible). Starting with the composition and recording of "Like a Rolling Stone," followed by the creation of *Highway 61 Revisited* and the launching of a world tour combining solo and band performances, Dylan's ambition pranced free and achieved miracles. The drugs were more than fun—neither fun nor escape ever seem to have been of primary importance to Dylan—they were a means to sustain the energy necessary to the realization of the (palpable if not articulatable) dream.

And as Dylan pranced freely, shouting to the heavens with the world at his feet, the times and especially the generation of young Westerners coming of age danced with him, whether coincidentally or because he was supported by and giving voice to a larger movement or because he was making possible and in some sense helping create the movement (or, probably, all three), and things just became wilder and headier and ever more intense—exhausting and unbearable and insupportable, certainly, but nothing remotely like the lifelessness, the dead-end feeling, that had earlier told him it was time to let it all go. This was not a plateau but running up a mountain, with of course a sense of dramatic finale, death, explosion, apocalypse, inevitably coming—this can't go on but you keep leaning into it because the feeling is fantastic (and addictive), and the end, whatever shape it takes, is certain to be glorious.

Faster!

And then the crash, and unexpectedly, in fact extraordinarily, what crashed in July 1966 was not Dylan but his ambition. He walked away and left it there to die, otherwise there would have and could have been no cancellation of the tour, no abandonment of the public arena, no detoxification from the substances that aided this mere mortal in sustaining his more-than-human role. The ambition had to die first—and it's true so often in human history, public and private, that it happens like this, that it's the little blow, the bump on the head in the backyard, whatever, rather than the huge dramatic sledgehammering, that is most transforming, that acts as a catalyst for an authentic change of heart, change of course.

And so the Basement Tapes may be considered the first Dylan performances not driven by the particular ambition or ambitions that made Bob Dylan who he was (and, given the immortality of myth, who he always will be seen to be). No doubt he had some new ambitions (more modest ones, for example to amuse and impress and be accepted by his companions, Danko, Robertson, Hudson and Manuel), but they weren't continuous with what had gone before. That wheel had exploded. Goodbye.

What follows the crash defies explanation. The rich creativity of the Basement Tapes/*John Wesley Harding* period unquestionably reflects a great healing taking place. Dylan was rediscovering the joys of music—old songs, improvised songs, crafted songs, they all provided him with evident satisfaction and pleasure as he performed them. It was a time when the distinctions that divide musical categories seemed to melt, and widely diverse realms such as traditional folk, country, rock and roll, blues, rockabilly, gospel, pop all became contiguous and Dylan and the Band could move from a boisterous sea chantey to an Elvis Presley pop ballad without missing a beat or shifting realities. You are what you feel like singing and playing, and you can sing and play anything you like.

In retrospect, the big question is why this creative flowering didn't last. Dylan wrote and performed at least 34 new songs in the latter half of 1967, some of them rough or unfinished but all of them bursting with musical and lyrical inventiveness. But in 1968 he wrote nothing that we know of, and performed almost nothing; indeed, Dylan's total output of new songs in the five years following 1967 seems to have been less than what he produced in these few months. Why? I don't know. But it must be acknowledged that liberation from burning ambition not only gives one the freedom to sing and write whatever one feels like, it also gives one the freedom to not sing or write at all. Or, if one does create, to not share those creations with the world.

Still, it's a mystery. The 1967 songs sound like they herald a great recovery and the beginning of a new, ground-breaking, abundantly creative period in Dylan's career as a performing artist. Instead, in hindsight, they mark the high point in a sequence of brief oases amidst a seven-year desert of creative energy.

None of the performances on the Basement Tapes was meant

to be released to the public. But, since it is well established that Dylan's preferred method of recording his albums (i.e., stuff that is intended for possible public release) is to perform live with musicians who are playing the song in question for the first time (it's hard to believe, but over and over through the years musicians who've been on Dylan sessions report they were asked to play a song not only without charts but without rehearsal, often with no information but the starting key), the question is, what difference does it make that this stuff wasn't for the public, since Dylan always "wings it" anyway? And the answer is, there's a shift in Dylan's intent that is audible in these performances. Maybe this shows up in Dylan's voice. Maybe it doesn't show up anywhere that can be pointed to. But the difference is there.

We can hear a difference in his voice in some of the performances of other people's songs: Dylan's trademark accent, the ever-shifting but always present matrix through which all his past singing had been done (since 1960 or so), is missing, and at first it's hard to recognize the singer as Dylan. There is an accent in the voice, a projected identity and texture, but the "Dylan" accent is absent—for example, "Don't You Try Me Now" has thick country blues textures in the vocal, and "Young But Daily Growing" projects an appropriate ballad-singer persona, but there's no identifiable "Bob Dylan" persona or texture underneath, as there had been in almost all his earlier performances, even of other people's material. The effect is startling, and a little scary.

In the songs written by Dylan, the difference in intent is perhaps noticeable in an ambivalence that I don't think was there in earlier work. Dylan's songs had often been ambiguous, elusive, but subjectively at least their intent was unmistakable. The song as performed provoked powerful and generally unambiguous feelings. The Basement Tapes songs provoke powerful feelings, but they are surprisingly open-ended. This isn't necessarily bad. The impact is like looking at a series of brilliant sketches, captured by the artist's hand but not yet integrated (if they can be) into his vision.

Sometimes the sketches are obviously unfinished, and then what is fascinating is how very much they manage to communicate in spite of everything that's missing. "I'm Not There," an unreleased Basement Tapes track that *Telegraph* editor John Bauldie believes is "one of Dylan's greatest vocal performances," has lyrics that can't be transcribed because they don't really exist: Dylan makes slurred noises that only sound like words, like the dummy copy in a rough of an advertisement that only looks like text. Further, when Dylan does use real words, they don't fit with the other words—but they do a good job of *sounding like* sentences; the transitions in particular are powerful and convincing.

What's astonishing here is that we can feel with great intensity and specificity what the singer is talking about, because of the expressiveness of his voice, even though 80% of the lyrics of the song have not been written yet! It's as though we're listening to Dylan in "Visions of Johanna" sing "Louise, she's all right, she's just near/She's delicate and seems like the mirror" and we're experiencing all the subtle, conflicting feelings of the situation, communicated through the inflections in the singer's voice, only he hasn't found the words for the feeling yet, just the inchoate sound of it, so he's actually singing "Louise, Saturday, under cheer/It's wafflish, she slumps out of fear"—and the second word is slurred, it could be "slaughterhouse" or "samurai" for all we know. But the sound of the singing and the sense of the song are so moving and so clear it brings tears to our eyes.

It's bizarre. It's as though when Dylan writes, the finished song is not constructed piece by piece as we might imagine, but tuned in, there in its entirety from the first but still out of focus, like the photograph of a fetus, a blur whose identifying characteristics are implicit but not yet visible—not because they're obscured but because they haven't yet taken shape. "I'm Not There" is a performance complete in feeling—"Dylan's saddest song," says Bauldie—achieved without benefit of context or detail. It's like listening to the inspiration before the song is wrapped around it.

It's a performance with a lot of words in it, the protagonist is just pouring out his heart; but every sentence trails off, or is filled with words that don't add up to phrases. The real words he's saying undoubtedly will never be written. But they have been sung, and that turns out to be the important thing. It's like the experience Plato describes, of seeing reality in its eternal, underlying forms, rather than its surface manifestations. "I'm Not There" in this sense is more than an unfinished sketch; it's a trip inside, a look at the beating heart that precedes and will survive the universe we see around us.

"I'm Not There" is a song Dylan probably intended to work

on but never got around to. "Apple Suckling Tree," on the other hand, is clearly in its final form (on the album take), even though it too has lyrics that are slurred and indecipherable and, when they can be heard, don't seem to mean anything. But in this case, that's perfectly appropriate, because this is a nonsense song. Dylan is singing in tongues, and no amount of messing with the lyrics could make the song more joyous or more universal than it already is.

The breadth of "Apple Suckling Tree" is remarkable. First of all it demonstrates exuberantly the universal musical principles that underlie and unify folk music and rock and roll. Lyrically it pulls together children's nonsense rhymes, and the genre of songs in which lovers anticipate reuniting after the war's over, and maybe just a little Garden of Eden imagery as well. Unquestionably it draws on that great reservoir of mystery that Dylan has spoken of as a characteristic part of traditional folk music. His piano-playing, Robbie's drumming, and Garth's organ on this track are sheer delight, a tonic for depression, a definition of comradeship, an affirmation of the healing power of music and demonstration of how it can be simultaneously totally mystifying and disarmingly simple and direct.

Two other favorite performances of mine from this period, "Yea! Heavy and a Bottle of Bread" and "Lo and Behold!," can also be considered nonsense songs. Unlike the verses of "Apple Suckling Tree," though, these songs have lyrics that are audible and play an important part in the songs' success. Thanks to the lyrics (the *sound* of "get the loot, don't be slow, we're gonna catch a trout"; the evocative humor of "boys, I sure was slick," and "Gonna save my money and rip it up!"—possibly Dylan's best pun ever), as well as two magnificent vocal performances, and some inspired back-up work (instrumental and vocal) by the Band, "Yea! Heavy" and "Lo and Behold!" qualify as two of the most charming performances Dylan has ever recorded. He has never been more crazed or more lovable ("Now pull that drummer out from behind that bottle!") or more dead-on; there's a sparkling appreciation of the ineffable here comparable only to Lewis Carroll's Alice books and the comic art (especially circa 1967) of R. Crumb.

Dylan does amazing things with his voice (I mean, his tone of voice, his inflection, the identities his voice projects) in many of these songs; perhaps having no particular end in mind left him free to have fun, to entertain the guys (it's like he's making faces), to lay a few tricks on 'em. "Lo and Behold!" is one good example; "Please, Mrs. Henry" is another (one of a handful of male-bonding songs featuring crude and playful sexual humor); "Clothes Line Saga" 's another. The latter song is like the door to a whole new genre Dylan never explored further: a vignette, a mood piece, rich in characterization and humor, understated all the way. Dylan's vocal presence on this one makes me smile and gives me chills both at once.

The open-endedness of the Basement Tapes songs, this sense that Dylan isn't necessarily singing to anyone but the people he's performing with, and yet at the same time he knows he is recording, his cleverness isn't just vanishing into the air, so there's a purposefulness and a freedom from purpose in his communication somewhat different from anything he's done before, this freedom for songs to add up or not add up or be immortalized or forgotten just depending on how he feels as he's singing them, has the effect of encouraging every song and performance to take off in a different direction, even when they start with similar concerns. "Goin' to Acapulco" is every bit as bawdy—and indeed, rather more explicit—in its lyrics as "Please, Mrs. Henry" and "Don't Ya Tell Henry," but the mood of the vocal is totally different. Dylan cracks up at the outrageousness of "Please, Mrs. Henry" in the middle of singing it, but there's never a smirk in his voice in "Acapulco," even when he's boasting "I can blow my plum, and drink my rum, and then go on home and have my fun" (you'll search in vain for these words in *Lyrics*—as so often happens throughout that book, the performed lyrics have been rewritten, replaced with purposeless doggerel, Dylan thumbing his nose at or trying to erase—"improve"—his art even as he anthologizes it, still eating the document).

Dylan doesn't smirk when he sings "Goin' to Acapulco" because, perhaps unexpectedly (he didn't know this would happen till they started performing it), it's a love song, his most heartfelt expression (during the Basement Tapes sessions) of his appreciation of the woman who takes care of him (sexually and every other way), the friends who hang out with him, and the way of life that's overtaken him (let's say a modest hedonism, a world where fun and security can coexist, where it's possible to fantasize because one no longer feels obliged or able to act out every fantasy). The key to what the song says is in Dylan's voice, specifically the interaction or connection between the sound of his voice and the sound of the band (mostly what one thinks one hears is the organ, but in fact it's a composite sound created by bass, guitar, drums, organ and maybe piano, I can't tell—magnificent in its complexity and expressiveness). Dylan's voice here is directly connected to his heart; all kinds of feelings flood out of him with every note he sings, and he just lets them through, rides the wave, gives and gives and gives and still there's so much more he wants to give, a desire crystallized and breathed out in the climactic "Yeah!" near the end of each chorus. The privileged listener feels the universe shudder, then realizes it's his own lungs breathing it in, his own heart beating in time.

All this expressiveness can't help but have some reflection in the lyrics, given Dylan's particular talent for letting feelings flow out of him as words—poet or no, he's a born languager, like Shakespeare or Thoreau or Conrad or Yeats—and although most of what the song says is in the articulation of the four syllables Ac-A-Pul-Co, and the affection with which he speaks Rose Marie's name, still it's interesting to note that "If someone offers me a joke" is presumably about being offered a joint, and "I just say no thanks" in hip 1967 context is an extremely frank comment, almost a confession: "I try to tell it like it is" (I hear this as actually being about seeing it like it is, getting off on experiencing the world unstoned for a change) "and stay away from pranks." "Every time you know when the well breaks down, I just go pump on it some" is a cute remark any married man can appreciate; the way it's sung and with "Rose Marie" showing up in the next line, "waitin' for me to come" [!], and following the "no thanks" section, this also could be heard as an acknowledgement that sometimes masturbation is a more mature or effective solution to horniness than infidelity.

And does Dylan intend to talk about these things in his song? Has he carefully salted this material in here like a riddle to be deciphered? I think it just comes through spontaneously, not unconsciously but just from the heart as words are invented to fit the sound and mood of the song, the way someone else might hear themselves say something quite intelligent and surprisingly honest and well-said during casual conversation.

Earlier in the song Dylan answers every possible question anyone could have about what he's doing now with his life and art and why: "It's a wicked life but what the hell/Uh, everybody's got to eat/And I'm just the same as anyone else/When it comes to scratching for my meat." (Neat pun there—image of working to support self and family, or just generally taking care of needs, including creative ones, combined with image of scratching his balls—hey, I shit and pick my nose too.) And then the tension/release as the song moves from verse to chorus, which is what makes a song an anthem: "*Goin'* to *Acapulco*..." That transition says everything. Incidentally, it's "soccer," not "some girl," they're going to see, despite the songbook; gives the song a kind of worldliness, doesn't it? There's worse ways to spend an (imaginary) lazy afternoon.

The relationship between voice and instruments, and between the heart behind the voice and the collective heart behind the instruments, is what fuels the wondrousness of these Dylan/Band performances at their best. Going beyond what might seem reducible to something interpersonal, this relationship can also be perceived as one between the chords, the musical texture, of the song, and the attack, the outbreath and vocalizing, of the singer, or perhaps more accurately as a three-way relationship between the singer and the key the music is in (almost a color) and the rhythm of the song, whether that rhythm is provided by drum or bass-and-drum or guitar or the singer's beating foot.

Something in Dylan leaps to respond to a certain nostalgic mysteriousness in the tune of a suitable song, and his instinctive response, when captured, creates an unforgettable musical moment. There are several examples of this among the old (and not-so-old) country/folk/blues songs that Dylan and the Band try out on the (unreleased) Basement Tapes, the most startling and ecstatic of which is a whaling song called "Bonnie Ship the Diamond." Dylan sings and strums this with fierce enthusiasm, in a voice filled with impenetrable mystery, maybe like being 150 days out and seeing Saint Elmo's fire for the first time while riding out a winter storm: "Cheer up, my boys!/Let your hearts never fail/When that bonnie ship the Diamond goes/Fishing for the whale." One recalls that this singer and these musicians had been on a comparable adventure together, sailing around the world into hostile and unknown waters. But it is the unique, spine-tingling quality of the singer's voice here, expressing something provoked in him by the melody and rhythm of the song as well as its setting, that makes this performance exceptional. One may imagine that Dylan's primary inspiration for writing the new Basement Tapes songs was hearing how great this other stuff sounded when he and the Band had a go at it.

Not all of the songs are successful. "Too Much of Nothing" sounds from the title like an autobiographical look at Dylan's period of inactivity, but it descends into self-parody, especially in the chorus. There's a big difference between inspired nonsense and bad writing, although a better tune on this might have encouraged a better performance, and brought it back to life. On the album version, Dylan tries a bit of rising-pitch melodrama on the verses that only makes things worse; the straightforward singing on the outtake has a texture to it that is quite attractive, but it's still evident that neither singer nor musicians could get excited about this one.

At least two of the Basement Tapes songs were typed out by Dylan before he found music for them (very unusual; he almost always writes words and music together, although as we shall see *John Wesley Harding* is an exception to this rule). These became his first collaborations: Richard Manuel wrote the music for "Tears of Rage," and Rick Danko for "This Wheel's on Fire." The two songs (which, along with "I Shall Be Released," were included on the Band's first album, released summer 1968) are among the most powerful compositions of the Basement Tapes period, and Dylan performs them with great conviction. One can never quite be sure, with either song, just what it is he's convinced of; but both performances are deeply moving in spite of or maybe even because of this uncertainty.

"Tears of Rage" is about love and regret, history and injustice—this much is clear just from the sound of Dylan's voice (what a stunning tune Manuel wrote for this, densely layered with anguish and affection and dignity). The lyrics are teasingly specific, drawing the listener into the game of solving each impossible riddle ("What daughter would treat a father so?" "What kind of love is this?"). I always come back to my first impression, based on the opening lines ("We carried you in our arms/on Independence Day"), that the song is about the American nation as seen from the perspective of the founding fathers, an expression of their pain at how she (personified as female, Liberty) has turned her back on the ideals in which she was conceived.

This would make the song a companion to "As I Went Out One Morning" on *John Wesley Harding*, which climaxes with Tom

Paine running up to say "I'm sorry for what she's done." Certainly Paine was among the most radical and idealistic of the Founders (although Thomas Jefferson talked a good show); perhaps Dylan had recently read Howard Fast's biography, *Citizen Tom Paine*. "Why must I always be the thief?" could easily be the lament of Paine in his later years. But the rest of the chorus of "Tears of Rage," though hugely evocative ("Come to me now, you know we're so alone/And life is brief"), doesn't quite fit this interpretation. And the advantage of that, I suppose, is it leaves the song open to be about any of the dozens or hundreds of things it means to different listeners at different times. Just bringing together rage, grief, loneliness, fathers and daughters (and reintroducing the dirge to popular music) is pretty good for starters.

"This Wheel's on Fire"—the album version adds some 1975 overdubs (drums, piano) to the original recording, but either way it sounds great—is a beautiful and chilling bit of double-talk, or dream-talk, working off of the recurring phrase "if your memory serves you well" and punctuated by the fabulously dramatic "wheel's on fire" chorus (which works even though there's no obvious connection between the words of the verses and the words of the chorus). The song is really circular, chorus breathlessly tumbling into verse and each verse opening and closing with the same words, rolling forward in an ever-increasing tension, releasing again and again and yet still building, still unresolved. What does it mean? It's like a dream. It does and doesn't have to do with certain things that happened; does and doesn't refer to events that still may happen, or are happening now. What does it mean? Maybe nothing. Some songs don't have meanings; they overflow with feelings instead.

A recurrent theme in the Basement Tapes songs (and in much of Dylan's work, from "A Hard Rain's A-Gonna Fall" to "Slow Train Coming") is anticipation. More than half the songs Dylan wrote at this time include the word "gonna," usually in reference to some big thing that's on the horizon: "gonna be the meanest flood that anybody's seen"; "when Quinn the Eskimo gets here, everybody's gonna jump for joy"; "it's just gonna be you and me"; "tomorrow's the day my bride's gonna come"; "we're all gonna meet at that million dollar bash."

The ultimate hymn of anticipation, of course, is "I Shall Be Released," and now the coming event takes on an obviously spiritual (and poignantly personal) aspect: "I see my light come shining/From the west unto the east./Any day now, any day now/I shall be released." Dylan cleverly makes the setting of the song a prison (or does he?), tugging on the strings of our desire for freedom so successfully that we're forced to realize that if we want it so bad we must not have as much of it already as we sometimes think. His vocal on the Basement Tapes recording is exquisite, and should be made available to the public (the version on *Greatest Hits Volume II* was recorded later, in 1971). The first verse is about desire for revenge, the second about faith, and the third about acceptance (implicit, by contrast with the man "next to me" who "swears he's not to blame"), and each verse is followed by the chorus, which is about desire for, faith in, and finally acceptance of, deliverance. This is not a song we can imagine showing up on *Blonde on Blonde* or *Highway 61 Revisited*. It's the humblest performance of all the Basements, and the least ambivalent; Dylan could be sly here too if he wished, but he chooses not to be; he has something he wants to say.

Which brings us to the unreleased "Sign on the Cross," which addresses the issue of Christianity much more overtly but also much more ambiguously than "I Shall Be Released." This is one of Dylan's strangest and most moving performances. Like "I'm Not There" it has some slurred words, but not as many; like "Goin' to Acapulco" it's been rewritten here and there for its *Lyrics* appearance, most notably when Dylan as editor tries to throw a little obfuscation into the impassioned monolog at the center of the song: *Lyrics* says "the bird is here and you might want to enter it," presumably an effort to pass the song off as nonsense, whereas what Dylan actually sings is, "later on you might find a door you might want to enter, but of course the door might be closed." (A fairly clear allusion, as Bert Cartwright points out, to Luke 13:25.)

The whole point of this absolutely brilliant, totally over-the-edge musical (one of the prettiest tunes and chord progressions you'll ever hear) and vocal and instrumental tour de force is that the singer is aware of, worried by, can't forget about, that sign on the cross. But who is the singer? Dylan takes on a persona partway between late-night radio preacher and aged backwoods wise man, and his voice sounds alternately soothing and deranged; one imagines the song simultaneously having roots in the comedic monologs of Lord Buckley and in classic folk/country spirituals like "Old

Rugged Cross" and in Dylan's authentic fascination with the Bible and identification with other teachers and performers who've leaned on it successfully for comfort in the storm.

In light of Dylan's conversion to a particularly Bible-oriented, apocalyptic form of Christianity in 1978-79, this song takes on added significance and mystery. It seems unlikely, in retrospect, that it was meant simply to be a put-on. Rather, it's a kind of confession of attraction; Dylan solves the problem of how to talk about his unfashionable and ambivalent feelings by assuming an identity that is at once the recognizable voice of madness and the undeniable voice of truth and wisdom. It's like you turn on the radio late at night and suddenly you hear God talking to you, but the old guy's obviously half-drunk or tripping on some powerful acid, but on the other hand you've never heard anything quite so weird or so sweet as the way his voice leans into the guitar accompaniment, and you find yourself turning up the volume and, eventually, singing along.

"Sign on the Cross" is built like a symphony, with four separate movements. The first is deliberate and elegant, Dylan singing with sublime slowness while Robbie Robertson plays gorgeous grace notes all around him. The second movement starts with an inspired bridge (could be the chorus, but we never hear it again), rousing and passionate, transitioning into a restatement of the musical theme from the first movement. The third movement is the spoken/sung monolog—Dylan's vocal performance on this is nothing short of genius, and the improvised music is dazzling in its complexity and accuracy. Another great segue takes us to the concluding movement, which starts with echoes of the bridge but immediately moves onto new structural ground, the music just as fresh and surprising now as when the song started, while successfully incorporating everything that's happened so far.

The song ends with Dylan singing, in the most manic, disturbing voice you're ever likely to hear recorded, these almost-comforting words: "...I mean to say you're strong/Yes you are, if that sign on the cross/If it begins to worry you/Well that's all right, you c'n just sing your song/And all your troubles'll pass right on through."

Who was that masked man? We'll never know, but what is clear is that he and the musicians with him, when suitably inspired, are capable of feats of spontaneous musical and verbal virtuosity that will confound and delight appreciators of fine art for centuries to come, even as the perpetrators invent 'em and forget 'em in an afternoon.

And that voice. Every inch, every moment of Dylan's singing on "Sign on the Cross" spills over with a truly frightening aliveness. What are we to make of this? In the end, the only thing we may be able to say about greatness is that it exists. There is a moment, on the outtake of "Nothing Was Delivered," when Dylan, after singing the lines "Now you must provide some answers/For what you sell that's not been received," suddenly bursts out with this spoken interpolation: "Yes you must—you must do that—you must get those answers!" Something about the way he says this—the rhythm, the earnestness, the space he's just created in the music, the sound of his voice—makes it stick in my mind, I can't forget it, sometimes I hear it echoed in phrases and sounds in my daily life. Why? What is it in the artist's performance that gives it such specific and universal power, and why do some artists have or express so much more of it than others?

These questions may not be answerable. But because of accidents (if there are any accidents) like the Basement Tapes, performances like "Sign on the Cross" exist, and will endure. A moment—a symphony—of aliveness, of inquiry, of creative energy, has been captured on tape.

"Johnny's in the basement, mixing up the medicine." Between June and October of 1967, Dylan and the Band mixed up quite a batch of the stuff, enough to last a good long while. And then the moment passed. Dylan went to Nashville without the Band in October and November and recorded an album, all new songs, something different, something intended for release to his public.

19.

"Then I went back and wrote just real simple songs...There's only two songs on the album [*John Wesley Harding*] which came at the same time as the music. The rest of the songs were written out on paper, and I found the tunes for them later. I didn't do [that] before, and I haven't done it since. That might account for the specialness of that album."
—Bob Dylan, 1978 (Matt Damsker interview)

"Right through the time of *Blonde on Blonde* I was doing it unconsciously. Then one day I was half-stepping and the lights went out. And since that point, I more or less had amnesia...It took me a long time to get to do consciously what I used to be able to do unconsciously.

"It happens to everybody. Think about the periods when people don't do anything, or they lose it and have to regain it, or lose it and gain something else. So it's taken me all this time, and the records I made along the way were like openers—trying to figure out whether it was this way or that way, just what is it, what's the simplest way I can tell the story and make this feeling real...

"*John Wesley Harding* was a fearful album—just dealing with fear [Dylan laughs], but dealing with the devil in a fearful way, almost. All I wanted to

237

do was to get the words right. It was courageous to do it because I could have not done it, too."
    —Bob Dylan, 1978 (second Jonathan Cott interview)

"Before I wrote *John Wesley Harding* I discovered something about all those earlier songs I had written. I discovered that when I used words like 'he' and 'it' and 'they' and talking about other people, I was really talking about nobody but me. I went into *John Wesley Harding* with that knowledge in my head. You see, I hadn't really known before, that I was writing about myself in all those songs."
    —Bob Dylan, 1971 (Anthony Scaduto interview)

"I used to think that myself and my songs were the same thing. But I don't believe that any more. There's myself and there's my song, which I hope is everybody's song...
    "I only look at them [my songs] musically. I only look at them as things to sing. It's the music that the words are sung to that's important. I write the songs because I need something to sing. It's the difference between the words on paper and the song. The song disappears in the air, the paper stays. They have little in common. A great poet, like Wallace Stevens, doesn't necessarily make a great singer. But a great singer always—like Billie Holiday—makes a great poet."
    —Bob Dylan, on *John Wesley Harding*, Feb. 1968 (Hubert Saal interview)

"We recorded that album, and I didn't know what to make of it...So I figured the best thing to do would be to put it out as quickly as possible, call it *John Wesley Harding* because that was one song that I had no idea what it was about, why it was even on the album. I figured I'd call attention to it, make it something special...People have made a lot out of it [the album], as if it was some sort of ink blot test or something. But it never was intended to be anything else but just a bunch of songs, really. Maybe it was better'n I thought."
    —Bob Dylan, 1985 (Cameron Crowe interview, for *Biograph*)

Dylan has had a lot to say about *John Wesley Harding* over the years—the album *has* been something of an ink blot test for him, as it has certainly been for his listeners and critics. Amazing things have been found in these songs, which is a tribute to the power and suggestiveness of their language; at least part of Dylan's intent here, certainly, is to tease, to provoke the analytical mind and then dance away from its net, which of course only provokes it more.

For myself, I'm quite certain that most of the songs do not contain specific messages (in the way that most of the analyses, such as Scaduto's in his biography, imply); rather, they are meant to stimulate thoughts and (more importantly) feelings in certain thematic directions. Like the not-yet-written words of "I'm Not There," many of these songs are not-yet-written essays about history, spirituality, moral values and other subjects that the songwriter clearly has a sincere interest in. They sound like finished constructs, puzzles ready to be solved, but in fact they are for the most part unsolvable, because the songwriter either has not tried to or has consciously chosen not to resolve the contradictions arising from his spontaneous techniques of generating phrases and images.

For example, I doubt that he knew or cared that St. Augustine was not a martyr; he needed a saint's name, and "Augustine" fit the tempo, as did "John Wesley Harding" when he needed the name of a historical outlaw. Various considerations do come into play—i.e., "Francis" wouldn't work not just for metrical reasons but also because the associations Dylan and the public have with him are too clear and don't fit here—but in the end the point is that the song is not about Augustine, to Dylan, nor is it necessarily about martyrs. It's about the feelings that the tune and the performance and the lyrics evoke. Dylan may not know what those feelings are, even for him, let alone for the listener. But he knows when it goes *thunk!*, because that's his gift (and something he has experience in—something he's learned, gotten better at, over the years, even if he's forgotten some other things along the way).

This is not to say that we can never say what "I Dreamed I Saw St. Augustine" is about, or judge whether or not it succeeds. It succeeds extraordinarily well, because of (not in spite of) its elusiveness; and one of things it unquestionably is about is guilt. We have the image of waking from a dream, guilty ("I dreamed I was amongst the ones who put him out to death"), angry, alone and scared, completed by this exceptional sentence: "I put my fingers against the glass, and bowed my head and cried."

What is the glass? It is a barrier, a feeling of claustrophobia, of being trapped, like Sylvia Plath's bell jar, although it can be a wall rather than an enclosing sphere or globe, simply depending on what fits the listener's own fears and imaginings. The words are so well chosen (and sung) that the image need not be imagined visually to be felt. And there is a powerful correlation with the penultimate line in "I Pity the Poor Immigrant," later on in the album: "Whose visions in the final end must shatter like the glass." This glass, which is related though not the same in the two songs, is terrifying whether it is felt as unbreakable or as shattering. Dylan's economy of language leaves room for the rest of us to write volumes.

Regarding technique: John Cohen asked Dylan, in their summer 1968 interview, to "talk about some of the diverse elements which go into making up one of your songs." Dylan answered, "Well, there's not much we could talk about—that's the strange aspect of the whole thing. [Notice that he's not being elusive here. He's simply saying what is true to him.] There's nothing you can see. I wouldn't know where to begin."

Cohen: "Take a song like 'I Pity the Poor Immigrant.' There might have been a germ that started it." Dylan: "Yes, the first line." When he does know where to begin, in other words, it comes to him whole cloth, and he makes a song of it. It isn't always the first line, probably, although he's told us that for most of the *John Wesley Harding* songs it wasn't the tune, because he started, atypically, with words alone. So "I Dreamed I Saw St. Augustine" could have been inspired when those words, followed by "alive as you or me," jumped into his mind, obviously as a reworking of the phrase that starts the most famous song from the Wobbly movement, "Joe Hill." Indeed the melody of Dylan's song, whether it arrived then or later, is closely related to that of the I.W.W. anthem. But the point is that Dylan took the phrase, which I imagine came to him unbidden, and went on to write the words that had to follow it, in terms of meter, tempo, rhyme, and implied subject matter, a set of words that turns out to be a vision of a passionate long-ago saint, running, searching, crying out to the people... and then becomes a song about dreaming, and how it feels to awaken from the dream.

The song that results is a work of art, extremely moving, totally original. What we need to understand about Dylan's technique in creating such a song, which he has explained over and over again in interviews and by example in his work, is that he lets it flow out of him from a point of inspiration, and what is in the song is what's left after the false starts, the lines that don't work, are discarded, and a successful course from starting point to felt conclusion is found. He knows the song is over when it sounds like it's over, and probably values a song like "St. Augustine" more than a song like "John Wesley Harding" specifically because he can feel the former go *thunk* at the end, with a certain resonance of greatness and a clear sense of completion, whereas the latter trails off adequately but with no sense of inevitability, no warm feeling of having fulfilled the original moment of inspiration.

In *Lyrics* the song "St. Augustine" is accompanied by a full-page drawing by Dylan, dreamer lying on his back smoking a cigarette, huge image of a severe St. Augustine, clutching a blanket, above him. The cigarette interestingly says this is a daydream rather than the kind that occurs in full sleep. Augustine looks like a priest, and one's attention is drawn to the blanket. But we must remember that this drawing is not from 1967, when the song was created, but, probably, from 1972. At best, it is the songwriter's own reinterpretation of the song, like a later performance of it.

And suppose we ask, what does the blanket symbolize? Why, in the song as well as the drawing, does he have "a blanket underneath his arm, and a coat of solid gold"? One can come up with very good answers, such as the blanket suggesting poverty and the gold coat material wealth, together in the same person, the paradox of the Christian church, etc. bullshit bullshit. Bullshit even if it's "correct interpretation," because if we think about it too much it takes us away from our experience of the song and seduces us into throwing a "meaning" matrix over it. The thing to keep in mind, without rejecting those images and feelings the blanket authentically stimulates for you, is that songs need words, stories and drawings need images, and therefore whatever else the blanket is, it is primarily a prop, something for the character to hold, something that can be used by singer and listener to contain or further the action/motion of the song.

If the word "blanket" didn't work, the songwriter would have tossed it out and just as quickly grabbed something else. It did work, so he kept it. That doesn't mean it doesn't symbolize poverty, but it does mean (to me) it wasn't consciously inserted with that in mind (i.e. "here's what I want to say, what image can I find to convey it?"). Instead it was tossed up by the subconscious and approved by the conscious, maybe in recognition of some specific connotation, maybe not, but certainly also because it sounded right, as a word, and looked right, as a visual image.

In any case, "I Dreamed I Saw St. Augustine" is a lovely song, a thing of beauty, performed like most of the songs on the album with a certain tentativeness, a caution, that doesn't limit the album but rather is part of its expression of who Dylan was at the time, particularly in relation to his audience. It may be true, as Dylan seems to remember, that the words were typed out before he put a tune to them; but I suggest that this was less a radical break with his past song-creating techniques than a kind of trick played on Dylan's conscious mind by his unconscious (for the very good purpose of helping him past an obstruction)—because in fact the tune was there in the words as Dylan wrote them (especially in this case, given the "Joe Hill" inspiration, but also I think in every song on this album) whether Dylan knew he was feeling it, sensing it, not quite humming it, as he wrote, or not. We the listeners can hear this in the song (even just by reading it). It is a song, not a poem. The words flow to fill the tune, and they do their job extremely well.

It is in fact Dylan's tunes more than anything else that make this album so wonderful—the tunes, and some of the finest bass-playing ever recorded. Take a bow, Charlie McCoy. Musicians (and not just bass players) will be returning to this record for hundreds of years to borrow ideas, and to renew their enthusiasm and love for their art.

It's a sweet record. Listen to the repeating bass run McCoy uses to punctuate "As I Went Out One Morning" (as pretty as Bruce Langhorne's embellishments on "Mr. Tambourine Man"), and the way Ken Buttrey's drums gallop after. Listen to the joy beneath the surface of Dylan's deadpan vocal on "Drifter's Escape," joy at the incredible rhythmic groove the three musicians have going here. Listen to the inspired harmonica fills between almost every verse of almost every song. Listen particularly to "Down Along the Cove," which absolutely captures what it is Dylan loves about performing music with other people. Here is ensemble expression of ensemble feeling, joy unbounded and cool as country water, group heart.

Dylan's use of the harmonica on this album is intriguing. He plays harmonica on eleven of the twelve songs, more than on any of his other albums except *Bringing It All Back Home*. This comes immediately after the Basement Tapes sessions, on which Dylan does not play harmonica at all.

He uses the harmonica here (very effectively) as an extension of his voice, his personality, as if to fill up and control the spaces in the songs when he's not actually singing. After the first verse of "John Wesley Harding," we hear Dylan's harmonica before and after every verse of the first four songs (except between the first and second verses of "St. Augustine"), the sixth song, and the eighth, ninth, and tenth songs. The absence of harmonica throughout most of the fifth song, "Frankie Lee," makes the song stand out, and then when the harp does come in before and after the last verse it has a special impact, dramatizing the words "nothing is revealed" and giving emphasis to the "moral" at the end of the story, a la Aesop's Fables. The harmonica is so omnipresent on this album that a tension is created when it's withheld (less so on "Dear Landlord" because there Dylan is playing piano instead of guitar).

Further confirmation of Dylan's song-creating techniques can be found in his comments on "Dear Landlord" in the *Biograph* notes: " 'Dear Landlord' was really just the first line. I woke up one morning with the words on my mind. Then I just figured, what else can I put to it?" If this is so, then Dylan presumably did not have a preconceived notion as to "who" the landlord was, who he was singing the song to. As in a dream, the person perceived or addressed could change identities, or unselfconsciously represent several people at once, or be the feeling of a kind of person rather than a specific individual. And we listeners in turn are free to hear the song as being about not one but a variety of different "landlords" in our own lives.

"Dear Landlord" is Dylan's most heartfelt performance on the album, the most liquid, open-throated—most of the songs are sung with a kind of cramped discomfort (appropriate, especially on "All Along the Watchtower," and the rogue's symphony of "Hobo," "Immigrant," and "Messenger"), suggesting that when Dylan says it "was a fearful album...all I wanted to do was to get the words right," he is referring to his remembered experience of the singing, not the songwriting. His voice is powerfully expressive throughout the album; he truly rises to what is required of him by the situation, and the fact that he felt free performing the Basement Tapes for and with friends, and somewhat trapped composing and performing *John Wesley Harding* for his creditors (manager, record company) and his expectant audience, does not of itself make one set of performances better than the other. Each set of circumstances creates its own artistic possibilities; Dylan's triumph is his honesty, his commitment to being himself in each situation and finding a way to speak his heart.

Some of the landlords we can reasonably imagine Dylan singing to here include his manager, his record company, his audience; in the context of the rest of the album and the subjects it touches on and evokes, we may also hear him singing to his country, to the powers that be, and not just in this town or this nation but in this world, this life. "I'm not about to move to no other place." Why not? some have asked, hearing this (with "I'm not about to argue") as an acquiescence to the Vietnam War. But I hear it as an expression of a deeper awareness that moving to another record company or another country or another manager, attractive as it may seem at times, won't actually change the situation.

"I'm not about to argue," because contending doesn't work; but "please heed these words that I speak," because, powerful as you are (the essence of the landlord/tenant relationship is the power of one over the other), there might be something you can learn from me. This may not seem to some a very strong position to take in relation to vested power; others may see it, as I do and I think Christ did, as the very strongest position one can take in the long run. It is interesting that Dylan as an artist, as one who is true to himself, has outlasted virtually all of his contemporaries, in the sense of both physical survival and going on with his work on his own terms.

"Dear Landlord" features some great drumming. Dylan's piano playing is fiery; we can hear a rock and roll/Chicago blues orchestra in his head as he beats out the riff and shouts into it, and just as they do on the "amplified folk" performances, McCoy and Buttrey pick up on the energy of the song and run with it, unconcerned that whatever is happening here doesn't fit the parameters of any kind of rock or folk or country or gospel or blues or jazz session they've ever heard or played on. Doesn't matter—the music itself tells them what to do, and they jump to it.

"The Ballad of Frankie Lee and Judas Priest" is one of many songs here that deal with guilt, betrayal, foolishness and regret—it doesn't seem too farfetched to see young Dylan as the rube who greedily accepts the money offered by his "best friend." The debt is then immediately called in, but in a mysterious way—the Judas who gave him money now sets him free in a world of unlimited sex and power, lets him bop till he drops, which he does. The end. If Frankie Lee is Dylan (and Judas Priest his manager, Albert Grossman), neither one is portrayed as a sympathetic character. The guilty little neighbor boy must also be Dylan, in this reading, maybe the side of him that knew better but said nothing. Of course, as in the other songs, the characters play other roles at the same time, and also exist by themselves, mythical like Stagger Lee and Billy, and Judas and Jesus, characters that just dance in our minds and memories and do strange things in dreams and songs. We don't know who they are; they've just always been here. Doesn't stop us from singing about them.

The most striking song on the album when it first came out, and the one that's been most enduring in terms of popularity (the number of times it's been played by Dylan and other artists—Dylan himself acknowledges he thinks of it as Jimi Hendrix's song now as much as his own) is "All Along the Watchtower," another extraordinarily successful interaction between Dylan (composer, voice, harmonica, guitar) and rhythm section (bass and drums). This brief tune features some of the best cinematography in modern songwriting, when the camera pulls back high above the ramparts, and we see the two lead characters approaching in the distance, about to start the scene we've just watched them play. The words that open and close their conversation beautifully express the dominant moods of the album—"there must be some way out of here" and "let us not talk falsely now." It is a case of Dylan once again expressing his personal moment so accurately and exquisitely that we as listeners immediately realize he's expressing the collective moment, not necessarily because he wants to but because he can't help it, it's the same moment, this is the peril and reward of telling the truth. What is most personal is most universal. And it's ironic, because surely this—being "the voice of his generation"—is what Dylan is most frightened of at this point in his career, along with the inevitable companion fear, which is of not being the voice of his generation any more.

One thing that does seem different about the composition of this album, and that definitely relates to the issue of conscious/unconscious creation, is that Dylan perhaps for the first time uses aids (other than amphetamines, alcohol and marijuana) to keep the flow going. I believe "I Pity the Poor Immigrant" was inspired by the title line itself, but there can be no question that Dylan had the

Bible open to the Book of Leviticus as he wrote the rest of the song. "Strength spent in vain," "heaven [as] iron," and "eats but is not satisfied" are directly from Leviticus 26, verses 20, 19, and 26, as Bert Cartwright points out. This incidentally leaves little doubt who the "I" is in this song, at least in the second verse. And yet in no way does the melody chosen for this song (borrowed from an old folk tune, a throwback to early Dylan methods of composition) or the voice Dylan sings it in fit with the persona of the God of the Old Testament. Subjectively, the "I" here is not the Lord, but Dylan as empathetic (human) observer. Mystery. I think it's a matter of left hand *choosing* not to know or care what right hand's doing. Half-stepping indeed.

And the song and performance that result are wonderful; Dylan's choice must be considered a wise one, for its moment.

"The Wicked Messenger" ("A wicked messenger falleth into mischief"; Proverbs 13:17) should be ironic, but again with Dylan, especially in this period, one never knows. I've always heard the closing lines ("he was told but these few words, which opened up his heart") as sarcastic, bitter—Dylan, perceived as a message singer, confronted by people complaining about the contents of the visions he shares: "If you cannot bring good news, then don't bring any." But I'm forced to admit that Dylan could just as well have been sincere about this. In any case, this after-the-crash album of his is full of, if not good news, then at least encouraging messages (and ones I'm sure he meant literally, as if to say, if people expect wisdom of me I'll do my best to tell them something helpful, to share some of the simple folk truths that are helping me get through it all): "Stay free from petty jealousies, live by no man's code, and hold your judgment for yourself" (i.e., don't be quick to judge others); "Don't go mistaking Paradise for that home across the road"; "There are many here among us who feel that life is but a joke, but you and I we've been through that and this is not our fate"; and "Each of us has his own special gift, and...if you don't underestimate me, I won't underestimate you." Poor Robert's Almanac. A little flat on the printed page, perhaps, but inspired and inspiring (and truly helpful) when enclosed in music and performed with heart.

The last two songs on *John Wesley Harding* exist almost at right angles to the style and subject matter of the other performances; it's a daring (especially given the musical monotheism of Dylan's fans, who have always demanded that he be folk but not rock, rock but not country, etc.) experiment, and it works (the programming, putting these songs at the end, and using the bluesy "Down Along the Cove" as a bridge to "I'll Be Your Baby Tonight," is very well considered). "I'll Be Your Baby Tonight" is as charming as Woody Guthrie singing "Take You Riding in My Car Car." A classic. (Some Dylan fans had never heard a steel guitar before.) This song, like "Dear Landlord" and "Down Along the Cove," is from the last of the three sessions (October 17, November 6, November 29), and the relaxed richness of Dylan's voice tells us a true healing has taken place in the course of recording the album. Good news, indeed. The harmonica-playing alone is evidence of transformation.

Seven weeks later, the album out and already a huge success, Dylan made his first public appearance since Royal Albert Hall twenty months earlier. Woody Guthrie had died (after fifteen years of illness) on October 3, 1967, and, apparently at Dylan's suggestion, plans were made to hold a benefit concert in his honor. The concert took place January 20, 1968, at Carnegie Hall; Dylan appeared backed by the Band (other performers included Odetta, Pete Seeger, Jack Elliot, and Judy Collins), and played three Woody Guthrie songs: "Grand Coulee Dam," "Dear Mrs. Roosevelt," and "I Ain't Got No Home." These performances were later released on a Columbia album called *A Tribute to Woody Guthrie, Part 1*.

Dylan and the Band are in fine form here—their performances are inventive, exuberant, and sublimely musical. Dylan seems to twit the audience by starting with a loud, joyous, rockabilly performance of "Grand Coulee Dam," a highly patriotic ditty ("always a flying fortress, that flies for Uncle Sam") at a time when anti-government and anti-war activism were at their height, and Dylan was still regarded as the patron saint of protest. Turning Guthrie's topical folk song into rock and roll was outrageous but entirely appropriate, a tribute to the timelessness and energy of Woody's work. It's a fine arrangement. The Band is ragged at times, but Robertson's guitar work is as delightful as it was on the '66 tour, and Dylan sings with great gusto, totally projecting himself into the song, spitting out Guthrie's 16-syllable lines as if they were watermelon seeds.

Dylan's second song is another unlikely and inspired choice, Guthrie's tribute to FDR on the occasion of his death, written like a letter to his widow. The arrangement is swing rockabilly, wonderfully honky-tonk (Richard Manuel's piano-playing is spot on), and Dylan sings his heart out, his genius for phrasing and for getting inside the dynamics of each musical moment much in evidence. What comes through is his genuine love for Woody Guthrie—"this world was lucky to see him born." Very moving.

A third example of Dylan's brilliance as a singer and song re-creator closes the set, a new arrangement of "I Ain't Got No Home (in This World Anymore)," which Dylan performed quite differently on the Minnesota hotel tape in 1961. Dylan makes good use of Rick Danko's skills as a back-up vocalist on the other two songs as well, but the harmonic refrain Dylan and Danko invent for this one is a pure triumph (and a precursor of Dylan's employment of back-up singers in his shows from 1978 on). Great piano. Great music.

The crowd (I was one of them) screamed for more, but it was not to be. The next public performance by Bob Dylan and the Band was in July of 1969.

20.

Dylan was virtually silent for the rest of 1968. In June and July he taped a sincere, thoughtful interview with John Cohen (an old friend) and Happy Traum, which was published in *Sing Out!* magazine in October. The Band's first album was released in early summer, with a Dylan painting (primitive, surrealistic, quite delightful) on the cover. Another Dylan painting, presumably a self-portrait (sitting man with hat and guitar), showed up on the cover of *Sing Out!* Shelton says Dylan recorded in Nashville in September, but if so no tape has emerged as yet.

On February 13 and 14, 1969, Dylan recorded nine new songs in Nashville, working with the same musicians as on *John Wesley Harding*, plus two other guitar players (Norman Blake and Charlie Daniels) and a piano player (Bob Wilson). On February 17 and 18, Dylan and his friend Johnny Cash recorded together for at least three hours, sharing vocals on old songs by Cash and Dylan plus a number of country standards. One of these performances was added to the nine from earlier in the week to make a new Bob Dylan album called *Nashville Skyline* (released in early April).

Nashville Skyline is a very pretty album. That is the best thing one can say about it, and at times it's quite enough. The worst thing one can say about it is that if Dylan had stayed at this level of originality and commitment as a performer, it would be difficult today to make an argument for him as a great artist. He would be instead what he sometimes has claimed is all he ever wanted to be, a good entertainer. But regardless of what he may or may not have wanted, he *couldn't* stay in this particular place, any more than he's been able to stay in any other place (identity, musical self-concept) for very long, any time in his career. This is closely connected to what makes him an artist; and whatever it is, it's involuntary. In some ways he directs and shapes it, but mostly it just happens to him.

Part of it is a compulsion to escape, to move on. *Nashville Skyline* was Dylan's most popular album to date in terms of sales, one of his most popular ever (the success of "Lay, Lady, Lay" as a hit single, and the growth both of Dylan's reputation and of the overall market for lp records since Dylan's earlier hits, were factors in this). Perhaps the most telling response to suggestions that Dylan was primarily interested in making money and/or pleasing a mass audience at this time is to note that after the great success of *Nashville Skyline*, Dylan made no effort to record a similar album. He had mass success and secure "entertainer" status in the palm of his hand, and he threw them away.

John Wesley Harding was apparently conceived of by Dylan as a collection of very simple songs; when the critics and the public received them as being anything but simple, Dylan responded (a year later) with a whole higher level of simpleness. There is an interesting process of simultaneous retreat and advance going on here. In this case, Dylan is retreating from the supposed meaningfulness of his words, from the oppression of his much-trumpeted (by others) influence and power as a cultural hero, while advancing into new concepts of who he might be as a performer and of what music-making is all about.

One of the many aspects of this is the idea of "the enemy of my enemy." Dylan, oppressed by hippies and intellectuals and rock and rollers and political radicals (all of whom are loudly putting him on a pedestal, all of whom act like he owes them something), turns to what he thinks the hippies see as their antithesis: the patriotic rednecks, the country music fans. Not that this is premeditated or insincere on his part—he's always loved country music, since he was a young boy; Hank Williams and Lefty Frizell were singing to him at night before Elvis Presley and Little Richard first arrived on the airwaves. But there is a certain satisfaction in pursuing something that's bound to upset most people's expectations of him. Keep them guessing. He even invents a new voice for himself—another retreat from people's ideas of who Bob Dylan is, another assertion of his identity as someone independent of who you think I am.

No one could reasonably say Bob Dylan was playing it safe with this record—it was a radical move, in the context of his career so far, a great risk. But there's also an aspect of this music, and of the image or public identity Dylan was toying with at the time, that suggests that he was running from something, looking for a place to hide. As elusive as he'd been up to now, he seemed to be searching for a kind of performing that would expose even less of himself, specifically of what he might be feeling inside. I think he wanted music to write and sing that wouldn't confront him with his inner feelings, wanted to escape the enemy (restlessness might be one name for it) within.

Did he succeed? No, I don't think so. He just forced himself into a corner where he had less and less energy for performing, not that that was necessarily inappropriate for his life situation, his very real commitment to his role as father and homebody. But he did turn out a series of extremely opaque albums—*Nashville Skyline*, *Self Portrait*, and *New Morning*—over the course of the next two years, and then just about gave up making records (or any kind of public music) after that.

Meanwhile, for better and worse, we have the stops along the way. Advancing and retreating. In *Nashville Skyline* he gives his fans as little of the "old Dylan" as possible (his refusal to rebel itself an act of characteristic rebelliousness), but at the same time is almost obsequious in his desire to be accepted as one of the gang in this new (to him) world in which he fantasizes himself some kind of a) good old boy and b) enduring songwriter and performer creating classic love songs, a cross between Jimmie Rodgers and Irving Berlin.

Inevitably, what Dylan ends up creating is nothing like what he seems to be reaching for. The *Nashville Skyline* album is almost inconsequential (only ten songs, all short, one an oldie, one an instrumental, and half of the remaining eight could be considered filler). And Dylan the country performer is singularly lacking in projected identity—it's as if he's used himself up just getting here—sure, he sounds relaxed, but that's striking only by contrast with who we've known him to be, it doesn't stand by itself. There are no great turns of phrase on the record, which means none of these songs will be country classics (nothing remotely approaching "your cheating heart will tell on you"). There are no real standout moments in the vocal performances, nothing that provokes awe or sends shivers down the spine. And yet...

And yet this is a magical album. It creates and sustains a unique mood, from the first note on side one to the last note on side two. The whole is tremendously greater than the sum of its parts, as if Dylan conceived of a certain color and texture and feeling he wanted to project musically, and invented a vocal and lyrical and rhythmic and melodic tone (or set of tones) just for this purpose, set the whole thing up and ran through it and succeeded totally, turning out a record that's like a little hologram projector, you put it on the stereo and this particular happy playful relaxed slightly wistful feeling generates and generates, a presence, an enduring musical environment. Scratch the surface and there's nothing underneath, but explore the surface and it's a fascinating web of complex and imaginative musicality, with the vocal parts almost a foil for the instrumental riffs that link them together, sounds-from-the-back-of-my-mind stuff—these were not invented spontaneously by the musicians, you can almost hear Dylan saying, "play something that sounds like *this*, 'dum-dee-dee-dah-diddle-dah-dee.'" And they stare at him blankly, and then suddenly they're in the groove, reading his mind, and magic happens.

The standout song here for me, the track that best captures (and transcends) the mood of the whole set, is "Tonight I'll Be Staying Here with You." (This is one of four Dylan albums that end with a song that has the word "tonight" in the title, each song a thematic—musical, lyrical—reworking and anticipation of the other three.) It's all here: piano, drums, steel guitar, rhythm guitars, each at least as eloquent as the human voice that unites these other voices into song structure, all adding immeasurably and indeterminately to the story conveyed in the lyrics. "Throw my ticket out the window!" They could have done another take and removed most of the sloppiness, but the heart of the performance would have disappeared with it. Dylan has a gift for stopping at the right moment.

Dylan visited Nashville again for a series of recording sessions in late April and early May; on May 1 he taped the Johnny Cash Show, his first television appearance in five years. The television performances (he sings "I Threw It All Away" and a new song, "Living the Blues," and then duets with Cash on "Girl from the North Country") reveal a scared, very stiff Dylan who obviously wishes he were someplace else. He relaxes a little when Cash sits beside him, and even manages to smile at the end of the duet. There are moments in each song when Dylan's voice comes alive— but these flashes of musical energy are immediately choked by his overriding discomfort, all the thoughts that seem to be going through his head.

The April/May sessions resulted in ten known tracks. "Living the Blues" is the only Dylan composition; the other recordings are songs associated with performers like Elvis Presley, Johnny Cash, and the Everly Brothers. Possibly Dylan had an idea about the kind of performer he'd like to become, the kind of songs he'd like to be writing, and hoped that by performing these songs in the studio he'd get a sound or a groove going that in turn would inspire him, open the door to his next burst of creativity. But nothing really happened.

Dylan the performer seems dazed here; he sets up situations but fails to take advantage of them. His arrangement of "Take a Message to Mary" is imaginative, but his vocal is flat and emotionless; when the piano player and the rhythm section get something going in the second verse, Dylan doesn't notice, doesn't respond. The guitar playing at the start of "Ring of Fire" is wonderfully deranged, and one can easily imagine Dylan breaking the song open now and taking it into uncharted realms of excitement and mystery, but no. "Take Me as I Am (or Let Me Go)" is a great lyric for Dylan to sing, his eternal message (and quite timely as the critics and fans respond to *Nashville Skyline*) presented with the hoariest, most venerable set of country chord changes, but Dylan sings it completely straight, never even hinting that he knows that you know what he's saying. It's as though (in these recordings) there's a wall in him that comes down whenever a lyric or a tune veers even remotely close to what he'd really be feeling at this instant if he let his emotions show. His conceit of the moment is that he can be a great music-maker without descending into the muck of un-disciplined private feelings—a desperate and perhaps worthy ex-periment that is of course doomed to failure (but if you're not letting yourself feel anything, it might take a while to notice).

These sessions did produce one track that, to my taste, is fully successful on its own terms: a loose, loving, energetic performance of Elvis's 1959 hit "A Fool Such as I." Dylan sings with great comic spontaneity, freeing the band to follow suit—I smile every time I hear this one. ("A Fool Such as I" was left off of 1970's *Self Portrait*, which does include six other songs from these sessions; it eventually appeared in 1973, on Columbia Records' unauthorized *Dylan* album.)

In late June Dylan sat for a lengthy interview with *Rolling Stone* editor Jann Wenner; he seems every bit as uncomfortable as on the Johnny Cash Show, except that there he was a sympathetic figure, your heart went out to him in his distress. In this print interview, though, he just comes across as weird. He later told Anthony Scaduto that the interview was a result of him having his mind on other things and "not paying much attention to what I was saying." He also says the interview came at a time when he didn't have the energy to concentrate on it.

Lack of energy seems to have been a continuing problem for Dylan as performer in the years following his motorcycle accident. Carlos Castaneda insists that taking responsibility for children robs a warrior of his (or her) energy; that may be a dramatic way of putting it, but certainly it does redirect one's attention. Sara Dylan had given birth every year since 1966; by the fall of 1969 she and her husband were the parents of two girls and three boys (including Dylan's stepdaughter, Maria). Children were coming faster and easier than albums at this point in Bob Dylan's life.

Sometime in the spring of 1969 Dylan's contract with his manager Albert Grossman came up for renewal; Dylan declined to sign it. It had been some years since he'd let Grossman make commitments in his name, but now a further bridge had been crossed. From this time on Dylan managed his own professional career, talking to the record companies and the promoters himself, making his own decisions, answering to no one.

On July 14, 1969, Dylan made a surprise appearance at a concert by the Band in southern Illinois. He came onstage during their encore and was introduced as "Elmer Johnston"; they performed four songs together, including Little Richard's "Slipping and Sliding" and Woody Guthrie's "I Ain't Got No Home."

On August 31, 1969, Bob Dylan and the Band performed at a music festival in Great Britain, on the Isle of Wight. Dylan sang 17 songs; his performance lasted slightly more than an hour, which made it significantly shorter than his 1966 appearances. As in 1966, he started with "She Belongs to Me," this time accompanied by the Band; he followed with "I Threw It All Away" and "Maggie's Farm." The next four songs were solo performances: "Wild Mountain Thyme," "It Ain't Me Babe," "To Ramona," and "Mr. Tambourine Man." Then the Band returned, and backed Dylan on "I Dreamed I Saw St. Augustine," "Lay, Lady, Lay," "Highway 61 Revisited," "One Too Many Mornings," "I Pity the Poor Immigrant," "Like a Rolling Stone," "I'll Be Your Baby Tonight," "The Mighty Quinn," "Minstrel Boy," and "Rainy Day Women."

It's a good Dylan performance, not a great one, but very interesting in view of the silences that precede and follow it, and much more alive and spirited than his studio performances at this time. If this had been the (somewhat awkward, but heartfelt) opening night of an extended tour, it's easy to imagine the same song list, same arrangements, same general approach to the music (same colors and textures, same sort of chops), evolving into something quite wonderful, a rich musical tapestry filled with beauty, excitement, surprise. All that's needed is a little more time playing together in front of an audience, a little more forgetfulness of time and place.

As it is, the tape of the concert is quite rewarding, especially "I Threw It All Away" (deeply felt, full of love and dignity), "Maggie's Farm" (great arrangement, with the memorable "No more!" chorus never heard before or since), and "Wild Mountain Thyme," Dylan's quavery-voiced tribute to his melodic roots in the British Isles. "Like a Rolling Stone," included on *Self Portrait*, is the weakest performance of the evening, although the new arrangement is imaginative, clearly a sincere (and bold) attempt to re-create the song as an expression of what Dylan is feeling now. But he doesn't seem to have the energy to bring it off. The limp vocal betrays (or courageously shares) his ambivalence.

On the other hand Dylan does have the balls to sing improvised lyrics on "Minstrel Boy," and I love the sound of the song's chorus. It's as though he's laughing at and acknowledging his relationship with his audience: "Throw some more money at me folks—it's true we have closets full of the stuff already, but how else can I be sure that you love me?" Bargaining for salvation one more time.

The Isle of Wight concert is a pleasure to listen to, and all the more so when contrasted to the listless studio performances Dylan put in during the rest of 1969 and into early 1970. He sounds like he's in the recording studio because he has a record contract (and maybe his wife wants him out of the house), and for no other reason, like a kid who's in school only because of the existence of truant officers. Bored, he tries various amusing tricks: singing harmony with himself on Simon & Garfunkel's "The Boxer" (a good song, which might have been quite moving if Dylan had done it straight), conducting "instrumental" jam sessions in the studio, bringing in a wide variety of instruments and studio musicians and proceeding to offer them no leadership or musical inspiration (just the opposite of great Dylan sessions of the past, as though his personal presence is now completely inverted), and writing a song (the only original Dylan song from these seven months of sessions) consisting of one line, which in turn is sung not by Dylan but by a female chorus: "All the Tired Horses" ("all the tired horses in the sun, how'm I s'posed to get any riding done?"). The latter song is the only memorable performance in the lot; I suspect its success comes from the fact that it has something to say that was real for Dylan at the time, an anthem about the absence of energy, comparable to (but, admirably, much less energetic than) Ray Davies's "Sunny Afternoon" and Hoagy Carmichael and Johnny Mercer's "Lazybones."

All of the ten known studio performances from fall 1969 are included on *Self Portrait* (there must be outtakes, but they're not circulating), as are four more generally credited to February or March 1970. The fall sessions were apparently in Nashville and Los Angeles, the winter ones in New York. When Dylan was interviewed by Jann Wenner in June 1969, he spoke of going on tour in "November…possibly December," but it never happened. (Dylan and his family moved back to New York City at the end of 1969.)

Dylan was reluctant to share his feelings with his listeners at this time; the difference between the Isle of Wight and the 1969-70 studio performances is that in live performance his feelings come through anyway, which I suppose is why he was willing to keep going into the studio even as he avoided any further live appearances. One example: in "Highway 61 Revisited" at the Isle of Wight, Dylan sings, "God said to Abraham, 'give me a son,' " which suggests to me that, with his wife pregnant and small children all around him, he couldn't bring himself to sing "kill me a son." This is a poor decision, I think, but it does show that he feels the words he's singing, that they make a difference to him. By contrast, in the fall of 1969 Dylan recorded a folk song called "Little Sadie" which appears (twice) on *Self Portrait*. The song begins with the singer murdering a woman for no apparent reason; he runs away, is caught and sent to jail. It's a cheerful, jaunty tune, as performed by Dylan and his band, and it climaxes in the confession: "Oh yes, my name is Lee; I murdered Little Sadie in the first degree; first degree, second degree; if you've got any papers will you serve 'em to me?" Dylan sings the song with no trace of remorse or self-consciousness—it's all just words and chords to him, fun to mess around with. Ambivalence doesn't stop him this time, because he's totally asleep to what he's saying or communicating.

Self Portrait was released in June 1970. It's a double album, deliberately perverse in its contents, Dylan's emphatic "fuck you!" to his audience, his record company, and his own artistic pretensions. For example, the four live songs from the Isle of Wight include two of the worst performances from that show; it is ballsy but not particularly enlightening to put on your album a live take in which you forget the words to one of your best-loved songs. If it had been a great performance in spite of the goofs, that would be something else; but it wasn't. Including "Blue Moon" on a Bob Dylan album is also ballsy (and got a lot of attention); but what is achieved by singing the song so lifelessly?

What gets in the way of interpreting *Self Portrait* simply as an attempt to be outrageous, to irritate people, to refuse to knuckle under to the pressure to be a musical and cultural leader, is that it represents a full year of effort in the studio. If Dylan had this in mind from the outset, he didn't have to take so long or work so hard at it. I have to assume that along with its defiant (and depressing) cleverness, the album is also an admission of defeat. Dylan tries to shatter his own myth here not just because it oppresses him but also because his efforts to come up with something both outrageous and musically meaningful have failed. Presidents stand naked, and even Bob Dylan must have to come up empty sometimes.

Dylan did manage, in 1985, to offer a plausible alternate explanation for *Self Portrait*. In the *Biograph* booklet, he says most of the *Self Portrait* songs were things recorded at the start of sessions just to get a sound, to loosen up and see how this studio and this group of musicians sound today. "Then we'd go on and do what we were going to do." So in the spring of 1970, when a lot of Dylan bootlegs were in stores featuring strange combinations of old practice tapes and live recordings, "I just figured I'd put all this stuff together and put it out, my own bootleg record, so to speak." Okay. Just one question: what happened to the stuff he actually went to the studio to record at all those sessions, the songs that these other tracks are just warm-ups for? It's possible, I know, that Dylan like Picasso may turn out to have a treasure trove of unseen, unheard major works that he's kept for himself—and if so, a very different history of this period in Dylan's artistic career may someday be written.

May 1, 1970, George Harrison was in New York, and he joined Dylan at a relaxed session which also featured Charlie Daniels on bass and producer Bob Johnston on keyboards. With Harrison playing guitar and joining on an occasional back-up vocal, Dylan (on the circulating tape) sings an interesting selection of his own songs ("Song to Woody," "Mama, You Been on My Mind," "Just Like Tom Thumb's Blues," and the omnipresent "One Too Many Mornings," Dylan's favorite piece of plastic in this era, here given its fifth or sixth totally different arrangement, quite a good one too), plus a couple of covers ("Da Doo Ron Ron" and the Beatles' "Yesterday"). Listening to this tape after listening to the *Self Portrait* sessions is a great relief; whatever conceptual weight was sitting on Dylan's shoulders has lifted, and he's just a singer making music with friends. "Song to Woody" is particularly moving—Dylan sings and plays harmonica with unaffected sincerity, and Charlie Daniels's soulful bass playing speaks Dylan's heart, telling us Dylan's special ability to project his feelings through the musicians around him isn't dead after all (he just had the gain turned down on his amps for a while there).

Also in May, as far as we can tell from the ambiguous information available, Dylan started recording the songs that ended up on his next album after *Self Portrait*, *New Morning* (released in October 1970). Two or three of these songs were recorded in New York in the spring ("If Not for You," "Time Passes Slowly," and maybe

"Went to See the Gypsy"); the rest are from a New York studio session in August. Clinton Heylin identifies various songs as being from these same August sessions based on the distinctive sound of Dylan singing while suffering from a head cold. On this basis he feels "Mr. Bojangles," "Mary Ann," "Big Yellow Taxi," and "Can't Help Falling in Love," all from the 1973 *Dylan* lp, are from August 1970, as is the version of "Spanish Is the Loving Tongue" which was released in 1971 as the B-side of a single. More warm-ups. "Spanish Is the Loving Tongue," performed solo at the piano, is the standout track here, passionate, full of naked feeling—as if Dylan were apologizing for the extravaganza he made of the song a year earlier and is now sharing what it really means to him. A trunkful of Dylan performances like this one would be a treasure trove indeed.

The songs included on *New Morning* are all Dylan originals. The album has a feeling of "starting over" about it, as the title and the back cover photo (Dylan with blues singer Victoria Spivey in 1961—he looks very young) both suggest. The usual critical assumption is that *New Morning* represents "damage control" (or even a sort of apology) after the overwhelmingly negative press response to *Self Portrait*. And certainly Dylan was very quick to put out a new album of original songs, one of them carefully designed to distance him from his politically unpopular decision to accept an honorary degree from Princeton University (which he did in June 1970). Dylan of course has a different story, no doubt equally true: he explains in the *Biograph* notes that he recorded "New Morning," "Time Passes Slowly," and "Father of Night" for a Broadway play written by Archibald MacLeish, and then backed out of the production after a misunderstanding. So "I took those songs and some others and recorded *New Morning*."

New Morning to me is a scary album. Unlike *Nashville Skyline* and *Self Portrait* it's not a conceptual experiment (Dylan goes country; Dylan sings other people's songs). It is not a half-hearted effort—there is energy and humor in the singing and musical accompaniment, cleverness and intelligence in the lyrics, personality and imagination in the music, the sound. It should be, in short, the return of Bob Dylan, and was hailed as such by fans and critics at the time. And that's the scary part. *New Morning* is Bob Dylan pretending to be Bob Dylan, not in any obvious way (like writing a sequel to "Mr. Tambourine Man") but in a very subtle way: he goes through all the motions and touches all the bases, but leaves out Ingredient X.

The songs and performances on *New Morning* are somehow inauthentic. This is certainly not intentional on Dylan's part; and I think his own dissatisfaction with what resulted when he went into the studio to make a straightforward album like he used to do was a major factor in his unwillingness or inability to complete another album of new songs until fall 1973, three long years later. The thing is that the inauthenticity is not superficial nor a result of laziness or disinterest. Rather, it is as though he's trying to be honest and is sabotaged by an invisible enemy, a deep inner resistance or fear.

It is as though the singer, the artist, is communicating from behind a barrier, a glass wall, whose existence he never acknowledges. He smiles and tells stories and acts like everything's fine. I start to wonder if there is no barrier (I must be imagining it), or if it's something that I'm creating, maybe an expectation, an idea. But then I play "Spanish Is the Loving Tongue" (the solo version, not the track from the *Dylan* album) immediately before or after whatever *New Morning* song I've been listening to, and the difference is astonishing. This one performance proves that Dylan *could* share his heart through music at this moment in his life, and gives the lie to everything on *New Morning*, with the possible exception of a few moments in the middle of "Sign on the Window." (I don't know what "Brighton girls are like the moon" means, but I can *feel* it, and that's what's missing for me throughout the rest of the album.)

The next recorded Dylan performance is a bit of video from an educational TV documentary on Earl Scruggs—Dylan sweetly sings "East Virginia" with Scruggs and his sons, circa December 1970. And then, March 1971, a breakthrough: Dylan went into the studio and recorded two terrific new songs, "Watching the River Flow" and "When I Paint My Masterpiece." The first was released as a single in June 1971 (with the solo "Spanish Is the Loving Tongue" on the back); both songs are included in the late 1971 collection, *Greatest Hits Volume II*. Leon Russell produced the session (the first Dylan recordings not produced by Bob Johnston since the two started working together in 1966) and plays dynamite piano—bass, drums, guitars, and back-up vocals are also featured; according to *Rolling Stone*, the session was "well-oiled."

Perhaps it was the booze and camaraderie; perhaps it was the simple honesty of the first words of "Watching the River Flow" ("What's the matter with me? I don't have much to say"); in any case *something* has loosened up our hero and (at least momentarily) set his genius free. "Watching the River Flow" is a wonderful performance—it has everything one could want from a Bob Dylan single, including lots of humor, universally applicable lyrics, and demonically brilliant lead guitar riffs (by Joey Cooper or Don Preston or Jesse Ed Davis; the credits are vague).

Most of all the performance exemplifies a key element of Dylan's genius: his timing. In a 1984 radio interview Dylan commented on this: "When I do whatever it is I'm doing, there is rhythm involved and there is phrasing involved. And that's where it all balances out…It's not in the lyrics. It's in the phrasing and the dynamics and the rhythm." Dylan scholar Ian Woodward adds, "I couldn't agree more…It's in the intonation, the pauses, the speeding up and slowing down, the lengthening of sounds, the timing, the inflection and other vocal tricks." These are not skills, which is why when Dylan makes a conscious effort to apply them (as on *New Morning*) he can fall flat—they are aspects of a gift Dylan has, a gift that shows up not on demand but as a function of that unpredictable quality called inspiration.

When Dylan is inspired, he sings as though every lyrical and rhythmic and melodic phrase in a song is subdivided into thousands of parts, and he can intuitively move among those parts, emphasizing, extending, combining, holding back, shaping each moment of the song as he sings it. The mechanism by which he achieves this is his sense of timing and his use of inflection. In "Watching the River Flow" Dylan establishes a mood and creates a fictional character, defines the implicit relationship between this character (the person singing) and the listener based on tone of voice, and implies an attitude and understanding about the world, about life, all in the first few lines of the song; this is accomplished entirely through the spin he puts on each word and phrase as he speaks it with his voice.

This is called inflection, I suppose (the way he says "matter," the way he says "me," the way he says "say"), but it's also timing because every word exists in a rhythmic context, the spin depends on the dynamic tension of the performance, a kind of energy that vibrates between singer and musicians and has a forward motion on it, a relentlessness, just as the spin on a pool ball depends on the fact that it's being set in motion in a straight line and has a weight and an inertia of its own. So you hit the ball in a certain (ever-shifting) place with a certain amount of energy and a certain built-in twist, and no way you can do that equation in your head, instead you go by color and texture and instinct, you learn to feel it. On a good day your timing is impeccable and just won't quit, no one knows where it comes from and no one with any sense ever pauses to ask. On a bad day you're dead in the water.

"Watching the River Flow" was recorded on a very good day. The magnificent false ending after the first verse (isolating it from the rest of the song like a sandbank in a river delta) is just the most obvious example of the musical humor and intelligence that rocks through every moment of this performance. Dylan when he's on has an uncanny ability to inspire the musicians he works with, and they in turn inspire him; a song like this is proof that you can come up with more worthwhile ideas in a good hour than in a bad year. Along with good timing the song exemplifies another essential Dylan quality, which is timelessness. "Mr. Tambourine Man" is a classic evocation of that part of our experience which happens outside of time, and Dylan himself has pointed out his consciousness-expanding manipulation of the listener's time assumptions in songs like "Wicked Messenger" and "All Along the Watchtower." "Watching the River Flow" evokes dawn in an all-night cafe (dawn after being up all night is Dylan's quintessential timeless moment) on some anonymous highway by an anonymous river, and places us inside the spirit of someone who can "wish I was back in the city" and "sit here so contentedly" both at once, and it's like snapping fingers and awakening into a sleepy reality more familiar and more certain than wherever we were before we came back here.

This is very good songwriting, and the question arises: Which comes first?—a good performance in response to the writer coming up with a good song, or maybe (and more likely) the songwriter noticing the performer is awake and hastening to (feeling inspired to) turn out something worthy of the singer's talents and the mood he's in this afternoon. Something he can lean into a little.

"When I Paint My Masterpiece" is a rare case of Dylan being so hoarse it actually bothers me, but it's still an outstanding song and performance. Again Dylan creates a fictional character and dazzles us with geography; again there's a wonderful feeling of being outside of time as the story is telescoped—one moment it's today and I'm in Rome, next moment I left there weeks ago. "Train wheels running through the back of my memory," indeed. The subject of the song is "someday" and the huge, laughable, poignant role it plays in our lives; Dylan makes fun of himself as an artist in such a sweet way it sounds like he's comfortable with his own aspirations again, for the moment.

August 1, 1971: Bob Dylan made a surprise appearance at the Concert for Bangladesh, at Madison Square Garden, New York, performing a five-song set at both the afternoon and the evening shows; Dylan played acoustic guitar and harmonica, with some tasteful back-up (embellishment, not a full band sound) from George Harrison on electric guitar, Leon Russell on electric bass, and Ringo Starr on tambourine. The evening set is included on the record album *The Concert for Bangladesh* and in the film of the same name. Dylan sings "A Hard Rain's A-Gonna Fall," "It Takes a Lot to Laugh," "Blowin' in the Wind," "Mr. Tambourine Man" (not included in the film), and "Just Like a Woman." There is also a circulating tape of the afternoon set, which features the same songs except that he does "Love Minus Zero" instead of "Tambourine Man."

This was Dylan's first live performance in two years. Harrison had to twist his arm to get him to take part in the benefit concert, and we can be very glad he did: it's a stunning performance (both shows), modest, confident, richly textured, with Dylan feeling and communicating genuine love for the music he's playing (in the case of "Blowin' in the Wind" this was his first public performance of the song in seven years). Most of all, Dylan's voice on this midsummer afternoon and evening has a rare, penetrating beauty that is immediately noticeable to almost anyone who hears it. This is, in a very real sense, the Dylan a large part of his audience dreams of hearing; this is the voice to fit the stereotyped or mythic image of Bob Dylan, guitar strumming poet laureate of the 1960s. Dylan could fill halls forever playing this set of songs with these close-to-the-original arrangements, alone or with a few back-up musicians, a fact that has always been either terrifying or simply of no interest to him; this is what the mass audience and many of his avid fans most want from him. He very seldom obliges, and for good reason—but this time he does, and with no cynicism at all, just heartfelt enthusiasm for the music that's flowing through him (and the other musicians) and real pleasure, even astonishment, at the warm response of the audience.

Dylan's greatness arises from the fact that each of his performances is different, each is new, each expresses (consciously and unconsciously) the musical and emotional possibilities of the situation, the moment. When he sings "Mr. Tambourine Man" or "It Takes a Lot to Laugh" at the Bangladesh concert he is *inventing* them, in some ways they're old friends rediscovered but at the same time the spirit that's moving through him is something that's never moved through him before; watching the film you can almost see him stepping aside to let this spirit through, and marveling at the results. This climaxes at the very end of the set, the last notes of "Just Like a Woman"; everything Dylan and the audience have shared comes together in the last word of the song ("...girl"), and it is clear that he knows it. His satisfaction and happiness are audible and visible. Bruce Cockburn once wrote, "Let me be a little of Your breath." Dylan looks like he's just had that experience, and is humbly giving thanks.

21.

Soon after the Bangladesh concert, in September or early October 1971, Dylan went into the studio to re-record some of his "Basement Tapes" songs for a new collection of *Greatest Hits* (Columbia had released his first *Greatest Hits* album in 1967). He recorded "I Shall Be Released," "You Ain't Goin' Nowhere," and "Down in the Flood," accompanying himself on acoustic guitar and harmonica, with Happy Traum on bass, banjo, second guitar and vocal harmony. The three songs close the two-record set (the order of songs on the album was determined by Dylan, who has acknowledged that he worked carefully at this task and felt proud of the result), a modest and very rewarding mini-symphony to follow "When I Paint My Masterpiece."

I call it a symphony because there is a unity of sound and an interaction between the rhythms and personalities of these three performances that seems to me to create a whole that is larger than the sum of the parts. If we forget about earlier versions of these songs (it's easy to be distracted by the radical change in mood of "I Shall Be Released" and by the flippant, delightful rewriting of "You

Ain't Goin' Nowhere"), and just open ourselves to the sound of the present performance, I believe we can hear a surprisingly happy Dylan reasserting the expressive power and rich musicality of his own work. The soulful harmonica playing, the striking two-part singing, the confident and inventive guitar rhythms, the strong conveying of individual consciousness and specific feelings in the vocalizing of words and phrases, all work together to communicate the artist's renewed confidence in the value of his work and in his ability as a performer to share something unique with the world.

This also is the statement that comes through in Dylan's choice of songs for and sequencing of *Greatest Hits, Volume II*. He seems pleased at how well these songs from different eras flow into and work alongside each other (all of his albums except the first and third are represented, and there are five previously un-released performances, four of them recorded in 1971), and at the rich interplay of musical and lyrical themes revealed in this compilation, which has the feeling of a painter's retrospective. Indeed, the dominant impression in this selection is of the vivid textures and colors (with emphasis on the melodic at least as much as the verbal) in Dylan's work. It is noticeably not a protest or rock and roll album, nor is it primarily surrealistic. Sex is not a major theme. The album gives a strikingly different picture or image of Dylan than that presented by most of his other albums at the time of their release.

What we have here is encapsulated by the opening song, "Watching the River Flow": a portrait full of dynamic energy yet surprisingly static, not in a negative sense but in the sense of self-contained, a world complete as it is, not really needing or wanting to go anywhere. Dylan's relationship with his own ambi-tion seems to have reached a plateau of maturity where he can feel proud of what he's achieved and can enjoy performing and sharing his music with people in the moment, without judging himself or his audience or feeling a need to equal or one-up whatever has come before.

The sequencing is excellent. The high point of the album for me comes when the first notes of "When I Paint My Masterpiece" burst forth from the applause at the end of "Tomorrow Is a Long Time." The timing, the thrill of the transition from one mood to the other, could not be more perfect. This suggests to me that Dylan does know who he is, in spite of *Self Portrait*, and appreciates as we do that mysterious realm where musical energy touches and transforms human lives.

On November 4 Dylan went into the studio again, for a very interesting session: his first topical song since 1963 (literally, a song about a topic in the news; this was the sort of composition that first brought Dylan great attention). Black author and political activist George Jackson had just been murdered by guards in what seemed a phony uprising (staged somehow by the state) in a California prison. Dylan wrote a song in response ("I woke up this morning, there were tears in my bed; they killed a man I really loved, shot him through the head"), recorded it, and had his record company release it, all in less than ten days. He put a solo acoustic performance of "George Jackson" on one side of the single, and a "big band version" (drums, steel guitar, bass, and two back-up singers) on the other side.

These are odd performances. Many commentators at the time questioned Dylan's sincerity, which seems cruel, since he clearly was genuinely saddened by Jackson's death (it must have been frustrating to Dylan that the issue raised by the song became his intentions rather than Jackson's fate, and I imagine this was a factor in his renewed disinclination to make records or otherwise share himself with the public). But it is understandable, because both performances are an odd mixture of energetic musicianship (the guitar riff in the solo version, a couple of technically beautiful harmonica solos in the big band one) and a sort of uncommunicative blankness, as though Dylan, going in to have a lively, creative, intimate session like the one with Happy Traum, finds himself unexpectedly struggling with what I call "inauthenticity" again—each performance is partly inauthentic, partly heartfelt. Dylan recorded another song at this session, a simple country waltz called "Wallflower," and a line from that song perhaps sums up his confusion: "Just like you I'm wondrin' what I'm doin' here; just like you I'm wondrin' what's goin' on."

In any case, Dylan as far as we know did no more recording for the rest of 1971 and all of 1972, except for some work as a sideman (harmonica, guitar, even an occasional shared vocal) for friends like Allen Ginsberg, Doug Sahm, Steve Goodman, and Roger McGuinn. He made one live appearance: four songs with the Band during their New Year's Eve concert, December 31, 1971, in New York. Of all Dylan's lost weekends and periods of silence,

1972 seems to have been the furthest gone. At one point he went to Arizona "to cool out for a while," and according to a 1985 interview he imagined himself pursued by Neil Young's hit song "Heart of Gold": "I used to hate it when it came on the radio; I'd say, 'Shit, that's me. If it sounds like me, it should as well be me.' "

After a year of being lost in one sort of desert or another, Dylan stumbled into something even stranger, a movie set, and ended up writing the soundtrack for and acting in Sam Peckinpah's movie *Pat Garrett & Billy the Kid*. Dylan plays a character named "Alias," a sort of sidekick or hero worshipper of Billy the Kid, who is played by Dylan's friend Kris Kristofferson.

Dylan's performance as Alias is eccentric and intriguing. All of the parts in the film other than Garrett and Billy are cameo roles; Alias is seen more and takes part in more scenes than any of the other minor characters, but his role in the story remains ambiguous. "Who are you?" Garrett asks him early in the film; "That's a good question," Alias answers, and Garrett drops the subject, uncertain whether he's being put on or not. Later, when Billy meets Alias and hears his name, he asks, "Alias what?" "Alias anything you want," is the reply. This would be unbearably and inappropriately cute except for the fascinating look on Dylan's face in each case; the viewer can feel an intense nonverbal communication taking place between the characters. This occurs again, and most strikingly, after Billy shoots the other three strangers who came into town with Alias and comes within a hairbreadth of killing Alias but stops, not because Alias tossed his knife into the throat of one of Billy's assailants, but rather because of the look, the silly grin, on Alias's face. There's a shrug, and an answering, somewhat bewildered grin from Billy, who clearly lives and acts on his intuition and who seems to accept Alias, not exactly as a friend, but as a nonhostile, shy, ballsy, unfathomable fellow intuitive. Dylan's performance may not be acting in the normal sense, but it is consistent with the gifts he displays in his musical performing: the ability to assume, move around within, and project an affecting, incomprehensible, and somehow vitally relevant presence.

Dylan's soundtrack for *Pat Garrett & Billy the Kid* works well with the movie (perhaps surprisingly, since Dylan has complained that "the music seemed to be scattered and used in every other place but the scenes which we did it for"). Dylan does a good job of creating music that reflects and expresses the movie's emotional and thematic content without either becoming hackneyed or calling undue attention to itself. "Billy," the title theme, which can be heard throughout both the film and the soundtrack album (the latter contains one instrumental version and three vocal versions of the song), is not particularly striking lyrically, but Dylan sings it with just the right mixtures of love and sadness, empathy and detachment; his harmonica solos are especially moving. The soundtrack was recorded in one session in Mexico City in January 1973 (Dylan and his family moved to Durango and nearby Yucatan in November 1972 while the movie was being filmed) and several sessions in Los Angeles in February 1973, with help from a variety of talented musicians, including Booker T. Jones, Roger McGuinn, Bruce Langhorne, Byron Berline, Jim Keltner, and Terry Paul. All the music was composed (and presumably arranged) by Dylan.

Jonathan Cott calls the soundtrack album "a kind of beautiful, rough-hewn, mostly instrumental mantra album from the mythical Old West." I'll go along with that—it has a hypnotic soothing quality, quite different from most of Dylan's recorded output but clearly an expression of a musical and even a spiritual place very meaningful to Dylan. "Man of Constant Sorrow" from 1961 and "Rank Stranger" from 1987 are examples of other Dylan performances that tap this same vein. *Pat Garrett & Billy the Kid* (the album) is elusive, and seems inconsequential when listened to casually, but listen to it repeatedly and it can get into your bloodstream, sounding better and stirring up more buried emotions each time through.

The standout track is "Knockin' on Heaven's Door," which is easily the most popular of all the songs Dylan has written in the 1970s and 1980s, in terms of the number of different bands and singers who've performed and recorded it. It is also, amazingly, Dylan's only top 20 single in these two decades. It was released in August 1973 and very slowly made its way up the charts, reaching #12 by late November. The song, like the album, grows on people.

It seems fair to say that the song, while it speaks from and to a very deep place in singer and listener, is largely an accident. Certainly Dylan had no thought to write an anthem or a hit single—he was just responding to pressure to come up with some little snippet for the film besides "Billy" and its variations. The lyrics, simple enough in any case, are taken directly from events in the film: the dying Sheriff Baker refers to his wife (memorably portrayed by

Katy Jurado) as "Mama," and in the preceding scene she had fastened his badge on him. The lyrics not included in film or album but often sung by Dylan since, "Wipe these tears offa my face/I can't see through them any more," also derive from Peckinpah's portrait of Mama and her man saying goodbye. Dylan's singing on the track, the rhythm established by musicians and singers, the sweetness of the "ooh-ooh"s, and the power of the harmonies on "knock-knock-knockin'," phenomenal as they all are and especially in the way they move together, are all a natural outgrowth of what Dylan has been doing with the rest of the soundtrack, a reflection of emotions stirred up in him by the subject matter of the film and by his experience being there, in Durango, in Peckinpah-land, in Billy-the-Kid and goodbye-to-the-last-outlaw land. Song and performance were squeezed out of Dylan by some greater force, not without effort and certainly not without genius but still in a sense when he wasn't looking. Bing! There it was, just as accidental or anyway unplanned as Dylan's involvement with the movie itself, his interlude in Durango. Just listening to the song you know, without being able to explain, that something somewhere has broken through, has passed some kind of point of no return.

Dylan and his family did not return to New York City when the work on *Pat Garrett* was completed; instead they relocated in Malibu, an exclusive California beach community just north of Los Angeles.

At this time, just before and after the Mexico adventure, Dylan was completing a sort of magnum opus: a hardcover collection of his lyrics and miscellaneous writings, 1961-1971, published in 1973 by Knopf under the title *Writings and Drawings*.

Writings and Drawings is a wonderful book. It did not receive the attention it deserved when it was published; despite Dylan's enormous reputation, critics and public both were conditioned to think of his new work as coming in the form of recordings, and so a relatively minor collection of new songs like *New Morning* got vastly more attention than this major, almost definitive collection of writings, many of them not previously available to the public.

Although most of the work of assemblage and transcription was left to "the girls upstairs" referred to in the dedication, there can be no question that the decision to issue this book, and the basic choices as to content and form of presentation, were Dylan's. Most significant is his decision to acknowledge more than sixty songs that had not been included on his albums over the years, including such major works as "She's Your Lover Now," "I'll Keep It with Mine," "Lay Down Your Weary Tune," and "Sign on the Cross." Dylan is telling us that he sees these songs as part of his work as a whole, even though he never released them as recordings. *Writings and Drawings* also resurrects and makes available to the reading public a variety of non-song writings, including his liner notes for his own and other people's albums, the collections of poems first printed on his third and fourth album sleeves, "My Life in a Stolen Moment" and "Advice for Geraldine on Her Miscellaneous Birthday" (major essays first published as concert hand-outs), and his performed poem "Last Thoughts on Woody Guthrie." (Other significant writings are omitted, quite possibly because they were overlooked or copies were not easily obtainable, rather than because they were deemed unworthy. In the case of the song selection, there is no evidence that Dylan or his helpers ever said, "This song is too dumb or too trivial to go in the book"—they simply included what could be found.)

As a bonus (and to brighten the title of the book, which was originally to be called *Words*), there are 18 drawings by Dylan, probably done in 1972, most of them intended to illustrate specific songs. The skewed two-hole guitar used on the cover is perhaps the most satisfying aesthetically; a few of the drawings seem to express strong feelings, while most are light jokes, doodles, visual puns; but overall the effect of their inclusion is a very positive one. It gives us still another side of Bob Dylan, lets us pick up nonverbally a little more of who he is or how he sees the world. It also helps remind us that the songs too are sketches and associative word games, and we don't necessarily always have to take them so seriously.

And there's more. The truly sappy dedication shows us that even Dylan, master of the revitalized cliché, can occasionally go off the deep end. The handwritten quatrain that serves as prelude to the text stands as a neat summation of Dylan's artistic philosophy: "If I cant please everybody/I might as well not please nobody at all/(there's but so many people/an I just cant please them all)." And last but not least, Dylan generously shares six pages of manuscript with us: the previously-discussed draft of "Subterranean Homesick Blues"; a handwritten song fragment about Morris Zollar included as a sort of epilog (meant to be spoken rather than sung, and a revelation in the way it silently and joyously communicates inflection, sound, and tone of voice); and four pages of typed song-doodling (creative process in action) included inside the front and back covers. ("I needa new name/ got to make some money...& break out of this place.") Of the goodies mentioned in this paragraph, only Morris Zollar and the "Subterranean" manuscript survive in *Lyrics*, the expanded *Writings and Drawings* Knopf and Dylan published in 1985.

Alas, my enthusiasm for *Writings and Drawings* must be tempered by a very serious criticism: what should be the standard reference text for the lyrics to Dylan's songs has been rendered far less useful than it could be by the fact that the words of the songs have been extensively altered by their author, and almost never for the better.

The fact that Dylan changes the words to his songs when he sings them in concert doesn't bother me at all; indeed, it is part of the process by which the songs are re-created and made new in each performance—nothing about them is sacred, they are instead jumping-off places for the spontaneous art the performer is going to create today. Sometimes these changes are spur-of-the-moment; other times they seem to have been worked on at some point before the performance (some of Dylan's lyric changes in "Gotta Serve Somebody," "Tangled Up in Blue," and "I Shall Be Released" in recent years sound like they were at least partly written out before they were performed); and often a changed lyric in a song continues to evolve from performance to performance as Dylan plays with the song during a concert tour.

Given this, how can we even say what the "correct" lyrics to a song are, and why should I object to Dylan's little and big rewrites (a lot of them a matter of a few words, efforts to improve the grammar perhaps) in *Writings and Drawings*? The answer to the first question, I think, is that for reference purposes we need a collection of Dylan lyrics that is an accurate transcript of the songs as they are performed on their first "official" recordings. It would of course be wonderful to have a secondary volume that includes transcripts of significant alternate versions and notes as to minor interesting changes in songs as performed live (or, as in the case of "You Ain't Goin' Nowhere," when there are changes from one recording session to another). These volumes don't have to pretend that the lyrics they print are definitive or correct—they would

simply state that they are transcripts of these particular performances.

As for why the rewrites in *Writings and Drawings* are a problem:
partly it's because they destroy the book's usefulness as a reference
work, but mostly it's because the changes are so often inappropriate (most of them seem the work of someone with a tin ear, who
doesn't feel what the song's about, doesn't understand the rhythm
of the language, and doesn't remember what the song means as it's
sung). These changes were not made by a performer in the act of
performing, and it's hard to believe Dylan ever tried to sing these
songs with their "cleaned-up" or "fooled-around-with" lyrics.
Rather, he just thought they'd read better this way or that it would
be fun to make this change. (I recognize that a few of the changes
are errors in transcription, but only a few; there are also some cases
where Dylan has provided new words because the lyrics on the
available recording—for example, "Tell Me, Momma"—are unin-
telligible in parts, and there is no written-out song to refer back to.)

In performance any change can be worth trying, even when it
doesn't work; following such impulses keeps the art alive. In the
context of this book, however, these unperformed alterations,
though no doubt thought of as done in the same spirit of irrever-
ence and artistic freedom so appropriate on stage, are condescending, hostile, petty, and very seldom expressive of anything that
could be called an artistic impulse. Dylan is wise to do most of his
recording spontaneously, live in the studio in one or two takes. The
editor and second-guesser in him is not a very sensitive or trustworthy creature. For other writers and composers, of course, the
situation can be just the opposite. But Dylan's genius rests squarely
on his spontaneity and on his stubborn reliance on and trust of his
spontaneity. His gift, his calling, is to be a performing artist.

In June 1973 Dylan sang a new song, "Forever Young" (reportedly written the previous year, during his stay in Arizona), into
a tape recorder in the office of his song publisher. This moving,
unselfconscious performance was later included on *Biograph*. Dylan
comments in the *Biograph* notes: " 'Forever Young,' I wrote in
Tucson. I wrote it thinking about one of my boys and not wanting
to be too sentimental. The lines came to me, they were done in a
minute. I don't know. Sometimes that's what you're given. You're
given something like that. You don't know what it is exactly that

you want but this is what comes. That's how that song came out....I was going for something else, the song wrote itself."

In the summer of 1973, Dylan and Robbie Robertson and the other members of the Band began discussing a tour. By October stadiums were being booked, and informal rehearsals had begun. And in early November, Dylan went into a Los Angeles recording studio and, with the Band backing him on most of the tracks, recorded an album originally called *Love Songs*, then *Ceremonies of the Horsemen*, then, finally, *Planet Waves*.

Planet Waves marks Dylan's return as a committed artist, the first time since *John Wesley Harding* that he has truly allowed an album-in-progress to be an open canvas for the expression of whatever he is seeing, thinking, and feeling as he works on it. It is not that he's been consciously holding back during the intervening six years; rather it is as though he suffered amnesia—he honestly forgot how to create in this fashion or that such a thing might be possible or desirable. And in the content of the *Planet Waves* songs we find the reason, if there needs to be one, for this amnesia: the artist creates by attacking and destroying his own security. "How does it feel/to be on your own/a complete unknown?" Very scary. And inappropriate to your life-situation, when you see yourself as husband and father, rather than lover/poet/vagabond. What to do? Renounce. Forget. Lose your appetite for all that danger and romance.

But the curse and blessing of the true artist is that he or she cannot be satisfied indefinitely with shelter and safety; sooner or later the appetite returns, and cannot be ignored. "I could say that I'd be faithful," Dylan sings in "Something There Is About You," "I could say it in one sweet easy breath/But to you that would be cruelty, and to me it surely would be death." Dylan's awakening, as documented on this album, is initially sexual. But its tangible results are a renewed ability to express himself, and a willingness to become a performer before live audiences again. (Dylan explores these themes explicitly and very effectively in his 1977 film *Renaldo & Clara*.)

Planet Waves marks the beginning of the second stage in Dylan's relationship with his audience. The first stage, lasting from his first album through *Blonde on Blonde*, was one in which Dylan attempted to get the audience's attention, and then, confident of that attention, he steadily expanded his audience even as he ignored and defied their expectations. The audience, for their part, resisted and rioted yet ultimately accepted and embraced his work on its own terms (this is of course a generalization, a picture of the collective audience rather than of the individual listener, but as such I believe it's accurate and significant).

The first stage was the period in which most of the Bob Dylan myth—his enduring public identity—was established. It was followed by a hiatus or interregnum, 1967 to 1973, during which neither Dylan nor his audience could feel certain of their relationship. What distinguishes the second stage from this interregnum is Dylan's success at recommitting himself to his art. In effect it is a unilateral declaration of relationship: "I am doing my work, and those who can hear it will hear it." This is the stance he took during the first stage, too; the interregnum marked a period during which he attempted to renew this declaration a number of times but it didn't stick (the limits of a unilateral declaration are that although you don't need anyone else's agreement, you do have to convince yourself).

The second stage has lasted from 1974 to the present, and presumably will last for the rest of the artist's life. (It is inevitable that a third stage in the relationship will begin after the artist's death; a paradoxical stage in which, freed of the artist's living presence, his audience will become far more able to accept him for who he is and to appreciate his work as a whole.) What marks this second stage is a constant (often unconscious and even unwished-for) skepticism on the part of the audience, a measuring of present work against past achievements, and a resultant frustration on the part of the artist, an ebbing and flowing of his willingness to participate in the relationship. At the extreme, this can lead to periods when he feels unable to create, and also to occasions when he'll create great work and then consciously or unconsciously withhold it from the public. Of course, there will also be moments when he is moved to try to set the world on fire again.

The mature second stage creator is constantly building on the foundation of, yet laboring under the shadow of, the impact of his first stage accomplishments (and this was as true for Einstein, another prodigy, as it is for Dylan). The first words of Dylan's liner notes for *Planet Waves* are "Back to the Starting Point!" The last words of the album are, "now that the past is gone." But in this sort of relationship, the past is never gone; and so a dominant aspect of this second stage in the relationship between Dylan and his audience is the difficulty we, the audience, continually have in opening ourselves to and appreciating his new work on its own terms.

As a case in point, when *Planet Waves* came out I didn't like it. I wanted very much for it to be a major work, and for a few days I convinced myself that it was; but that initial enthusiasm was replaced by resentment when the album didn't grow on me as I listened to it. I felt keenly, almost bitterly aware of the distance between what I wanted from Dylan and what he seemed to be giving me.

Much later, I was able to appreciate a few of the songs for their ambiguous, autobiographical honesty; but I was still unable to hear the power and beauty of the album as a whole. I was certain, for one thing, that the Band's accompaniment was uninspired and inappropriate; and so that was what I heard on the rare occasions when I listened to the album. It sounded like there was a fog hovering over the whole project, only dispelled (and then only partially) on the acoustic tracks, "Dirge" and "Wedding Song."

Now (after 14 years) that fog has lifted, and since the record hasn't changed, the difference must be in me, in my listening. It cannot be emphasized enough, when we discuss music or literature or any created art, that the artist is only half the story; the creation and realization of great art depends also on the energy and integrity and commitment of the receiver—the viewer, reader, listener. And the point is not simply that I had an attitude that kept me from appreciating *Planet Waves*, but that I had that attitude in spite or even because of my sincere desire to like the album, and my earnest efforts to open myself to it. This is the recurring problem for Dylan's audience regarding his new work (new albums, new tours): we have trouble hearing it. Dylan is so inventive and so primitive, he operates so far outside anyone else's concept of singing, writing, and performing, that learning the language of one set of Dylan performances does not necessarily aid us in learning or acclimatizing to the language of another set. Indeed, it can be the primary obstacle in our listening: our attention is not innocent but expectant, and it's waiting (as it turns out) in all the wrong places.

What I hear now in *Planet Waves* (after my recent breakthrough) is a rich, variegated, consistent flow of attractive and inventive music and of playful, stimulating language describing marital anguish and innocent sexual joy, a sense of rediscovery of self combined with fear of loss, with the emphasis firmly on the necessity of being honest and of taking risks. The long fallow period just behind him, the spectre of renewed touring and performing rising up just before him, and the memories of a long-ago circus and his escape therefrom, are tangible throughout the album. The coming separation and divorce are also very much present, at least for the listener aware of Dylan's subsequent personal history. The album, like most of Dylan's albums, is a performance: quick, impromptu, urgent, full of the mood and energy of the particular moment when it was put together. It is meant to convey not eternal truth but immediate truth. Planet waves = tribal rhythms—the personal, universal news of our moment.

"The crashing waves roll over me," Dylan sings in what might be the most startling and seductive performance of the album ("Never Say Goodbye") were it not that all of these performances are so interrelated, it's hard to single one out (just as it's hard to single out one wave when the real joy of standing in the surf is how it keeps coming, wave splashing into wave, constant and ever-changing)—"as I stand upon the sand" (image of movement followed by image of solidity; also image of power and danger followed by an image of modesty and peace) "and wait for you to come" (anticipation) "and grab hold of my hand" (Zing! The essential *Planet Waves* themes are evoked, the excitement of an affair, the sanctity of the moment of union, and the maternal protection from fear—specifically fear of the big world—that a wife or close friend can offer, all in language that would be ordinary or even banal were it not for the earnestness of the singing and the wild energy and intelligence of the musical accompaniment). This was the first song recorded; Dylan and the Band were visiting the studio, checking it out, and they put this one down to see what kind of sound they could get. Levon Helm wasn't there that day so Richard Manuel played drums. Rick Danko's bass line at the beginning of the song holds the whole album together, in my opinion.

That was Friday, November 2, 1973; on Monday, Tuesday, and the following Friday Dylan and the complete Band recorded most of the rest of the album. Then on Saturday Dylan came in and told the engineer he had another song which wasn't quite ready. An hour later he sat down and recorded "Wedding Song," solo, in one take. He may also have done a solo "Dirge" on acoustic guitar at this session; in any case at a mixing session a few days later he was fooling around at the piano and decided to rerecord "Dirge." He played piano and asked Robbie Robertson, who says he'd never heard the song before this, to sit in on guitar. They did two takes, the second of which is on *Planet Waves*.

All of the songs on *Planet Waves* are "I/you" songs, Dylan singing in the first person to and about "you," with the exception of "Forever Young" (in which there is only "you" and no "I") and "Going, Going, Gone" (in which he talks to himself; there is an implied "you" but she is not addressed directly). It's arguable that Dylan has never made an album in which he was less conscious of or less concerned about his public audience. One reason for the quickness of Dylan's recording style (few or no warm-ups, few or no retakes) is to get the song out before self-consciousness sets in. This has therapeutic as well as aesthetic value—if the artist allows himself to question how much he really wants to reveal, he may end up not releasing/expressing those feelings and thoughts that press on him most powerfully, that most need to be let out. So, in Dylan's case, he blurts his songs onto tape quick before the self-censor can get hold of them. *Planet Waves*, an extremely personal album following a long period when Dylan's innermost feelings were not expressed in his writing and performing, is full of ambiguous images that seem to well up from deep inside, all of them relevant to who he is in the important I/you relationships in his life: husband/wife, boy/girl, child/parent, singer/audience, present me/past me. This immediacy and intimacy translates into powerful and affecting performances not because it's fun to psychoanalyze Bob Dylan but because the listener through identification becomes, variously or simultaneously, the "I" and/or the "you" in the song, and the unconscious material brought to the surface is our own.

Lyrically, there are interesting recurrences: "There is plenty of room for all/So please don't elbow me" in "On a Night Like This" and "Won't you move over and give me some room?" in "Tough Mama"; or "I stood alone upon the ridge and all I did was watch" ("Tough Mama") and "I just want to watch you talk" ("You Angel You"). He tells one woman her absence is "making me blinder and blinder" ("Hazel") and tells another (The same one? Possibly the characters the songs are addressed to are part real, part imaginary, or part one person, part several others) "you turn the tide on me each day and teach my eyes to see." The last line is from "Wedding Song," and is typical of the bizarre, even sinister undercurrents in that song: the first phrase a mixture of "turning the tide" (to reverse a condition; generally a pivotal event, as when the tide of a battle turns in one army's favor; not often thought of as occurring every day) and the usually hostile "turning the tables on [someone]." What is so disturbing about "Wedding Song" is that there is genuine love in it (you can hear it in his harmonica playing), and at the same time the resentment that comes through (presumably unconscious, unintended) is overwhelming. And the sad thing about the song is that the past isn't gone, and every time he uses the phrase "more than ever" he affirms its stifling presence.

Elsewhere in the multiple song that makes up the album the past has a different significance: "If I'm not too far off I think we did this once before" ("On a Night Like This") is a neat, specific evocation of timelessness (there's a fine general timelessness pervading "Never Say Goodbye," including the wild shift from frozen lake to crashing waves). Best of all is the couplet in "Something There Is About You," "Thought I'd shaken the wonder and the phantoms of my youth/Rainy days on the Great Lakes, walking the hills of old Duluth." This shows the past as an enriching force, a beneficent wound reopened by a new lover's presence—rediscovery and reaffirmation of self.

The reason I was unable to appreciate *Planet Waves* for so long is that I resisted and rejected the *sound* of the album, and that sound is the essence of the album's achievement and the key to everything else that's good about it. It's an energetic, innocent, warmly resonant sound; the musicians, including Dylan, seem to have left their thinking minds at the studio door, and are responding directly to the beauty of this new batch of songs and to the heartfelt, spontaneous music-making going on around them. The melodies of the songs are particularly well-suited to this kind of ensemble performing. "Tough Mama," "Hazel," and "Something There Is About You" sparkle with melodic and rhythmic hooks, insinuating themselves into the listener's heart and mind and demanding to be heard again and again, all three so interrelated but so dissimilar, another delightful mini-symphony.

The music evokes and shares a unique mood, a vibrant and poignant moment. This mood expresses itself emphatically, exquisitely, in the vocal bridges that burst forth in the middle of "Hazel" and "Going, Going, Gone" and "You Angel You": "Oh no, I don't need any reminder"; "Grandma said, Boy go and follow your heart"; "You know I can't sleep at night for trying." It positively shimmers in the guitar invention that completes each vocal phrase in "Something There Is About You" (a haunting riff that harks back to the harmonica solo in "Hazel," and still echoes in the opening of "Forever Young")—and it's achingly present in Dylan's voice when he says, "Suddenly I found you, and that spirit in me sings." That spirit sings throughout this album, and it's a real gift. It even manages to give life to "Forever Young," which I regard as a fairly banal bit of songwriting redeemed by the grace and sincerity with which it's performed. (Note that what distinguishes the slow version from the fast version is the repetition of the words "Forever young, forever young" in the chorus. This bit of crooning transforms the song from prayer to anthem and, since both versions are included here, neatly illustrates the awesome power of communication and emotional manipulation locked up in harmonic structure.)

"Wedding Song" and "Dirge" were the last songs recorded. "Wedding Song" seems to arise directly from Dylan's concern about Sara's likely reaction to the album; its title and content suggest that he wants to reaffirm his marital vows. He also seems at pains to argue that his need to go back out on the road (the forthcoming tour) does not have to be threatening to their relationship. When he sings, "It's never been my duty to remake the world at large/Nor is it my intention to sound a battle charge," I hear him reassuring her and himself about the nature of his reentry into the public arena.

"Wedding Song" has a quick, easy flow to it, lyrically and melodically, and the contradictory messages conveyed by both words and performance are fascinating. "When I was deep in poverty you taught me how to give" is a fine tribute. But the next verse is a catalog of horrors: "eye for eye and tooth for tooth" is a phrase that always refers to a pattern of retaliatory punishment; "your love cuts like a knife" is odd praise, odder still because it's sung without sarcasm or irony. "My thoughts of you don't ever rest, they kill me if I lie" says that his love for her has become a source of unending, self-flagellating guilt. The last line of the verse is particularly scary, given its form as part of a pledge of love: "I'd sacrifice the world for you to watch my senses die." What seems to be going on here is that, as so often in Dylan's songs, the time sense has been transposed—what he's really communicating is that at times it feels as though he has sacrificed the world for her and watched his senses die. Now he's no longer doing that, but the fact that he did means to him that he *would*, and so he wants credit for that. (More proof of his love.) Overall the song amounts to a plea for her to recognize his love and not let the marriage be threatened (by whatever might seem to be threatening it). But since "I hate myself for loving you" (as he states in "Dirge"), the more he says "I love you" the more hatred is dredged up. Unsurprisingly, the song did not succeed in its presumed purpose (Dylan and his wife did separate in the spring of 1974); but as the portrait of a moment, a painting of a particular aspect of marriage, it is unnervingly successful.

"Dirge" is a triumph for the penetrating beauty of Dylan's voice, the power of his rhythmic piano playing, and the richness of Robertson's guitar accompaniment, as he brilliantly and gently reads and expresses the singer's heart. The lyrics are a little like those on *John Wesley Harding* in that they deliberately tempt the listener to search for intention and purpose in what is actually spontaneous expression, free association. But maybe I just say that because try as I may I can't get a handle on who he might be addressing who praises progress and sings songs of freedom and "man forever stripped." I don't think it's any of the people that the other elements of the song seem to be addressed to: his wife, his audience, and his ex-manager (and the music business world he personifies). So I take comfort in the notion that this is a dream narrative, a riddle without solution, to be appreciated for itself alone. And I do love the way he sings, "It's a dirty, rotten shame."

But I'm no longer hoodwinked by the self-conscious artiness of "Dirge" into thinking it has more to offer than "Tough Mama" or "Something There Is About You" or even "You Angel You." The naked truth is present in all these songs. This is a very giving album.

The cover's wonderful. So's the handwritten, hand-drawn back cover, with the humor and energy and breathlessness of its liner notes. ("I dropped a double brandy and tried to recall the events.") ("We sensed each other beneath the mask.") You can make these notes mean anything if you put a little effort into it.

And then on January 3, 1974, Chicago, Illinois, Dylan sang "Hero Blues" and kicked off his first tour in seven and half years, the beginning of a whole new era.

Discography

I. Albums by Bob Dylan

All of the following (except *Masterpieces*) are available in the United States from Columbia Records. All were originally released by Columbia Records except *Planet Waves* and *Before the Flood*, which were first released by Asylum Records. All of the albums are available at present in lp and cassette formats, and most are also available as compact discs. For the purposes of this volume, it seems unnecessary to provide catalog numbers for the different formats. Date of first release is given, and the sequence of songs is the order in which they appeared on the original lp release. "A" indicates side one, "B" indicates side two.

1. *Bob Dylan*, released 3/19/62. A: You're No Good/Talkin' New York/In My Time of Dyin'/Man of Constant Sorrow/Fixin' to Die/Pretty Peggy-O/Highway 51. B: Gospel Plow/Baby, Let Me Follow You Down/House of the Risin' Sun/Freight Train Blues/Song to Woody/See That My Grave Is Kept Clean.

2. *The Freewheelin' Bob Dylan*, released 5/27/63. A: Blowin' in the Wind/Girl from the North Country/Masters of War/Down the Highway/Bob Dylan's Blues/A Hard Rain's A-Gonna Fall. B: Don't Think Twice, It's All Right/Bob Dylan's Dream/Oxford Town/Talking World War III Blues/Corrina, Corrina/Honey, Just Allow Me One More Chance/I Shall Be Free.

3. *The Times They Are A-Changin'*, released 1/13/64. A: The Times They Are A-Changin'/Ballad of Hollis Brown/With God on Our Side/One Too Many Mornings/North Country Blues. B: Only a Pawn in Their Game/Boots of

Spanish Leather/When the Ship Comes In/The Lonesome Death of Hattie Carroll/Restless Farewell.

4. *Another Side of Bob Dylan*, released 8/8/64. A: All I Really Want to Do/Black Crow Blues/Spanish Harlem Incident/Chimes of Freedom/I Shall Be Free No. 10/To Ramona. B: Motorpsycho Nightmare/My Back Pages/I Don't Believe You/Ballad in Plain D/It Ain't Me Babe.

5. *Bringing It All Back Home*, released 3/22/65. A: Subterranean Homesick Blues/She Belongs to Me/Maggie's Farm/Love Minus Zero-No Limit/Outlaw Blues/On the Road Again/Bob Dylan's 115th Dream. B: Mr. Tambourine Man/Gates of Eden/It's Alright, Ma (I'm Only Bleeding)/It's All Over Now, Baby Blue.

6. *Highway 61 Revisited*, released 8/30/65. A: Like a Rolling Stone/Tombstone Blues/It Takes a Lot to Laugh, It Takes a Train to Cry/From A Buick 6/Ballad of a Thin Man. B: Queen Jane Approximately/Highway 61 Revisited/Just Like Tom Thumb's Blues/Desolation Row.

7. *Blonde on Blonde*, released 5/16/66. 1A: Rainy Day Women #12 & 35/Pledging My Time/Visions of Johanna/One of Us Must Know (Sooner or Later). 1B: I Want You/Stuck Inside of Mobile with the Memphis Blues Again/Leopard-Skin Pill-Box Hat/Just Like a Woman. 2A: Most Likely You Go Your Way and I'll Go Mine/Temporary Like Achilles/Absolutely Sweet Marie/4th Time Around/Obviously 5 Believers. 2B: Sad Eyed Lady of the Lowlands.

8. *Bob Dylan's Greatest Hits*, released 3/27/67. A: Rainy Day Women #12 & 35/Blowin' in the Wind/The Times They Are A-Changin'/It Ain't Me Babe/Like a Rolling Stone. B: Mr. Tambourine Man/Subterranean Homesick Blues/I Want You/Positively 4th Street/Just Like a Woman.

9. *John Wesley Harding*, released 12/27/67. A: John Wesley Harding/As I Went Out One Morning/I Dreamed I Saw St. Augustine/All Along the Watchtower/The Ballad of Frankie Lee and Judas Priest/Drifter's Escape. B: Dear Landlord/I Am a Lonesome Hobo/I Pity the Poor Immigrant/The Wicked Messenger/Down Along the Cove/I'll Be Your Baby Tonight.

10. *Nashville Skyline*, released 4/9/69. A: Girl from the North Country/Nashville Skyline Rag/To Be Alone with You/I Threw It All Away/Peggy Day. B: Lay Lady Lay/One More Night/Tell Me That It Isn't True/Country Pie/Tonight I'll Be Staying Here with You.

11. *Self Portrait*, released 6/8/70. 1A: All the Tired Horses/Alberta #1/I Forgot More Than You'll Ever Know/Days of 49/Early Mornin' Rain/In

Search of Little Sadie. 1B: Let It Be Me/Little Sadie/Woogie Boogie/Belle Isle/Living the Blues/Like a Rolling Stone. 2A: Copper Kettle (the Pale Moonlight)/Gotta Travel On/Blue Moon/The Boxer/The Mighty Quinn (Quinn the Eskimo)/Take Me as I Am (or Let Me Go). 2B: Take a Message to Mary/It Hurts Me Too/Minstrel Boy/She Belongs to Me/Wigwam/Alberta #2.

12. *New Morning*, released 10/21/70. A: If Not for You/Day of the Locusts/Time Passes Slowly/Went to See the Gypsy/Winterlude/If Dogs Run Free. B: New Morning/Sign on the Window/One More Weekend/The Man in Me/Three Angels/Father of Night.

13. *Bob Dylan's Greatest Hits, Volume II*, released 11/17/71. 1A: Watching the River Flow/Don't Think Twice, It's All Right/Lay Lady Lay/Stuck Inside of Mobile with the Memphis Blues Again. 1B: I'll Be Your Baby Tonight/All I Really Want to Do/My Back Pages/Maggie's Farm/Tonight I'll Be Staying Here with You. 2A: She Belongs to Me/All Along the Watchtower/The Mighty Quinn (Quinn the Eskimo)/Just Like Tom Thumb's Blues/A Hard Rain's A-Gonna Fall. 2B: If Not for You/It's All Over Now, Baby Blue/Tomorrow Is a Long Time/When I Paint My Masterpiece/I Shall Be Released/You Ain't Goin' Nowhere/Down in the Flood.

14. *Pat Garrett & Billy the Kid*, released 7/13/73. A: Main Title Theme (Billy)/Cantina Theme (Workin' for the Law)/Billy 1/Bunkhouse Theme/River Theme. B: Turkey Chase/Knockin' on Heaven's Door/Final Theme/Billy 4/Billy 7.

15. *Dylan*, released 11/16/73. A: Lily of the West/Can't Help Falling in Love/Sarah Jane/The Ballad of Ira Hayes. B: Mr. Bojangles/Mary Ann/Big Yellow Taxi/A Fool Such as I/Spanish Is the Loving Tongue.

16. *Planet Waves*, released 1/17/74. A: On a Night Like This/Going Going Gone/Tough Mama/Hazel/Something There Is About You/Forever Young. B: Forever Young/Dirge/You Angel You/Never Say Goodbye/Wedding Song.

17. *Before the Flood*, released 6/20/74. 1A: Most Likely You Go Your Way and I'll Go Mine/Lay Lady Lay/Rainy Day Women #12 & 35/Knockin' on Heaven's Door/It Ain't Me Babe/Ballad of a Thin Man. 1B: five songs by the Band. 2A: Don't Think Twice, It's All Right/Just Like a Woman/It's Alright, Ma (I'm Only Bleeding)/three songs by the Band. 2B: All Along the Watchtower/Highway 61 Revisited/Like a Rolling Stone/Blowin' in the Wind. (live album)

18. *Blood on the Tracks*, released 1/17/75. A: Tangled Up in Blue/ Simple Twist of Fate/You're a Big Girl Now/Idiot Wind/You're Gonna Make Me Lonesome

When You Go. B: Meet Me in the Morning/Lily, Rosemary and the Jack of Hearts/If You See Her, Say Hello/Shelter from the Storm/Buckets of Rain.

19. *The Basement Tapes*, released 6/26/75. 1A: Odds and Ends/*Orange Juice Blues (Blues for Breakfast)/Million Dollar Bash/*Yazoo Street Scandal/Goin' to Acapulco/*Katie's Been Gone. 1B: Lo and Behold!/*Bessie Smith/Clothes Line Saga/Apple Suckling Tree/Please, Mrs. Henry/Tears of Rage. 2A: Too Much of Nothing/Yea! Heavy and a Bottle of Bread/*Ain't No More Cane/Crash on the Levee (Down in the Flood)/*Ruben Remus/Tiny Montgomery. 2B: You Ain't Goin' Nowhere/*Don't Ya Tell Henry/Nothing Was Delivered/Open the Door Homer/*Long Distance Operator/This Wheel's on Fire. (songs marked * are performed by the Band without Dylan)

20. *Desire*, released 1/16/76. A: Hurricane/Isis/Mozambique/One More Cup of Coffee/Oh, Sister. B: Joey/Romance in Durango/Black Diamond Bay/Sara.

21. *Hard Rain*, released 9/10/76. A: Maggie's Farm/One Too Many Mornings/Stuck Inside of Mobile with the Memphis Blues Again/Oh, Sister/Lay Lady Lay. B: Shelter from the Storm/You're a Big Girl Now/I Threw It All Away/Idiot Wind. (live album)

22. *Masterpieces*, released 2/25/78 in Japan, Australia, and New Zealand only. 1A: Knockin' on Heaven's Door/Mr. Tambourine Man/Just Like a Woman/I Shall Be Released/Tears of Rage/All Along the Watchtower/One More Cup of Coffee. 1B: Like a Rolling Stone (from *Self Portrait*)/The Mighty Quinn (Quinn the Eskimo) (from *Self Portrait*)/Tomorrow Is a Long Time/Lay Lady Lay (from *Hard Rain*)/Idiot Wind (from *Hard Rain*). 2A: Mixed Up Confusion/Positively 4th Street/Can You Please Crawl Out Your Window?/*Just Like Tom Thumb's Blues/*Spanish Is the Loving Tongue/*George Jackson (big band version)/*Rita May. 2B: Blowin' in the Wind/A Hard Rain's A-Gonna Fall/The Times They Are A-Changin'/Masters of War/Hurricane. 3A: Maggie's Farm (from *Hard Rain*)/Subterranean Homesick Blues/Ballad of a Thin Man/Mozambique/This Wheel's on Fire/I Want You/Rainy Day Women #12 & 35. 3B: Don't Think Twice, It's All Right/Song to Woody/It Ain't Me Babe/Love Minus Zero-No Limit/I'll Be Your Baby Tonight/If Not For You/If You See Her, Say Hello/Sara. (performances marked * are not available on any American album)

23. *Street-Legal*, released 6/15/78. A: Changing of the Guards/New Pony/No Time to Think/Baby Stop Crying. B: Is Your Love in Vain?/Senor (Tales of Yankee Power)/True Love Tends to Forget/We Better Talk This Over/Where Are You Tonight? (Journey through Dark Heat).

24. *Bob Dylan at Budokan*, released in the U.S. 4/23/79. 1A: Mr. Tambourine Man/Shelter from the Storm/Love Minus Zero-No Limit/Ballad of a Thin Man/Don't Think Twice, It's All Right. 1B: Maggie's Farm/One More Cup of

Coffee (Valley Below)/Like a Rolling Stone/I Shall Be Released/Is Your Love in Vain?/Going Going Gone. 2A: Blowin' in the Wind/Just Like a Woman/Oh, Sister/Simple Twist of Fate/All Along the Watchtower/I Want You. 2B: All I Really Want to Do/Knockin' on Heaven's Door/It's Alright, Ma (I'm Only Bleeding)/Forever Young/The Times They Are A-Changin'. (live album)

25.   *Slow Train Coming*, released 8/18/79. A: Gotta Serve Somebody/Precious Angel/I Believe in You/Slow Train. B: Gonna Change My Way of Thinking/Do Right to Me Baby (Do Unto Others)/When You Gonna Wake Up/Man Gave Names to All the Animals/When He Returns.

26.   *Saved*, released 6/20/80. A: A Satisfied Mind/Saved/Covenant Woman/What Can I Do for You?/Solid Rock. B: Pressing On/In the Garden/Saving Grace/Are You Ready.

27.   *Shot of Love*, released 8/12/81. A: Shot of Love/Heart of Mine/Property of Jesus/Lenny Bruce/Watered-Down Love. B: Dead Man, Dead Man/In the Summertime/Trouble/Every Grain of Sand. (later pressings include The Groom's Still Waiting at the Altar at the start of side two)

28.   *Infidels*, released 11/1/83. A: Jokerman/Sweetheart Like You/Neighborhood Bully/License to Kill. B: Man of Peace/Union Sundown/I and I/Don't Fall Apart on Me Tonight.

29.   *Real Live*, released 11/29/84. A: Highway 61 Revisited/Maggie's Farm/I and I/License to Kill/It Ain't Me Babe. B: Tangled Up in Blue/Masters of War/Ballad of a Thin Man/Girl from the North Country/Tombstone Blues. (live album)

30.   *Empire Burlesque*, released 5/27/85. A: Tight Connection to My Heart (Has Anybody Seen My Love?)/Seeing the Real You at Last/I'll Remember You/Clean Cut Kid/Never Gonna Be the Same Again. B: Trust Yourself/Emotionally Yours/When the Night Comes Falling from the Sky/Something's Burning, Baby/Dark Eyes.

31.   *Biograph*, released 11/4/85. 1A: Lay Lady Lay/Baby, Let Me Follow You Down/If Not for You/I'll Be Your Baby Tonight/*I'll Keep It with Mine. 1B: The Times They Are A-Changin'/Blowin' in the Wind/Masters of War/The Lonesome Death of Hattie Carroll/*Percy's Song. 2A: *Mixed-Up Confusion/Tombstone Blues/*The Groom's Still Waiting at the Altar/Most Likely You Go Your Way and I'll Go Mine (from *Before the Flood*)/Like a Rolling Stone/*Jet Pilot. 2B: *Lay Down Your Weary Tune/Subterranean Homesick Blues/*I Don't Believe You (She Acts Like We Never Have Met)/*Visions of Johanna/Every Grain of Sand. 3A: *Quinn the Eskimo/Mr. Tambourine Man/Dear Landlord/It Ain't Me Babe/You Angel You/Million Dollar Bash. 3B:

To Ramona/*You're a Big Girl Now/*Abandoned Love/Tangled Up in Blue/*It's All Over Now, Baby Blue. 4A: *Can You Please Crawl Out Your Window?/Positively 4th Street/*Isis/*Caribbean Wind/*Up to Me. 4B: *Baby, I'm in the Mood for You/*I Wanna Be Your Lover/I Want You/*Heart of Mine/On a Night Like This/Just Like a Woman. 5A: *Romance in Durango/Senor (Tales of Yankee Power)/Gotta Serve Somebody/I Believe in You/Time Passes Slowly. 5B: I Shall Be Released/Knockin' on Heaven's Door/All Along the Watchtower/Solid Rock/*Forever Young. (performances marked * are not available on any other American album)

32. *Knocked Out Loaded*, released 7/14/86. A: You Wanna Ramble/They Killed Him/Driftin' Too Far from Shore/Precious Memories/Maybe Someday. B: Brownsville Girl/Got My Mind Made Up/Under Your Spell.

33. *Down in the Groove*, released 5/31/88. A: Let's Stick Together/When Did You Leave Heaven?/Sally Sue Brown/Death Is Not the End/Had a Dream About You, Baby. B: Ugliest Girl in the World/Silvio/Ninety Miles an Hour (Down a Dead End Street)/Shenandoah/Rank Strangers to Me.

34. *Dylan & the Dead*, released 2/6/89. A: Slow Train/I Want You/Gotta Serve Somebody/Queen Jane Approximately. B: Joey/All Along the Watchtower/Knockin' on Heaven's Door. (live album)

35. *Oh Mercy*, released 9/19/89. A: Political World/Where Teardrops Fall/Everything Is Broken/Ring Them Bells/Man in the Long Black Coat. B: Most of the Time/What Good Am I?/Disease of Conceit/What Was It You Wanted/Shooting Star.

II. Singles by Bob Dylan

The intention is to list all U.S. 7-inch singles except reissues, plus overseas singles that include performances not otherwise available. All singles are on Columbia Records unless otherwise indicated. An * indicates performances not available on any of Dylan's American albums. Date is date of first release.

Mixed Up Confusion/*Corrina, Corrina	12/14/62
Blowin' in the Wind/Don't Think Twice, It's All Right	8/63
Subterranean Homesick Blues/She Belongs to Me	3/65
Like a Rolling Stone/Gates of Eden	7/20/65
Positively 4th Street/From a Buick 6	9/7/65
Can You Please Crawl Out Your Window?/Highway 61 Revisited	11/30/65

One of Us Must Know (Sooner or Later)/Queen Jane Approximately	2/66
Rainy Day Women #12 & 35/Pledging My Time	4/66
I Want You/*Just Like Tom Thumb's Blues	6/66
Just Like a Woman/Obviously 5 Believers	8/66
Leopard-Skin Pill-Box Hat/Most Likely You Go Your Way and I'll Go Mine	3/67
*If You Gotta Go, Go Now/To Ramona (released in the Netherlands only)	9/67
I Threw It All Away/Drifter's Escape	4/69
Lay Lady Lay/Peggy Day	7/69
Tonight I'll Be Staying Here with You/Country Pie	10/69
Wigwam/Copper Kettle	7/70
Watching the River Flow/*Spanish Is the Loving Tongue	6/3/71
*George Jackson (big band version)/*George Jackson (acoustic version)	11/12/71
Knockin' on Heaven's Door/Turkey Chase	8/73
A Fool Such As I/Lily of the West	11/73
On a Night Like This/You Angel You (Asylum Records)	2/74
Something There Is About You/Going Going Gone (Asylum)	3/74
Most Likely You Go Your Way and I'll Go Mine/Stage Fright (by the Band) (Asylum)	7/74
Tangled Up in Blue/If You See Her, Say Hello	2/75
Million Dollar Bash/Tears of Rage	7/75
Hurricane (part 1)/Hurricane (part 2)	11/75
Mozambique/Oh, Sister	2/76
*Rita May/Stuck Inside of Mobile with the Memphis Blues Again	11/30/76
Baby Stop Crying/New Pony	7/31/78
Changing of the Guards/Senor	9/78
Gotta Serve Somebody/*Trouble in Mind	8/79
When You Gonna Wake Up/Man Gave Names to All the Animals	11/79
Slow Train/Do Right to Me Baby	2/80
Solid Rock/Covenant Woman	6/80
Saved/Are You Ready	8/80
Heart of Mine/*Let It Be Me (Europe only)	9/1/81
Heart of Mine/The Groom's Still Waiting at the Altar	9/11/81
Union Sundown/*Angel Flying Too Close to the Ground (Europe only)	10/28/83
Sweetheart Like You/Union Sundown	11/83
Jokerman/Isis	2/20/84

Tight Connection to My Heart/We Better Talk This Over	5/85
Emotionally Yours/When the Night Comes Falling from the Sky	9/85
*Band of the Hand (Dylan is not on B-side) (MCA Records)	4/86
Silvio/Driftin' Too Far from Shore	6/88
Everything Is Broken/*Dead Man, Dead Man (cassette single only)	10/89

III. Other officially released recordings by Bob Dylan

This list attempts to include all officially released recordings on which Dylan is the primary singer. Recordings on which he only plays guitar or harmonica or sings back-up vocals have been omitted, with a few exceptions. Unauthorized recordings (i.e. bootleg records or collectors' tapes) are not included in this discography. The list starts with song names, followed by the album on which they appear, name of record company, and month of release.

Midnight Special (Dylan on harmonica), on Harry Belafonte: *Midnight Special*, RCA, 3/62.

I'll Fly Away/Swing and Turn Jubilee/Come Back, Baby (all Dylan on harmonica), on Carolyn Hester: *Carolyn Hester*, Columbia, summer 1962.

Rocks and Gravel/Let Me Die in My Footsteps/Rambling, Gambling Willie/Talking John Birch Paranoid Blues, on *The Freewheelin' Bob Dylan* (early promotional edition), Columbia, 4/63.

John Brown/Only A Hobo/Talkin' Devil (under the pseudonym Blind Boy Grunt), on *Broadside Ballads, Volume I*, Broadside/ Folkways, 9/63.

Only a Pawn in Their Game (live from the March on Washington, 8/63), on *We Shall Overcome*, Folkways, winter 1964.

Blowin' in the Wind/We Shall Overcome (ensemble performances from Newport Folk Festival, 7/63), on *Evening Concerts at Newport, Volume I*, Vanguard, May 1964.

Playboys and Playgirls (sung with Pete Seeger)/With God on Our Side (sung with Joan Baez) (from Newport 7/63), on *Newport Broadside*, Vanguard, May 1964.

Sitting on Top of the World/Wichita (Dylan on harmonica and background vocals, backing Big Joe Williams, late 1961), on Victoria Spivey: *Three Kings and a Queen*, Spivey, 10/64.

A Hard Rain's A-Gonna Fall/It Takes a Lot to Laugh, It Takes a Train to Cry/Blowin' in the Wind/Mr. Tambourine Man/Just Like a Woman, on *The Concert for Bangladesh*, Apple, 12/71.

Grand Coulee Dam/Dear Mrs. Roosevelt/I Ain't Got No Home (in This World Anymore) (from Carnegie Hall, 1/68), on *A Tribute to Woody Guthrie, Part One*, Columbia, 1/72.

Train A-Travelin'/I'd Hate to Be You on That Dreadful Day/The Death of
    Emmett Till/Ballad of Donald White (as Blind Boy Grunt) (recorded
    1962), on *Broadside Reunion*, Folkways, 1972.

Big Joe, Dylan and Victoria/It's Dangerous (Dylan on harmonica, backing Big
    Joe Williams and Victoria Spivey, late 1961), on Victoria Spivey: *Three
    Kings and a Queen, Volume 2*, Spivey, 7/72.

Wallflower/Blues Stay Away from Me/(Is Anybody Going to) San Antone
    (shared vocals), on Doug Sahm: *Doug Sahm and Band*, Atlantic, 12/72.

Buckets of Rain (shared vocal), on Bette Midler: *Songs for the New Depression*,
    Atlantic, 1/76.

Sign Language (shared vocal), on Eric Clapton: *No Reason to Cry*, Polydor,
    9/76.

People Get Ready/Never Let Me Go/Isis/It Ain't Me Babe (live from fall 1975),
    on *4 Songs from Renaldo and Clara*, Columbia (promotional disc), 1/78.

Baby Let Me Follow You Down (two versions)/I Don't Believe You/Forever
    Young/I Shall Be Released (live from 11/76), on The Band: *The Last
    Waltz*, Warner, 4/78.

interview with occasional guitar accompaniment, on *Dylan London Interview
    July 1981*, Columbia (promotional disc), 9/81.

We Are the World (shared vocal; Dylan's role is small), released as single and
    on USA for Africa: *We Are the World*, Columbia, 3/85.

Sun City (shared vocal; Dylan's role is small), released as single and on Artists
    United Against Apartheid: *Sun City*, Manhattan, 12/85.

The Usual/Had a Dream About You, Baby/Night after Night, on Fiona, Bob
    Dylan, Rupert Everett: *Hearts of Fire*, Columbia (soundtrack album),
    10/87.

Pretty Boy Floyd, on *Folkways: A Vision Shared*, Columbia, 8/88.

Dirty World/Congratulations/Tweeter and the Monkey Man (lead vocals;
    other tracks on the album also feature Dylan on shared vocals and
    guitar and keyboards), on *Traveling Wilburys, Volume One*, Warner, 10/88.

Filmography

I. Films by Bob Dylan

Eat the Document. Filmed 5/66 by D. A. Pennebaker, edited 1967 by Bob Dylan, Howard Alk, and Robbie Robertson. First shown publicly 2/8/71. Not currently available. Circa one hour.

Renaldo & Clara. Directed by Bob Dylan. Filmed fall 1975, edited 1977 by Dylan with Howard Alk. First shown publicly 1/25/78. Not currently available. Original is close to four hours with an intermission. A second, two-hour edited version was released in fall 1978.

II. Films about Bob Dylan

Don't Look Back. Directed by D. A. Pennebaker. Filmed 4-5/65. First shown publicly 5/17/67. Circa 90 minutes. Available on videocassette.

"Hard Rain." Live concert footage shot 5/23/76 in Fort Collins, Colorado, by TVTV (Top Value Television); edited by TVTV. Broadcast on NBC 9/14/76. Circa 55 minutes. Not currently available.

Hard to Handle. Live concert footage filmed by Gillian Armstrong in Sydney, Australia, 2/24 and 2/25/86. Edited by Armstrong. Broadcast by HBO 6/20/86. Circa one hour. Available on videocassette.

"Getting to Dylan." A one-hour segment of the BBC program "Omnibus." Directed by Christopher Sykes. Broadcast 9/18/87. Not currently available.

III. Films in which Bob Dylan appears as an actor

"The Madhouse on Castle Street." Dylan acted and sang in this British
television drama, made and shown by the BBC, 1/63.

Pat Garrett & Billy the Kid. Directed by Sam Peckinpah. Released 5/73. Circa
106 minutes. Available on videocassette (director's original version has
now been released).

Hearts of Fire. Directed by Richard Marquand. Released 10/87, UK only. Circa
90 minutes. Videocassette announced but not yet released.

IV. Films that include performances by Bob Dylan

Festival. Directed by Murray Lerner. Released 1967. Footage from Newport
Folk Festival, 7/64 and 7/65, including All I Really Want to Do/Maggie's
Farm/Mr. Tambourine Man. Available in film format.

The Concert for Bangladesh. Edited by George Harrison, with help from Dylan.
Released 3/72. Includes If Not for You (partial)/A Hard Rain's A-Gonna
Fall/It Takes a Lot to Laugh/Blowin' in the Wind/Just Like a Woman.
Available on videocassette.

The Last Waltz. Directed by Martin Scorsese. Released 4/78. Includes Forever
Young/Baby, Let Me Follow You Down/I Shall Be Released. Available on
videocassette.

V. Major television appearances

"The Madhouse on Castle Street." BBC, 1/63. (see above)

"The Times They Are A-Changin'," half-hour segment of the Canadian
Broadcasting Company program "Quest," recorded 2/1/64 and broad-
cast by CBC 3/10/64. Includes Restless Farewell and five other songs.
Archived in video form. Prior to this, Dylan made three known televi-
sion appearances in the U.S. in 1963, including one song on Johnny
Carson's "Tonight" show.

"Les Crane Show," live, WABC, New York, 2/17/65. Dylan sings two songs
accompanied by Bruce Langhorne and is witty and cutting in conversation. Archived in audio only. (Because of content, more significant than
his "Steve Allen Show" appearance a year earlier.)

BBC programmes recorded in BBC studios, 6/1/65, and broadcast in two
parts in 6/65. 12 songs, approximately 70 minutes. Archived in audio
only, apparently.

San Francisco Press Conference, KQED Studios, 12/3/65, broadcast by KQED later that day. Circa one hour. Archived in video form.

"The Johnny Cash Show." Three songs, taped 5/1/69, broadcast on ABC 6/7/69. All items from here forward are archived in video form.

"The World of John Hammond," part of the National Educational Television "Soundstage" series. Includes three songs by Dylan. Recorded 9/10/75, first broadcast 12/13/75.

"Hard Rain." NBC, 9/10/76. (see above)

"Saturday Night Live." Three songs. NBC, 10/20/79.

"Grammy Award Show." CBS, 2/27/80. One song: Gotta Serve Somebody.

"Late Night with David Letterman." NBC, 3/22/84. Three songs, including Don't Start Me to Talkin'.

Live Aid Concert. Three songs. 7/14/85. Broadcast live by satellite around the world.

Farm Aid Concert. 9/22/85. Four songs were broadcast live by the Nashville Network.

"Hard to Handle." HBO, 6/20/86. (see above)

Farm Aid 2 broadcast. 7/4/86. Three songs from Dylan's concert in Buffalo, New York were broadcast live by VH-1 TV; much of the concert was shot and transmitted live by satellite in preparation for the broadcast.

"Getting to Dylan." BBC, 9/18/87. (see above)

VI. Promotional Videos

Between 1983 and 1989 Dylan participated to some degree in the making of promotional videotapes to accompany the following songs. All of these are studio recordings attached to footage shot later, so there are no actual new performances on these tapes.

     Jokerman

     Sweetheart Like You

     Tight Connection to My Heart

     Emotionally Yours

     When the Night Comes Falling from the Sky

     Handle with Care (Traveling Wilburys; a second Wilburys video includes Dylan minimally if at all)

     Political World

Bibliography

I. Books by Bob Dylan

Tarantula. New York: Macmillan, 1971.
Writings and Drawings. New York: Alfred A. Knopf, 1973.
Lyrics, 1962-1985. New York: Alfred A. Knopf, 1985. (Expansion of *Writings and Drawings*.)

II. Key references used in preparing this text

Krogsgaard, Michael. *Master of the Tracks, The Bob Dylan Reference Book of Recording*, Copenhagen: Scandinavian Society for Rock Research, 1988. Lists all known recorded performances, including audience tapes of concerts, studio outtakes, etc., with full song lists for each performance. This edition is an update of his earlier book, *Twenty Years of Recording*. For information about availability of a (further updated) U.S. edition under the title *Positively Bob Dylan*, call Popular Culture, Ink. at 800-678-8828.

Heylin, Clinton. *Bob Dylan—Stolen Moments*, Romford, England: Wanted Man, 1988. A detailed chronology of Dylan's personal and professional life; more reliable than the biographies. Available from Wanted Man, PO Box 22, Romford, Essex RM1 2RF, UK.

Shelton, Robert. *No Direction Home, The Life and Music of Bob Dylan*, New York: William Morrow, 1986. Biography.

Scaduto, Anthony. *Bob Dylan*, New York: Grosset & Dunlap, 1971 (updated, 1973). Biography.

McGregor, Craig, ed. *Bob Dylan, A Retrospective*, New York: William Morrow, 1972. Includes 1966 *Playboy* interview, 1968 *Sing Out!* interview, 1969 *Rolling Stone* interview, plus watershed pieces by Robert Shelton, Nat Hentoff, Ralph Gleason, Irwin Silber, Jules Siegel and Jon Landau.

The Telegraph, issues #1 (1981) — #34 (1989). Edited by John Bauldie. A phenomenal amount of Dylan information, insight, and entertainment is contained in these pages; most of the back issues are out of print, alas. Currently publishing three 100-page issues a year, plus five newsy "*RTS*" supplements (written by Clinton Heylin). For subscription information, contact Wanted Man, PO Box 22, Romford, Essex RMI 2RF, UK.

The Wicked Messenger, issues #1 (1980) — #505 (1989). Dylan newsletter, written by Ian Woodward. Consistent, obsessive, indispensable. Now available only as a supplement to *Look Back* or *Isis* (see below for addresses).

III. Other sources used in preparing this text

Look Back, quarterly Dylan magazine, 23 issues through 1989, unpretentious, fun to read, *the* central meeting place for American Dylan fans. Edited by Tim Dunn and Rob Whitehouse. For subscription information (includes *TWM* supplement), contact Look Back, PO Box 857, Chardon, OH 44024.

Isis, bimonthly UK Dylan magazine, 28 issues through 1989, lots of news, oriented towards collectors. Edited by Derek Barker. For subscription information (includes *TWM* supplement), contact U.S. agent Rolling Tomes, PO Box 1943, Grand Junction, CO 81502.

Anderson, Dennis. *The Hollow Horn, Bob Dylan's Reception in the United States and Germany*, Munich: Hobo Press, 1981.

Bicker, Stewart P., ed. *Friends & Other Strangers, Bob Dylan in Other People's Words*, no publisher, 1985.

Bicker, Stewart P., ed. *Talkin' Bob Dylan 1984 & 1985*, no publisher, 1986.

Bowden, Betsy. *Performed Literature*, Bloomington: Indiana University Press, 1982.

Cable, Paul. *Bob Dylan, His Unreleased Recordings*, New York: Schirmer, 1980.

Cartwright, Bert. *The Bible in the Lyrics of Bob Dylan*, Bury, England: Wanted Man, 1985.

Cohen, Scott. "Don't Ask Me Nothin' about Nothin'" (interview), in *Spin*, December 1985.

Cott, Jonathan. "The *Rolling Stone* Interview with Bob Dylan," in *Rolling Stone*, 1/25/78 and 11/16/78.

Cott, Jonathan. *Dylan*, New York: Rolling Stone Press, 1984.

Crowe, Cameron. *Biograph* booklet and liner notes, included with album, 1985.

De Somogyi, Nick. *Jokermen & Thieves—Bob Dylan and the Ballad Tradition*, Bury: Wanted Man, 1986.

Diddle, Gavin. *Images and Assorted Facts*, Manchester, England: The Print Centre, 1983.

Diddle, Gavin, ed. *Talkin' Bob Dylan...1978*, Pink Elephant, 1984.

Dundas, Glen. *Tangled Up in Tapes, A Collector's Guide of Tape Recordings of Bob Dylan*, Thunder Bay, Canada: SMA Services, 1987.

Dylan, Bob. *In His Own Write*, the bob dylan archive unltd. (Unauthorized collection of hard-to-find writings from 1962-65; no city or date.)

Dylan, Bob. *Positively Tie Dream*, Forban, England: Ashes and Sand, 1979. (Unauthorized collection of interviews and fictions.)

Gans, Terry. *What's Real and What Is Not*, Munich: Hobo Press, 1983.

Gilmore, Mikal. "Positively Dylan," in *Rolling Stone*, 7/17/86.

Gray, Michael and Bauldie, John, editors. *All Across the Telegraph*, London: Sidgwick & Jackson, 1987. Anthology from the magazine.

Gross, Michael. *Dylan, An Illustrated History*, New York: Grosset & Dunlap, 1978.

Herdman, John. *Voice Without Restraint, Bob Dylan's Lyrics and Their Background*, New York: Delilah, 1982.

Heylin, Clinton. *Rain Unravelled Tales*, Ashes and Sand, 1985.

Jansen, Gerhard, ed. *Bob Dylan—Pressing On*, Lelystad, Holland: no publisher, 1980.

Kooper, Al. *Backstage Passes: Rock 'n' Roll Life in the Sixties*, New York: Stein & Day, 1977.

Kramer, Daniel. *Bob Dylan*, New York: Citadel Press, 1967.

Landy, Elliott. *Woodstock Vision*, Hamburg: Rowohlt, 1984.

Lawlan, Val and Brian, editors. *Steppin' Out*, Linfield, England: Steppin' Out Productions, 1987.

Miles. *Bob Dylan*, London: Big O, 1978.

Miles, ed. *Bob Dylan in His Own Words*, New York: Quick Fox, 1978.

Pennebaker, D. A. *Don't Look Back*, New York: Ballantine, 1968.

Pennebaker, D. A. "Looking Back on *Don't Look Back*," in *Fourth Time Around*, #1, August 1982.

Penrose, Roland. *Picasso, His Life and Work, Third Edition*, Berkeley: University of California Press, 1981.

Pickering, Stephen. *Bob Dylan Approximately, A Portrait of the Jewish Poet in Search of God; A Midrash*, New York: David McKay, 1975.

Ribakove, Sy and Barbara. *Folk-Rock: the Bob Dylan Story*, New York: Dell, 1966.

Rinzler, Alan. *Bob Dylan, The Illustrated Record*, New York: Harmony, 1978.

Roques, Dominique. *The Great White Answers*, Salindres, France: Southern Live Oak Productions, 1980. Guide to bootlegs.

Rosenbaum, Ron. "*Playboy* Interview: Bob Dylan," in *Playboy*, March 1978.

Rubin, William, ed. *Pablo Picasso: A Retrospective*, New York: The Museum of Modern Art, 1980.

Sloman, Larry. *On the Road with Bob Dylan*, New York: Bantam, 1978.

Thompson, Toby. *Positively Main Street*, New York: Coward-McCann, 1971.

Thomson, Elizabeth M., ed. *Conclusions on the Wall*, Manchester: Thin Man, 1980.

Van Estrik, Robert. *Bob Dylan: Concerted Efforts*, Netherlands: no publisher, 1982.

Von Schmidt, Eric and Rooney, Jim. *Baby Let Me Follow You Down: The Illustrated Story of the Cambridge Folk Years*, New York: Anchor, 1979.

Weasel, Verily E. *"Eat the Document,"* in *Endless Road*, #5, 1984.

Woodward, Ian. *"Planet Waves*—Dates of Recording," in *Occasionally Bob Dylan*, #4, January 1984.

*For assistance in locating and obtaining particular books, you may wish to contact one of the long-established mail order companies specializing in books about Bob Dylan:

> My Back Pages, P.O. Box 2 (North P.D.O.),
> Manchester, M8 7BL, England.

> Rolling Tomes, P.O. Box 1943, Grand
> Junction, CO 81502. (303) 245-4315.

Credits

Photographs

Copyright Citations

Acknowledgments

A great many people have helped and supported me during the research and writing of this volume of *Performing Artist*. (I want to apologize in advance to those whose names are not mentioned here but should be.) My heartfelt thanks, then, to Gunter Amendt, John Bauldie, Christian Behrens, Randal Churchill, Nancy Cleveland, Dave Dingle, Glen Dundas, Carlo Feltrinelli, Bob & Susan Fino, Frank Gironda, Bill Graham, Kirk Gustafson, Dieter Hagenbach, David G. Hartwell, Dave Heath, Clinton Heylin, Jon Kanis, Michael Krogsgaard, Jonathan Lethem, Paul Loeber, Bev Martin, Jim McLaren, Blair Miller, Chuck Miller, Marleen Mulder, John Pateros, Michael Pietsch, Pat Reday, Elliott Roberts, Jeff Rosen, Robin Rule, Gerhard Schinzel, Shasta, Jan Simmons, Heckel Sugano, Brian Stibal, Clyde Taylor, Cooky Tribelhorn, Jerry Weddle, Marcus Whitman, Sachiko Williams, and Ian Woodward.

Special thanks are due to my editor, Tim Underwood; my children, Erik Ansell, Heather Ansell, Taiyo Williams, and Kenta Williams; and my wife, Donna Nassar, whose patience, love, and enthusiasm have kept me going through the most challenging writing task I've ever undertaken.

And of course a word of acknowledgment is also due to the subject of this book, who, although a determinedly private person, has courageously and energetically shared himself through his music for thirty years now. "No one else could play that tune, you knew it was up to me." Thank you.

Index

Paul Williams was the founder of *Crawdaddy!*, the first American rock music magazine; he is the author of 18 books, one of which, *Das Energi*, is in its 21st printing. He is well known to Dylan appreciators as a respected scholar and writer in the field; in 1988 he was the featured guest speaker at an international gathering of Dylan fans in Manchester, England.

Williams's other books include *Nation of Lawyers, Remember Your Essence, The International Bill of Human Rights* (as editor), *The Map, or Rediscovering Rock and Roll*, and *Only Apparently Real: The World of Philip K. Dick*.